Self-Help, Inc.

Micki McGee

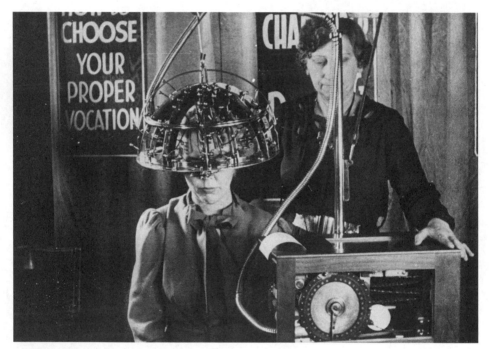

Self-Help, Inc.

Makeover Culture

in American Life

OXFORD
UNIVERSITY PRESS
2005

OXFORD
UNIVERSITY PRESS

Oxford University Press, Inc., publishes works that further
Oxford University's objective of excellence
in research, scholarship, and education.

Oxford   New York
Auckland   Cape Town   Dar es Salaam   Hong Kong   Karachi
Kuala Lumpur   Madrid   Melbourne   Mexico City   Nairobi
New Delhi   Shanghai   Taipei   Toronto

With offices in
Argentina   Austria   Brazil   Chile   Czech Republic   France   Greece
Guatemala   Hungary   Italy   Japan   Poland   Portugal   Singapore
South Korea   Switzerland   Thailand   Turkey   Ukraine   Vietnam

Published by Oxford University Press, Inc.,
198 Madison Avenue, New York, New York 10016

www.oup.com

Oxford is a registered trademark of Oxford University Press

Library of Congress Cataloging-in-Publication Data
McGee, Micki.
Self-Help, Inc. : makeover culture in American Life / by Micki McGee.
p. cm.
Includes bibliographical references.
ISBN-13 978-0-19-517124-2
ISBN 0-19-517124-1
1. Self-help techniques—United States.   2. Psychological literature—United States.
3. Success—United States—Psychological aspects.   I. Title.
BF632.M36 2005
158'.0973—dc22   2004024905

Cover and frontispiece image: The psychograph was a novelty device featured in department stores and theater lobbies during the depression of the 1930s. The machine was used to measure the bumps on an individual's head and, according to the principles of the pseudo-science of phrenology, said to reveal the subject's personality and most suitable vocation. The American Psychograph Company operated from 1929–1937. Photographer unknown. Collection: ROGER-VIOLLET.

9 8 7 6 5 4 3 2 1

Printed in the United States of America
on acid-free paper

For François and Mikaila

Acknowledgments

At the heart of this project is the notion that no one, try as they may, can invent themselves. The same might be said of just about any undertaking: very little, if anything, that gets done gets done alone. But the acknowledgments pages of first books are tricky: one can imagine the trajectory of assistance arching backward in time toward kindergarten teachers. While early childhood educators are always an influence, I will try to focus on those individuals and institutions that made specific contributions to this book, or to the thinking that shaped it. As a consequence, these thanks will be necessarily incomplete.

A generous circle of friends has sustained me in the writing of this project. Two women in particular—Carrie Sakai and Jeanne Newhouse—have made the invaluable contribution of reminding me, again and again, that what I have to say matters. Without that, one wouldn't even bother to start such a project. Once started, Allison Barlow and Anne Bergeron helped me sustain my momentum. In addition to providing regular doses of encouragement, each directed me toward consulting work that kept the wolves at bay without requiring that I put this project aside completely. Allison also volunteered to read the very first predraft from start to finish—an act of heroism if ever there was one—and shepherded the manuscript to its publisher. It wouldn't have happened without her. Diane Pacom offered her insights into the thesis-writing process and regular emergency telephone consultations. Joline Blais and Nancy Graham read the very earliest drafts of the writing that evolved into this project and asked all the right questions, chief among them Nancy's: "What's so great about productivity?" My friendship with Chris Ford has grown with this project, and the project grew through her thinking, as she challenged me to think more fluidly about the relationship of individual development to social and political transformation. David Martz has provided years of e-mailed comic relief. And Karl Willers has urged me onward. Through it all, my friendship with Hillel Schwartz has been a source of inspiration, advice, and fun, as well as delightful self-help cartoons, tips on the latest cultural history literature, and excellent punning.

Several individuals fostered my earliest consideration of these ideas. Judy DeVoss, Dick Dunlap, Larry Price, and Becky Price at the University of California, Santa Barbara, were the people who first suggested the question of life as work of art. Mary Linn Hughes, for many years a collaborator and co-conspirator in various art and life ventures, searched out antiquarian books, such as *Living the Creative Life* and *The Need for Art in Life*, that furthered my consideration of this topic. Sherry Millner and Ernest Larsen's healthy skepticism about the value of careers of any kind has been an ongoing source of inspiration. The artists, critics, and teachers Allan Sekula, Martha Rosler, Marge Dean, Newton and Helen Harrison, Fred Lonidier, Allan Kaprow, David Antin, Eleanor Antin, Jean Viala, and Jean Marie Allaux fostered my thinking at earlier, more germinal moments.

Friends, teachers, and colleagues at the Graduate Center of the City University of New York, where this project had its first iteration as a doctoral thesis, have provided remarkable support. The members of my dissertation committee—Stuart Ewen, Catherine Silver, Barbara Katz Rothman, and Robert R. Alford—each brought their own special qualities to the project. Through his work, Stuart Ewen has been an inspiration. While self-improvement books claim to change people's lives, my experience is that books such as Stuart's are much more likely to have that sort of impact. An early reading of his *Captains of Consciousness* certainly changed mine. Catherine Silver has been, in so many ways, a touchstone for my work at the Graduate Center, encouraging me at times when I could quite easily have given up, asking the right questions, and reminding me to think of a dissertation as a book draft. She was right: that's what it can be. Barbara

Katz Rothman has reminded me again and again how important it is for women scholars to write and to teach in their own voices—whole, complete, and embodied voices. And the recently departed Bob Alford taught me about a kind of collegiality I could never have imagined: an exchange of ideas and insights that proved conclusively that the best work is never done in isolation. His legendary Logics of Inquiry seminar provided the setting for many of the most fruitful conversations that informed this research. My fellow "logicians of inquiry" in Bob's seminar—among them Randall Doane, Ariel Ducey, Lorna Mason, Jennifer Smith, and Betsy Wissinger—offered suggestions, insights, and support. Camaraderie is key to accomplishing anything; their support was vital. Stanley Aronowitz, in many a sidebar conversation, has cajoled and provoked me into finishing this project, as well as provided valuable dialogue on the nature of immaterial labor. Neil McLaughlin offered detailed comments on the manuscript and shared his work on Eric Fromm; both were most helpful.

My colleagues at New York University have provided ongoing support. George Yúdice, first at the Graduate Center and later at New York University, has been a friend, a teacher, and, more recently, a colleague who has supported me and this project in countless ways. The Privatization of Culture Seminar that he convened with Vera Zolberg through New York University and at the New School University provided a collegial space for dialogue and sustenance. Toby Miller has provided support and encouragement and invited my participation in his lively intellectual community. The John W. Draper Interdisciplinary Master's Program in Humanities and Social Thought at New York University has offered me an institutional home for this project in its transformation from thesis to book. My colleagues there—among them Robin Nagle, Riaz Khan, Amy Ninetto, and especially Shireen Patell and Amy Ninetto in the "grotto"—have provided unwavering support. Special thanks go to Amy who read the page proofs with care, helping to eliminate many of the bugs. Frederich Ulfers's seminar on Nietzsche was filled with epiphanies for me. Chris Crowe at Bobst Library facilitated my ongoing research between academic appointments. Karen Jewett, Kathleen Hulley, and Bassam Abed, at the School of Continuing and Professional Studies, afforded me the opportunity to teach a course called "Success in the American Imagination," where I first floated many of the ideas elaborated here. My co-conspirators at the NYU Chapter of the American Association of University Professors—including Kathleen Hull, Andrew Ross, Anna McCarthy, Solo J. Dowuona-Hammond, Arvind Rajagopal, Stephen Duncombe, and the late Francis Tenywa—have been models of the benefits of thinking and acting collectively.

Some of my research on self-improvement culture was first published elsewhere. Work on *The Artist's Way* (elaborated in chapter 4 here) was initially presented at a February 2000 conference on developments in the arts and culture industries hosted by Erasmus University in Rotterdam, and subsequently published in the anthology *Trends and Strategies in the Arts and Culture Industries*. My thanks go to the organizers of that conference, in particular Susanne Janssen and Karlijn Ernst. My consideration of the general category of self-help literature, labor management, and theories of victimization (taken up in the conclusion and appendix) were first explored in an article that Randy Martin and Toby Miller invited me to contribute to *Social Text* 70. I want to thank them both, as well as Michele Sharon-Glassford and the *Social Text* Editorial Collective for their support of that work. Much of the research on artists as ideal workers that appears in chapter 4 was first presented at the 2001 meeting of the American Sociological Association, where Joy Charlton chaired the session on occupations and professions. I want to thank her for her comments and encouragement at that early stage.

During the early development of this project I was fortunate to be able to subsidize my writing with consulting work for a variety of national cultural and youth development organizations. One client, Girls Incorporated, deserves particular thanks for their flexibility while I juggled the multiple demands of research, writing, consulting, and new motherhood. Colleagues and friends at this organization—especially Heather Johnston-Nicholson, Jackie McCaffrey, Linda Haynes, and Jenny Lindstrom—were unusually responsive to my need to schedule writing time.

Others have not only offered their support; they've also taken out their checkbooks, literally or figuratively, to make this work possible. A Dissertation Year Fellowship in 1998–99 from the Graduate School of the City University of New York supported research costs, as well as time for thinking and writing. A summer residency at Blue Mountain Center in August 1997 and a miniresidency in 2004 made the initial and final readings for this project a lakeside pleasure and provided the inspired and inspiring company of Mel Rosenthal, Bobbie Perry-Mapp, Janet Zweig, Joseph Goldstein, Leslie Nuchow, Maggie Dubris, Laura and Neil Seldman, David Morris, and Eileen Myles. Harriet Barlow, Ben Strader, and the rest of the Blue Mountain staff created exactly the kind of quiet retreat that makes reflection possible. Back in New York City, Avec Incorporated provided an affordable office space in lower Manhattan. My parents, Dan and Pauli McGee, added their support, freeing me from taking on additional consulting work that might have stalled the project's completion.

Dedi Felman, my editor at Oxford University Press, has shepherded me through the publication process, urged me on to vital revisions when writer's fatigue had begun to set in, and believed wholeheartedly in the value of this project. She recruited a marvelous cast of reader-reviewers, including Arlie Russell Hochschild, Nina Eliasoph, Vicki Smith, and Toby Miller, all of whom provided fine-grained comments and generous suggestions that have enriched the project. Arlie's thoughtful comments suggested the consideration of social movement theory that emerges in the book's conclusion. Their comments have only enriched this project; any shortcomings herein are my own. Kim Robinson, Jessica Ryan, and Michele Bove, also at Oxford University Press, played key roles in making the book possible. Conversations and correspondence with Christine Whelan, who has been preparing a dissertation on self-help literature, have offered welcome provocations and empirical insights.

Practical support for research and writing comes in other forms as well. If Anthony Trollope famously had his "groom" attending to that critical cup of morning coffee, mothers have their childcare providers, Manhattan residents their mini-storage watchmen, and computer users their data recovery experts. Joan Perineau, Maria Elena Modica, and the children's Aid Society–Greenwich Village Center provided the kind of childcare that makes it possible to lose oneself in a project like this one. Victor Smith, at the ministorage where I kept my unwieldy collection of self-help books and research files, urged me on whenever I appeared to pull files or books: "Maggie, when ya gonna finish that book?" The friendly folks at Tekserve worked their magic to rescue my manuscript from a hard drive destroyed in the power surges and outages that followed the events of September 11, 2001. Steven Tamarin, Lauren Marcus, Lauren Gorman, Roy Boorady, Steven Forrest, and Todd Bresnick helped keep me well in body and mind. And my sister Danielle offered her frequent telephonic counsel and support. Thanks to all of them.

Finally, most of all, there are two others to thank—the two with whom I share my daily life—François Alacoque and our daughter Mikaila. They've lived with this project, the absences it's created and opportunities it's provided. This is for them, and for the living reality of a world where all you can be *is* all you can be and all you can be is enough.

[T]he serious artist is himself in much trouble,

and could well do with some intellectual and

cultural aid from a social science made sprightly

by the sociological imagination.

—C. Wright Mills

contents

Self-Help, Inc.

Covey's Daughter and Her Dilemma

The self-help author Stephen R. Covey is best known for his blockbuster *The Seven Habits of Highly Effective People*, but let's start this consideration of self-improvement culture with another of his books, *First Things First.*[1] Dr. Covey launches the book with a story about his daughter Maria, who had recently given birth to her third child. As he tells it, Maria expressed frustration, explaining that while she loved her new baby, the responsibilities of motherhood were taking all of her time: "I'm not getting anything else done, including many things that only I can do." Covey tells his readers that he can understand Maria's frustration, explaining that Maria is "bright and capable, and she's always been involved in many good things." As they talked, the time management expert had an epiphany: that Maria's frustration was simply a result of her expectations. His solution required her to adjust those expectations: "for now, only one thing was needful— enjoying that baby." Let us resume the story in Covey's own words:

> "Just relax," I said. "Relax and enjoy the nature of this new experience. Let this infant feel your joy in the role of mother. No one else can love and nurture that child the way you can. All other interests pale in comparison for now."

Maria realized that, in the short run, her life was going to be imbalanced . . . and that it should be. "There is a time and a season for everything under the sun." She also realized that as the baby grew and entered a different phase in life, she would be able to reach her goals and contribute in other powerful ways.

Finally, I said, "Don't even keep a schedule. Forget your calendar. Stop using your planning tools if they only induce guilt. This baby is the first thing in your life right now. Just enjoy the baby and don't worry. Be governed by your internal compass, not by some clock on the wall."[2]

Although several aspects of this anecdote will be of interest, what is particularly striking is the contradiction: the bestselling author and management consultant who has made his fortune advocating mission statements and marketing planning tools to structure every moment of the waking day concedes that these tools are of little use to those engaged in one of the most fundamental human activities: caring for one's offspring. The figure of a reasoning, self-inventing, and self-mastering individual—one that Covey certainly did not invent but usually embraces—simply falls short when confronted with this basic human activity (albeit one typically relegated to women). Even in Dr. Covey's world of highly effective people there must be some place, a sequestered domestic sphere—reduced here to the mother-baby dyad—that is best shielded from the ideal of a self-interested, rational, and calculating subject maximizing her individual opportunities through a regimen of time management.

Consider for a moment how Dr. Covey's advice would sound if offered to a distraught son rather than a distressed daughter:

"Relax and enjoy the nature of this new experience. Let this infant feel your joy in the role of *father*. No one else can love and nurture that child the way you can. All other interests pale in comparison for now . . . this baby is the first thing in your life for now."

Were this single factor changed, the whole tenor of Covey's advice would be transformed. Instead of a traditionalist advice book, *First Things First* might be counted among the most socially progressive in the genre. But of course Covey's advice is neither gender neutral nor socially progressive. Rather, the father of nine who enjoys the support of a stay-at-home wife finds that in order to advocate for first things first—for putting the care of the most vulnerable and dependent ahead of the desire for individual acclaim and the quest for financial rewards—he must fall back on conventional gendered and privatized arrangements.[3]

The solution Dr. Covey proposes—that women who are rearing children ought to cede (or at least postpone) their ambitions for self-determination—is legitimized through a robust sort of nostalgia that appeals to scriptural wisdom, traditional metaphors, and American myths. Although he substitutes "under the sun" for "under the heavens"—perhaps a turn of phrase to appeal to his more secular readers—Covey's paraphrase of Ecclesiastes ("to every thing there is a season")[4] aligns his advice with centuries of biblical wisdom.[5] The reference might also remind the close reader that Covey writes in a tradition that goes back to the introduction of Johannes Gutenberg's Bible in 1456, when the development of mass printing techniques made possible, for the first time, not only widespread literacy but also the codification of manners and the emergence of the genres of advice manuals or self-improvement books.[6] Some social observers have suggested that the Bible is perhaps the first and most significant of self-help books.[7] Others have argued that the success of self-improvement literature, whether secular or religious, is contingent on its ability to function as inspirational literature.[8] The role of spiritual and religious traditions, which have been both muted and persistent in an increasingly medicalized and psychological culture, will operate as an important background to my consideration of the literature of self-improvement culture. Certainly, *First Things First* and Covey's other advice books tap into the religious undercurrents in much of self-improvement culture.

As in any rhetoric, metaphor is crucial to Dr. Covey's story, as it will be in my analysis. When Dr. Covey concludes his advice to Maria, he urges her to be "governed by her internal compass, not by some clock on the wall."[9] This pair of dueling metonyms, the clock and the compass, also appears in the cover illustration of the paperback edition of *First Things First*, with the compass superimposed on the clock. The metonym of the compass reveals a centerpiece of Covey's metaphorical framework: the spatial analog of the journey is superimposed on the temporal phenomenon of a lifetime. Space is substituted for time during this period of unremitting speedup.[10] Given how compressed time is for women like Maria—women who imagine that they ought to cultivate both themselves and their offspring, pursue independent careers, and raise their children—the idea of a compass suggests the freedom to embark on adventures and explore new frontiers (long an American solution to social problems). And, of course, a switch from clock to compass suggests the metaphor of the journey in which life is understood in terms of geography: itinerary, crossroads, and cul-de-sacs, mapping a course, and getting somewhere. The road is (more or) less traveled. One searches for "a path" or, even better, "a path with heart." In a culture where, until recently, women were to stay home and mind the hearth while men ventured forth into the unknown, we must ask ourselves to what extent the image of being on the road or path of life reflects a gendered view of personal development. Perhaps other metaphors—of unfolding, of awakening, or of planting, blossoming and harvesting—have been less popular because they lack the narrative thrust of the adventure story.

Finally, there is a certain nostalgia in Dr. Covey's worldview—a longing for an elusive past where, it is imagined, men were governed by virtue rather than limited self-interest (by what Covey calls "universal principles") and women supported their men and raised their children, putting first things first. That nostalgia, as well as a mythic personage, is inscribed in the name of the company that markets Covey's products: the FranklinCovey Company, where Covey shares second billing with none other than Benjamin Franklin.[11] Franklin, with his little book of virtues, might well be considered the inventor of the day planner, as well as one of the grandfathers of the advice literature genre. Like Covey, he was a proponent of rational time management, yet not unaware of its limits. Although Franklin created a precise schedule for each hour of his day from the moment he rose at 5:00 a.m. until the moment he went to bed at 1:00 in the morning, he observed that the difficulty of adhering to a schedule—to his virtue of "Order"—varied depending on the functions one performed:

> My Scheme of ORDER, gave me the most Trouble, and I found, that tho' it might be practicable where a Man's Business was such as to leave him the Disposition of his Time, that of a Journey-man Printer for instance, it was not possible to be exactly observ'd by a Master, who must mix with the World, and often receive People of Business at their own Hours. [12]

Self-mastery—particularly the mastery of one's time—was central to the virtue of "Order." As the quintessential self-made man, Franklin noted that the making of the self-made man started with the control of the substance of his life, his time, his daily schedule: "do not squander Time, for that is the Stuff Life is made of."[13] Yet such mastery was severely constrained by

the necessity of responding to others—that is, by the necessity of responding to one's customers or market. The ideal of rational self-mastery to which
Franklin aspired is one that Western thought has inherited from the culture of classical Greece, where the citizen's capacity to master himself was
premised on the fact that the labor of women and enslaved persons supported his leisure. Self-mastery was a value to be cultivated in a citizen but
was deemed an impossibility for those whose labor produced the necessities of life—for those who were subject to orders imposed by others. Thus
if Franklin found it difficult to adhere to his schedule while trying to keep
his customers satisfied, one can only imagine how much more difficult it
would have been for his wife, his servants, and his slaves. How might Mrs.
Franklin have arranged her day if she was to be ever responsive to the needs
of others: of husband, of children, of household help, and shop assistants?
Indeed, Franklin makes mention of his wife, noting that "it is lucky for me
that I had one as much dispos'd to Industry & Frugality as myself. She assisted me cheerfully in my Business, folding & stitching Pamphlets, tend-
ing Shop, purchasing old Linen Rags for the Paper-makers, &c. &c."[14] How,
one might wonder, was Mrs. Franklin—aka Deborah Read Franklin—to
schedule all of those "etceteras"? It is the chasm between the clear and simple
imperatives of advice books, schedules, and to-do lists, and the "&c's" that
shape the fabric of social life, that will be of interest in the coming chapters.

The images of Franklin's wife and Covey's daughter, images that span
more than two centuries, are striking both for their similarities and for their
differences. Both women are represented as industrious: "given to Industry" in the former and "bright, capable, and involved in many good things"
in the latter. And both are playing important supporting roles, subordinat-
ing their own development in the service of others. Instead of "inventing
themselves"—as modern advice literatures suggest we must all do—these
women are engaged in the work of inventing and nurturing others. While
the mythology of the self-made man and the possibility of social mobility
may have been viewed as revolutionary ideas when they emerged in the
eighteenth century against the European background of traditional hierarchies and fixed social position acquired at birth, women and people of color
were largely excluded from the fantasy. The mythology of the self-made
man relied on their unacknowledged labor and servitude. Increasingly,
awareness of this fact permeates our popular culture. Consider a cartoon
by Roz Chast that appeared in the May 1997 issue of *Ladies' Home Journal*.
In honor of Mother's Day, Chast created what she called "Mother's Day

Cards In Reverse"—imaginary cards from mothers to their children. One, illustrated with snapshots of family life, read as follows:

> Here's all the food I lugged home from the store;
> Here's the apartment we rented;
> Here's all the clothes and the shoes that you wore;
> Here is the "self" you "invented."
>
> —Mother[15]

Humor can speak what might otherwise be verboten: the idea that one can make oneself, invent oneself, is not only fundamentally mistaken but also a profoundly alienating one that implies estrangement from the social position of one's origins as well as from those individuals who fostered one's development.

Despite the similarities between Franklin's wife and Covey's daughter, there is an important difference.[16] By Franklin's report his wife is cheerful, while Covey describes his daughter as frustrated. In the eighteenth-century account we find the image of a wife and helpmate whose cheerful assistance is readily available for her enterprising husband's success, while in the contemporary self-help text we find the image of a daughter-turned-mother whose "expectations" are getting in her way of "relaxing" and "enjoying" what Covey represents as a wondrous "new experience" of caring for a third baby. Born into a culture that takes for granted Betty Friedan's not-so-long-ago revolutionary idea that women are entitled to engage in satisfying careers outside the home, Covey's daughter (like the women she stands in for in this text) finds herself unwilling to readily relinquish other activities for selfless devotion to family. Women are both permitted *and* expected to develop themselves in occupations outside the home and family—to "realize themselves" in work outside the domestic sphere. But this once revolutionary ideal of individual autonomy and self-invention was extended to women with mixed and contradictory outcomes.

While the invention of selves—those of one's partner and progeny—was traditionally considered the primary if not sole arena for a woman's self-expression, now contributing to the invention of others is hardly valued at all, at least in economic terms. Not even the most minimal economic provisions are made for the activities of parenting: the family wage, where the usually male partner's salary was sufficient to support the childrearing activities of the other, has all but vanished; low-income women are characterized as lazy and idle when they are engaged in the activities of caring for their own children, and are forced into minimum wage or workfare labor; and professional women find that their own market value drops when they step out of the paid labor market to engage in the unwaged labor of caring for children and other dependents—when they participate in what is euphemistically known as "the mommy track." Even among those atypical American families that can indulge in the luxury of a full-time stay-at-home mother (or father), the specter of unexpected unemployment—downsizing, layoffs, and other forms of corporate restructuring—erodes any sense of security. And those few women who enjoy the possibility of staying at home with their children while a spouse provides financially face the ever-present possibility of divorce, which notoriously leaves women economically disadvantaged. Thus the suggestion that Dr. Covey offers Maria—that she relax, forget about her other priorities, and focus on her newborn—is one that is not widely available to American women and their families.

Like millions of other working Americans, Maria finds herself situated in a contradictory world that devalues the labors of caring for and shaping others in every practical material way while (and by) characterizing these labors as private and "priceless." She is encouraged to pursue an ideal of self-invention and self-mastery that hails from a culture where someone else's labors (that of wives and enslaved persons) would provide for the necessities of daily life. And she is urged to develop and "invent herself"—to accommodate herself to suit the shifting requirements of a volatile labor market while paradoxically finding some way of cultivating an "authentic self" that is unaffected by economic vagaries. Like millions of other working women and men, Maria finds herself belabored. [17]

From Self-Made to Belabored

The part I really don't understand is if you're looking for self-help,
why would you read a book written by somebody else? That's not
self-help, that's help.
—George Carlin

Imagine a self and then invent that self. Picture a life, then create that life. The ideal of self-invention has long infused American culture with a sense of endless possibility. Nowhere is this ideal more evident than in the burgeoning literatures of self-improvement—a sector of the publishing industry that expanded dramatically in the last quarter of the twentieth century, particularly in its final decade. The trade publication *American Bookseller* reports that self-help book sales rose by 96 percent in the five years between 1991 and 1996.[1] By 1998, self-help book sales were said to total some $581 million, where they constituted a powerful force within the publishing industry, shoring up profits in an era of bottom-line publishing faced with otherwise declining sales, unearned author advances, and hard cover return rates soaring to 45 percent nationally.[2] Indeed, the self-improvement industry, inclusive of books, seminars, audio and video products, and personal coaching, is said to constitute a $2.48-billion-a-year industry.[3] One-third to one half of Americans have purchased a self-help book in their lifetimes.[4] One New York City bookstore allocates a quarter mile of shelf space to the various subcategories of self-improvement literature.[5] And perhaps most impressively, between 1972 and 2000, the number of self-help books more than doubled, increasing from 1.1 percent to 2.4 percent of the total number of books in print.[6] Advice books—specifically self-improvement books, not simply the traditional didactic youth literature with life lessons or moral imperatives—are now available for every age group from early readers to the aged.[7] Self-improvement books are available to cover any and all issues, with titles specialized to address every market segment.

The appeal of this literature is understandable: the tremendous growth in self-help publishing parallels an overall trend of stagnant wages and destabilized employment opportunities for American workers. Americans face what some social observers have called a "new insecurity" in the wake of the end of the standard job and family.[8] With social welfare programs all but dismantled, and with lifelong marriage and lifelong professions increasingly anachronistic, it is no longer sufficient to be married or employed; rather, it is imperative that one remains marriageable and employable.[9] Sculpting one's figure to remain desirable to one's spouse and perfecting one's leadership techniques to remain valued by one's company are not options but imperatives in this new economy. A sense of personal security is anomalous, while anxiety is the norm. To manage this anxiety, individuals have been advised not only to work longer and harder but also to invest in themselves, manage themselves, and continuously improve themselves.

The less predictable and controllable the life course has become, the more individuals have been urged to chart their own courses, to "master" their destinies, and to make themselves over. In addition to actual hours spent on the job—which have increased dramatically—Americans are compelled to constantly work on themselves to remain competitive in the labor market.[10] Such additional toil includes, but is not limited to, retraining and reschooling for new types of work, maintaining one's appearance as youthful and vigorous, and searching for one's "true calling." Thus it comes as no surprise that one finds a marked increase in the number of self-help titles in this period of declining economic security. In the place of a social safety net, Americans have been offered row upon row of self-help books to boost their spirits and keep them afloat in uncharted economic and social waters. Yet the self-help net has its own traps. This book looks at how the promise of self-help can lead workers into a new sort of enslavement: into a cycle where the self is not improved but endlessly belabored. It examines the shifts in self-improvement culture in an era of dramatic economic and social changes and offers a glimpse of how the cultures of personal transformation, though largely a force for maintaining the status quo, might be mined for progressive political opportunities.

Self-Made Men, Belabored Selves

The ideal of individual success and self-invention, epitomized in figures such as Benjamin Franklin, Andrew Carnegie, and Bill Gates serves to cajole and encourage American workers.[11] The figure of the self-made man—and more recently that of the self-made woman—comforts and consoles us, suggesting that vast material, social, and personal success are available to anyone who is willing to work long and hard enough. The fantasy has maintained considerable appeal, despite its troubling corollary: if success is solely the result of one's own efforts, then the responsibility for any failure must necessarily be individual shortcomings or weaknesses.[12]

At the close of the twentieth century, the figure of the self-made man came under dual pressures. On the one hand, the extension of the possibilities of self-invention to women and to others who had been traditionally excluded from the possibility of reinventing their lives revealed the fundamental gendered fault lines in the idea of the self-made man: namely, that the labors of women's daily lives—the bearing and rearing of children, the care of the ill and the infirm, attending to myriad domestic activities—were largely incompatible with traditional notions of success through self-invention. And, on the other hand, changing economic circumstances—declining real wages and increased uncertainty about employment stability and opportunities—created a context in which constant self-improvement is suggested as the only reliable insurance against economic insecurity. Self-invention, once the imagined path to boundless opportunity, has become a burden under which a multitude of Americans hoping to fast track their careers, or simply secure their basic necessities, have labored.

The traditional ideal of the self-made man relied on the privileged positions afforded to men. Women had long been urged to support the "self-invention" of sons, husbands, and brothers.[13] The mid-twentieth-century cliché of the woman abandoned after supporting her husband to climb the corporate ladder or garner an advanced degree gained its hackneyed status because as men invented their new selves, their unwaged support staff could be changed accordingly. In addition to the actual support women provided to men's efforts at self-making, the image of individual success was closely tied to characteristics associated with masculinity: independence, strength, dominance, invulnerability, and muscular vigor.[14] Men were deemed self-made, while women, lacking the appropriate masculine characteristics for success, were, ironically, designated as the self-made man's invisible helpers.

Changes in gender roles in the late twentieth century began to undermine the narrow vision of the self-made man. In the wake of the civil rights and women's movements, the ideal of self-invention was extended more broadly. Resources that had been devoted almost entirely to cultivating the success of (usually white) men now had to be shared. Those who had been making it possible for men to "make themselves" were being encouraged to pursue their own self-fulfillment. Middle-class women entered the labor force in increasing numbers, not simply to pursue a livelihood (as working-class women had long done) or to shore up family finances, but in a quest for personal fulfillment. These changes would seem a good thing—equal opportunity had long been a basic tenet of American life in theory, however underrealized it was in practice. However, in the process of transferring the values associated with self-invention across gender lines, this ideological construction of the self-made man—what one might call a polite fiction or a taken-for-granted idea—came under enormous pressure from changing social and material arrangements. Of course no one has ever single-handedly invented or created a self, but now the individuals who had contributed to the making and shaping of others were demanding their own opportunities for self-invention.

Contemporaneous with these changes in women's roles and expectations, and with the related increases in women's participation in the paid labor force, an equally important transformation was reshaping economic life. While Americans had grown accustomed to living in an industrial society where manufacturing played a central role in the nation's economy, by the early 1970s economists and social theorists described and predicted dramatic restructuring of the economy and the labor force. Industrial capitalism, it was argued, was rapidly being replaced by what was variously called "monopoly capitalism," "postindustrial capitalism," "information" or "knowledge capitalism," or, in what might have been a moment of unbridled optimism, "late capitalism" or "post-capitalism."[15] Traditionally unionized jobs in manufacturing were lost as a national economy, once protected by tariffs, yielded to the rise of "multinational" or "transnational" capitalism. In the place of manufacturing work, low-paying service sector jobs, along with "knowledge work," played an increasingly important role in the economy. Moreover, corporate structures that had once relied on "vertical integration"—a multitiered hierarchy of management structures overseeing a relatively stable labor force—were increasingly flattened. Middle management positions were eliminated in waves of what came to be known in the early 1990s as "downsizing." Other members of the labor force found their jobs had grown woefully insecure, as efforts by management to remain competitive included the increased use of temporary, part-time, and other contingent forms of labor, as well as the export of jobs offshore to employment venues more favorable to management's interests in reducing the cost of wages and benefits. Simultaneously, greater participation by women in the paid labor force intensified competition for those jobs that were not outsourced or sent offshore. Some social theorists have called this phenomenon "the jobless future" or the "end of work."[16] But in a strange twist for American workers, the result has been something akin to work without end.

When social and economic structures—gender role expectations and employment conditions, in this particular case—undergo dramatic changes, individual and interpersonal change is inevitable. Social structures and individual identities are mutually constitutive: interconnected to such an extent that changes in the former necessarily produce changes in the later, and, some would argue, vice versa. Indeed, a central premise of social theory is that various economic systems correspond with varied cultural, social, and interpersonal formations. For example, the social theorist Max Weber argued that the emergence of European and American entrepreneurial and industrial capitalism was made possible by the frugality and industriousness fostered by the rise of Protestantism. Assuming Weber's central insight to have been correct, then in the face of the dramatic transformation in the forms of contemporary capitalism, some new ethos ought to be unfolding right before our eyes. One might reasonably expect that new modes of being, new individual identities, and new conceptions of selfhood would abound. And such does seem to be the case.

While "postmodernism" has been the umbrella term for the cultural formations of advanced capitalism, the proliferation of recent academic and scholarly books on the topic of "the self" suggests how contested identity, selfhood, or "subjectivity" has become. The self has been described variously as mutable, protean, autotelic and evolving, multiple, marginal, postmodern, narcissistic and minimal, hungry and empty, saturated and seeking, invented and enterprising, well-tempered, playing, and "decentered."[17] This abundance of theories of the self suggests that the self under advanced capitalism is nothing if not belabored. The self is a topic of preoccupation in both academic and popular literatures, as well as—and most important—a site of effort and exertion, of evaluation and management, of invention and reinvention. The introduction of another portrait of the contemporary self into what is clearly a well-populated gallery is not without its risks. One might be accused, perhaps justifiably, of belaboring the subject. But I would argue that this notion of the self is both necessary and new. In the place of the traditional notion of the self-made man—a construct that is gendered in its basic formation, patriarchal in its assumptions of how individuals come into being, and self-congratulatory in its tone—the belabored self presents itself as overworked both as the subject and as the object of its own efforts at self-improvement.

The concept of the belabored self operates on two levels. First, the belabored self describes an actually occurring phenomenon: workers are asked to continually work on themselves in efforts to remain employable and reemployable, and as a means of reconciling themselves to declining employment prospects. Second, the concept of the belabored self offers a new way of framing what the historian and social critic Christopher Lasch misunderstood as the "narcissism" of late-twentieth-century American culture. Rather than understanding the individual's preoccupation with the self in psychological terms—a move that created an analytical cul-de-sac for Lasch[18]—the idea of the belabored self asks us to reconsider the cultural preoccupation with the self in terms of labor. Not only is extensive and ongoing labor on the self required of working people under advanced capitalism, but the labor of caring for others and managing the details of domestic life collides head-on with the imperative that everyone—man, woman, and child—focus on inventing an autonomous or self-sufficient self. While mutable gender roles have made the stress points in the idea of a self-making individual ever more apparent—clearly no one gets to the top without help from others—changes in the nature of the labor market have made efforts at self-making and self-invention increasingly urgent. Paradoxically, the imperative of inventing the self that is found in the literatures of self-improvement is often cast in the form of discovering or uncovering an authentic, unique, and stable self that might function—even thrive—unaffected by the vagaries of the labor market.

The combination of these forces has created tremendous pressures on the figure of a masterful, self-governing self. These pressures, I will argue, represent a unique opportunity to revisit our concept of the self and its making, not in psychological terms but as features of political and economic forces. Contradictions in the ideal of the self-made man—pressure on the cracks in this cultural icon—may also present particular political opportunities. But before one can explore the political possibilities available in such a moment, it's important to remember that long-held ideological constructs, such as the idea of a self-inventing self, do not crumble easily, whatever their cracks and strains.[19] Instead, as these ideals are contested, there seems to be an ongoing effort to shore them up—to buttress them against their own internal contradictions. The ubiquitous culture of self-improvement that burgeoned in the late twentieth century—and continues in the present— represents one aspect of this buttressing, and offers a rich source of materials for tracing changing notions of the self and for charting the emergence of the belabored self. The popularity of this literature, and the variety of specific advice it offers its readers, goes a long way toward explaining how we have come to be not simply overworked but also belabored.

Belaboring the Self: Makeover Culture in American Life

Although Americans turn to self-improvement literature for inspiration in times of despair, for specific advice on how to conduct their lives, and for reassurance in the face of enormous social, political, and economic changes, paradoxically this literature may foster, rather than quell, their anxieties. The proliferation of self-improvement discourse—in magazines, newspapers, tabloids, talk shows, bookstores, and internet sites—may have consequences not unlike the rise of advertising in the early twentieth century.[20] Just as the emergence of consumer advertising fostered social anxiety by focusing on an array of supposedly embarrassing corporeal "problems" such as halitosis or dandruff—problems that could be addressed through the purchase of various toiletries—today's retinue of self-improvement experts, motivational speakers, and self-help gurus conjure the image of endless insufficiency. Makeover television programs have proliferated: *Extreme Makeover* pitches plastic surgery, diet, exercise, and improved grooming as the best means of self-transformation, while *What Not to Wear* offers wardrobe advice as the fastest way to a "new you." *Extreme Makeover Home Edition* and *Trading Spaces* suggest home improvement as a route to self-improvement. *Queer Eye for the Straight Guy* advocates a multifaceted makeover; everything from wardrobe and grooming to interior design and home entertaining tips are revamped. In many cases, these makeover television shows are organized on the premise of "the ambush": the person to be "made over" has not volunteered, rather his or her friends and family have "turned them in." *Ambush Makeover*, *What Not to Wear*, and *While You Were Out* all operate on this structure. While you might have thought you looked just fine, or that your home was pretty comfortable, the people closest to you have been making some rather different, even scathing, assessments. No one is ever completely safe from the critical gaze of a culture steeped in the makeover ethos. Makeover programs, and the literatures of self-improvement (which will be the focus of this book), serve as constant reminders of our ostensible insufficiency even as they offer putative solutions. Works of contemporary advice literature—even straightforward "how-to" books—do not stop at simply offering advice; rather, they impugn the individual. Whereas once one might have consulted an advice book on "personal finance" or "wine tasting," now such books are marketed as *Personal Finance for Dummies* or *The Complete Idiot's Guide to Wine*.[21] The literature of self-improvement defines its readers as insufficient, as lacking some essential feature of adequacy—be it beauty, health, wealth, employment options, sexual partners, marital happiness, or specialized technical knowledge—and then offers itself as the solution. The resulting contagion of insufficiency constitutes the self-improvement industry as both self-perpetuating and self-serving. While the purchase of a commodity—mouthwash or dandruff shampoo—was once the route to some sense of interpersonal social security, today the simple purchase of a commodity is insufficient: altogether too easy. Instead, one must embrace a lifestyle, a series of regimes of time management or meditation, of diet and spiritual exploration, of self-scrutiny and self-affirmation.

Mutual Aid and Moral Values

Fostering self-doubt and insecurity has not always been a hidden function of self-help culture. Over the course of the last three decades of the twentieth century, there has been a significant shift in the meaning of "self-help." As recently as the 1970s (and particularly in the contexts of international aid, human services agencies, and grassroots healthcare), "self-help" referred not to individual self-improvement practices but to cooperative efforts for mutually improved conditions on the part of a community of peers.[22] Mutual aid, which had at one time been primarily fostered by religious and church-based charitable organizations, was increasingly professionalized, much as the counseling functions of clergy were increasingly handled by secular psychiatrists and psychotherapists. In the face of this professionalization of care, "self-help" groups reclaimed the authority previously ceded to "professionals" and "experts." A prominent example is that of the self-help medical care of the Boston Women's Health Collective, which provided an alternative to the authority of typically (at that time) male medical "experts" and resulted in the publication of the 1971 bestselling *Our Bodies, Ourselves*. But this engaged, collective, and political notion of self-help has largely eroded. Consider a *New York Times* article from 2000 discussing the publication of the first Spanish-language edition of *Our Bodies, Ourselves*. The article notes that *Nuestros Cuerpos, Nuestras Vidas* emphasizes "*mutual help over self-help* and a woman's need to take care of herself so she can better care for others" (emphasis added). [23] This observation might seem a hopeful one for anyone committed to a notion of collectivity: after all, the idea of mutual aid is mentioned rather than ignored or rejected. But the latent content of the quote reflects a less heartening shift in the use of the word "self-help." In less than thirty years, "self-help"—once synonymous with mutual aid—has come to be understood not only as distinct from collective action but actually as its opposite. [24] The changes in the literatures of self-improvement over the course of the last quarter of the twentieth century that will be considered in the coming chapters reflect this trend as well. The self is imagined as increasingly isolated, and "self-help," with some exceptions, is represented as a largely individual undertaking.

Some social critics would argue that this move toward an increasingly isolated individualism had been underway for some time—at least since the middle of the twentieth century, when psychoanalysis had infused the ideal of individual self-making with a new psychological component. Emotional well-being, the subjective experience of happiness, and the pursuit of pleasure, rather than, say, the accumulation of wealth, community involvement, and moral rectitude, began to be equated with success. This focus on self-fulfillment constituted a departure from the traditional criteria for evaluating success. While the self-made man of the nineteenth and early twentieth centuries aimed to achieve success in terms that were largely external and measurable—for example, accumulations of wealth, status, or power—late-twentieth-century self-making involves the pursuit of the rather more elusive and variable state of self-fulfillment. With the emergence of an emphasis on self-fulfillment, one finds there is no end-point for self-making: individuals can continuously pursue shifting and subjective criteria for success. This new psychological culture, it was argued, constituted a "triumph of the therapeutic" over religious and moral imperatives. [25] Some argued that it also provided new means of "governing the soul."[26] But the reputed triumph of the therapeutic was both partial and short-lived. Not only does the resurgence of religious fundamentalism suggest that traditional moral values continued to retain and attract numerous adherents, but the self-help and advice literature of the late twentieth century demonstrates that traditional religious and moral values are interwoven in the literature of self-improvement. One sociologist suggests that self-improvement literatures operate by "shrinking God," another characterizes self-help culture as a "thin" culture—a desiccated, juiceless version of thicker traditional cultural values—while yet another has called self-help literature an "an oracle at the supermarket."[27] These observations were borne out in my reading of self-help literature from the late twentieth century. Some strains of self-help culture do provide a kind of secularized religion—a sort of moral values lite.

The Aesthetic Turn in Self-Improvement Culture

The rise of a self-improvement culture that is focused on subjective, internal criteria for success and that is spiritual without necessarily embracing traditional theistic or moral values has contributed to the emergence of the idea that one ought to consider one's life as a work of art. Although this metaphor has its roots in the nineteenth-century Romantic ideal of "living the creative life," the new emphasis on the proposition that each individual imagine his or her life as a work of art is largely a late-twentieth-century phenomenon.[28] Even as individuals are urged to pursue their unique imagination and creative vision in books such as Julia Cameron's *The Artist's Way*, the phenomenon of "extreme makeover" television presents a conformist vision of aesthetic preoccupations in which the lines and wrinkles born of individual experience are erased to yield as generic an image of beauty as possible. The aesthetic turn in the self-help literature of the late twentieth century, like the emergence of the belabored self, is in part a consequence of the changing nature of the labor market and the blurring of the boundaries between the commercial and intimate spheres.

With the increased participation of women in the paid labor force (and their demands for recognition of their work in both the home and the workplace) the already suspect idea that public and private life, commercial and domestic spheres, could be sequestered from each other was further eroded. The boundaries between an intimate domestic sphere governed by affective values and a commercial sphere governed by the market values of productivity and profit were increasingly blurred. Ideals and values that had once been applied largely to the commercial arena—for example, ends-driven, profit-motivated rationality—were transferred to the private, intimate arena of personal life. For example, as the sociologist Arlie Russell Hochschild points out, the market values of maximizing profit offered the ideal of applying a kind of cost-benefit analysis to interpersonal relationships when the concept of codependence emerged in the early 1980s.[29] One could reasonably expect that if a blurring of boundaries between the commercial and the intimate spheres were taking place, that this would presage a migration of values in both directions. While the intimate sphere would be increasingly dominated by commercial values, so, too, the commercial realm would come to include an increased emphasis on interpersonal care and nurturance. And to some extent this has occurred. Examples include the "total quality management" advocated by the popular management expert Tom Peters, whereby managers are encouraged to cultivate their work "teams" as one would a family, and the emergence of what cultural theorists from varying perspectives have called the "no-collar" or humane workplace.[30] A number of advice books on women and management argue that women can operate more effectively as managers because they can, for example, emulate the collaborative behavior of dolphins rather than the ruthless individual character of sharks.[31] But the interchange between the commercial and intimate spheres has not been entirely reciprocal. Perhaps because the imperatives of the market so often come into direct conflict with the values associated with the care of others, the systems have not operated in perfect symmetry. Instead, because a profit-driven commercial sphere cannot accommodate the values of nurturance and care associated with the intimate sphere, aesthetic values—for example the pursuit of the "creative life"—have served as a ready, ethically neutral buffer for these tensions, helping to balance the asymmetries that emerge as the distinction between the commercial and intimate spheres blurs. In the literatures of self-improvement, aesthetic values were offered to women who were dissatisfied with the application of market values to private life and unlikely to realize significant economic advances, as well as to workers faced with both decreasing employment stability and economic rewards.[32]

While the ideal of life as work of art served as an alternative to the pecuniary metaphor of life as a business and to the rational, ends-driven thinking associated with the commercial sphere, in the late twentieth century the Romantic idea of the artist sequestered from the demands of the market gave way to a new model of the artist as an entrepreneur. Aesthetic and commercial values are merged—most famously in the work of Andy Warhol, who asserted: "Being good in business is the most fascinating kind of art"[33]—but also in the emergence of what the journalist David Brooks calls a culture of "bourgeois bohemians."[34] This idea of life as a work of art found its corollary in the emergence of the figure of the artist as the ideal, self-motivating, self-monitoring, and even self-employing worker.[35] This aesthetic self operates according to the principles of the marketplace and emerges fully formed in the figure that Tom Peters calls the "CEO of Me, Inc."—the fully commodified self that incorporates both capital and labor in its model for individual development but identifies itself solely with capital.

The incorporation of aesthetic values into the overall logic of the marketplace represents something of a setback for certain strands of radical political thought that had suggested that aesthetic values could provide an alternative to the ends-driven instrumental rationality of advanced capitalism.[36] Instead, in its most recent iterations, the ideal of life as a work of art turns out to be not an alternative but rather a trap: a model perfectly suited to the conditions of advanced capitalism, where the intimate sphere becomes a site of ongoing and tireless production, a design studio for reinventing one's most marketable self. Through this emphasis on the aesthetic, the impulse toward individual self-determination—a value that has long served as a catalyst for progressive social change—has been harnessed in the service of accelerated consumption and production. For example, the visual aesthetics of ever-changing fashions spur consumption while the ideal that one ought to work without concern for rewards or compensation—a characteristic long associated with artistic obsession—is encouraged among contemporary workers, particularly those in creative professions. Whether there is a way to counter such a tendency and restore progressive, even radical, possibilities to the ideal of self-invention is at the heart of this investigation.

The Ends of Self-Improvement Culture

To what extent the idea of individual self-invention offers opportunities for progressive or even radical political movements has been a question addressed by a number of social theorists, critics, activists, and historians. Some theorists have argued that the late-twentieth-century preoccupation with the self serves as a tool of social control: soothing political unrest and hampering the possibilities for political organizing.[37] Self-improvement literature has, it is argued, focused on individual concerns in ways that are largely incompatible with collective political action, and thus contributes to maintaining the status quo. Others contend that, on the contrary, the pursuit of individual self-fulfillment can serve as a catalyst for social change: that individual transformation can and does spur social and political advances. Seeking one's own desire, inventing a life of one's own, creating a self, these scholars and activists argue, can be seen as a necessary, if usually insufficient, factor in social and political change.[38]

The extent to which either of these positions proves valid depends on how one understands both the self and the constitution of ideology. If one understands the self as an autonomous, largely self-forming and self-governing individual, as has been the tendency under the radical individualism of Western thought, then the idea of self-invention is invariably a conservative and masculinist notion because this idea of the self conceals the labors of care—often, but not always, the labor of women—in the making of other selves. On the other hand, if one understands the self as both embedded in *and* at least in part constitutive of others and of a social sphere—as a contributor to the making of both self and others, as well as an outcome of the efforts and actions of others—then the pursuit of individual self-invention continues to hold radical political possibilities, particularly when one's own pursuit of self-invention confounds existing societal expectations.[39] The example of an individual such as Malcolm X in making over his life—from illiterate convict to articulate national leader—suggests that self-making can hold profound political possibilities. Typically the scholars and activists who hold the view that self-making offers political possibilities have a greater optimism regarding the individual's role in social change—that is, they argue that individual and personal transformations can and do affect social formations.[40] Rather than viewing ideology as monolithic, ideologies are understood as something that individuals can work to inscribe and perform or to subvert. Thus the culture of self-improvement is seen as fragmented, varied, mutable, and, at least in theory, potentially emancipatory.[41] Self-help culture is seen as a prepolitical form of protest: as evidence of individual dissatisfactions that could be channeled toward political participation.[42] Perhaps promises of boundless opportunity will begin to ring hollow when constantly frustrated by growing economic inequality, increased work time, and decreased access to basic necessities such as affordable healthcare, quality education, and secure retirement.

What this examination of self-improvement culture will show is that although the idea of individual self-determination remains a potent political force, the versions of self-invention offered in the preponderance of popular self-help literature typically maintain the status quo. On the other hand, the ideas that self-improvement literature is premised on—self-determination and self-fulfillment—continue to hold political possibilities that might be tapped for a progressive, even a radical, agenda. Realizing these possibilities requires dual trajectories. One must attend to developing new models of the self and self-making that recognize the labor of others in the making of each and every individual. And one must recognize that the desire to invent a life is no longer either evidence of narcissistic self-involvement or an emancipatory countercultural impulse, but rather is increasingly required as a new form of "immaterial labor"—mental, social, and emotional tasks—required for participation in the labor market.[43] Managing, promoting, and advancing oneself are critical to remaining simply employable.

Toward these dual ends, I want to consider the emergence of the idea of vocation and calling, and how it has been adapted to various economic circumstances (chapter 1). Then I will outline what models or metaphors of the self are proposed for women and for men in the literatures of self-improvement, comparing the general unisex "conduct of life" literature (chapter 2) with advice written for women in particular (chapter 3). This analysis reveals how the literatures addressed to women have been necessarily more innovative, perhaps because women's roles have been at the center of the radical transformations of the commercial and intimate spheres. Chapters 4 and 5 consider labor in particular, with chapter 4 examining changes in job search advice literature over the course of the last three decades of the twentieth century—particularly the emergence of the artist as the ideal laborer in the postindustrial labor force. Chapter 5 examines more completely just how laborious the work of "inventing a self" can be, and how the ideal of individual self-mastery—which is at the heart of most self-help literature—relies on the unacknowledged servitude of others. Finally, chapter 6 suggests—in a provisional way—how the cultures of self-improvement might be mined for more progressive political opportunities. Rather than abandon the idea of individual self-determination to conservative political forces, I argue that the recognition of the labor inherent in the making of selves in itself offers political possibilities. The forced labor of self-making, the belaboring of our selves, is at the center of this discussion.

chapter 1

From Calling to Vision

Spiritual, Secular, and Gendered Notions

The idea of duty in one's calling prowls about in our lives like the ghost of dead religious beliefs.
—*Max Weber*

One hundred years after the publication of Max Weber's celebrated thesis on the rise of Protestantism and the emergence of modern capitalism, the idea of pursuing a calling—of having a central purpose in life—remains fundamental to the American culture of self-improvement. Most recently, the bestseller lists include titles such as *The Purpose-Driven Life* by Rick Warren, and *What Should I Do with My Life?* by Po Bronson. Although much of what Weber observed has proven correct, he erred somewhat in characterizing the religious beliefs associated with the concept of calling as "dead." In fact, the religious and spiritual dimensions of "calling" have remained quite lively, morphing and mutating to accommodate changes in the organization of economic and social life. Often these adaptations have taken the form of the therapeutic imperative that one find self-fulfillment in work and variations on the Romantic belief that one ought to pursue one's life as a creative enterprise—as a work of art. These transformations have been vital to the development of a new work ethic that infuses work discipline with pleasure.[1]

Weber's premature post-mortem on the religious and spiritual dimensions of calling emerges from his emphasis on the rational and productive dimensions of social life. At the center of Weber's thesis regarding the

Protestant ethic and the rise of a "spirit of capitalism" was his observation that the idea of a divinely ordained vocation or calling was transplanted to the secular sphere of everyday work rather than sequestered within the specifically religious domains of, for example, monasteries and convents. To make his case, Weber overstated the shift, arguing that the idea of "calling" or vocation had become synonymous with God-given work that, when pursued with zeal, would yield worldly evidence of one's position as a member of "the elect," the only souls predestined to enjoy everlasting salvation:

> Now it is unmistakable that even in the German word *Beruf,* and perhaps still more clearly in the English *calling,* a religious conception, that of a task set by God, is at least suggested. The more emphasis is put upon the word in a concrete case, the more evident is the connotation. And if we trace the history of the word through the civilized languages, it appears that neither the predominantly Catholic peoples nor those of classical antiquity have possessed any expression of similar connotation for what we know as a calling (in the sense of life-task, a definite field in which to work), while one has existed for all predominantly Protestant peoples.[2]

While pursuing one's divinely ordained workplace vocation was an important piece of the concept of calling, this was *not,* as had been suggested in Weber's 1904 thesis, its sole, or even its primary, meaning. The idea of "calling" was a dual concept, split between spiritual, otherworldly dimensions and the material, workaday world. The conflation of "life-task" and "field in which to work" oversimplifies the Protestant innovation, in particular the Puritan construct that serves as the source of American traditions regarding work. When Weber maintained that "calling" had taken on a completely occupational emphasis, he overlooked some of the primary texts of Puritan thinking on the topic. Consider the following description of the dual nature of a Christian's calling, from a 1701 sermon by the Massachusetts Bay Colony clergyman Cotton Mather:

> There are *Two Callings* to be minded by *All Christians.* Every Christian hath a GENERAL CALLING; which is, to Serve the Lord Jesus Christ, and Save his own Soul, in the Services of *Religion,* that are incumbent on all the Children of men. God hath *called* us, to *Believe* on [*sic*] His *Son,* and *Repent* of our *Sin,* and observe the Sacred Means of our *Communion* with Himself and bear our

Testimony to His *Truths* and *Wayes* in the World: And every man in the world, should herein conform to the Calls of that God, who *hath called us with this Holy Calling*. But then, every Christian hath also a PERSONAL CALLING; or a certain *Particular Employment*, by which his *Usefulness*, in his Neighborhood, is distinguished. God hath made man a *Sociable* Creature. *We* expect Benefits from *Humane Society*. It is but equal, that *Humane Society* should Receive Benefits from *Us*. We are Beneficial to *Humane Society* by the Works of that Special OCCUPATION, in which we are to be employ'd, according to the Order of God.

A Christian at his *Two Callings*, is a man in a Boat, Rowing for Heaven; the *House* which our Heavenly Father hath intended for us. If he mind but one of his *Callings*, be it which it will, he pulls the *Oar*, but on *one side* of the Boat, and will make but a poor dispatch to the Shoar of Eternal Blessedness.[3]

Mather, a figure of considerable influence in colonial Massachusetts, was attempting to resolve a critical tension of the early colonial period when he presented this image of symmetry in the rower, rowing toward both sacred and occupational destinations.[4] Competing spiritual and material values emerged in debates over what were known as the Covenant of Works and the Covenant of Grace. In the former, good works would be rewarded both on earth and in the afterlife, but in the latter only divine intervention in the form of grace could save a man from eternal damnation. The Covenant of Grace, with its ironclad determinism—and the sense of futility and power-lessness it provoked—led to the problem of antinomianism: if nothing one can do will help one gain salvation, then what is one to do? Although Mather denied that he was proposing a Covenant of Works, his emphasis on good works sought to mitigate this crisis.[5] For Mather, conscientious good works, though a necessary part of salvation, were not in themselves sufficient: good works would be rewarded only if performed by a man who had already been saved.[6] Mather's "man in a boat rowing to heaven" illustrates how the doctrine of calling was both religious and secular in its scope: lest one row in circles, the Puritan needed to pursue both the general and particular, spiritual and workaday callings, with equal vigor.

Rather than reflect on the contradictory nature of the New England Puritan experience, Weber emphasized the significance of Benjamin Franklin, whose own focus was decidedly worldly rather than spiritual.[7]

Indeed, the historian Judy Hilkey comments that Franklin's emphasis on the accumulation of wealth would have shocked the Puritans in Mather's community.[8] By overlooking the influence of figures such as Cotton Mather, as well as Jonathan Edwards—the New England clergyman whose evangelism characterized the period of spiritual revivalism known as the First Great Awakening—Weber neglects the profoundly expressive, emotional, and charismatic dimensions that are central features of the evangelical Protestant tradition.[9] The choice of Franklin's writing as a major source of evidence was what sociologists of our period might call a sampling error. It was also inspired, as it bolstered Weber's controversial thesis: by selecting a character who has been aptly described as "an avant-garde of one," Weber provided a grim, if accurate, glimpse of the future of a rationalist capitalism applied to every aspect of life.[10] But to ignore the expressive and spiritual dimensions of daily life would be to reproduce Weber's bias toward the productive commercial sphere and its rational imperatives.

Life under capitalism contains complementary, mutually reinforcing elements: the rational, calculating dimension exemplified by Franklin's orderly, reasoned, and self-disciplined approach to the accumulation of wealth that has come to be understood as the Protestant ethic and the expressive, charismatic dimension that the sociologist Colin Campbell calls the Romantic ethic and that has its antecedents in the sensation-oriented fire-and-brimstone evangelism of figures such as Jonathan Edwards.[11] While it might at first appear that these elements are in direct opposition—the frugal, calculating asceticism of the Protestant ethic opposed to the indulgent sentimentality and sensation-seeking of the Romantic ethos—their emergence at the moment when the Industrial Revolution split human affairs into productive and consumptive spheres allowed them to operate as complementary opposites, each governing their respective realms, the public and private spheres.[12] Typically these spheres are understood as gendered: a masculine public sphere and a feminine private sphere. Although the premise of a gendered public and private sphere (and, indeed, the idea of a public sphere) has been subject to some debate, in general the rise of industrialization in the United States, and to a lesser extent in western Europe, emphasized this division of labor and values.[13] Men were pulled from farms and villages that had been the sites of productive labor to work in urban factory settings. Women, particularly middle-class women, were to a large extent sequestered at home, which was no longer a center of production but was instead focused on the work of reproduction (both biological and cultural) and the newly emerging work of consumption that was vital to sustain industrial growth.[14] The market values and "masculine" rational principles of accumulation that dominated in the public sphere were countered by the moral values and emotional and expressive dimensions that governed the private and were said to be the province of "true womanhood."[15]

The partition of the social world into masculine and feminine spheres that emerged in the mid-nineteenth century gave rise to competing ideals for individual development. The sociologist Robert N. Bellah and his co-authors in *Habits of the Heart,* call these distinct sets of values utilitarian and expressive individualism.[16] Although Bellah and his colleagues don't align these distinctions specifically with gender, others have.[17] Utilitarian values are primarily associated with a masculine public world, while expressive values are associated with a feminine private or familial sphere. In the case of utilitarian individualism, human life is understood as a struggle in which individuals aim to advance their own self-interest narrowly defined in terms of attaining advantages of wealth and power. Man is understood as an economic animal—*Homo economicus*—an instrumentally rational creature engaged in calculations and strategy to advance his position. Cost-benefit analysis serves as the model for decision-making. This unsentimental and instrumental approach to the questions of daily life has come to be understood as a "masculine" worldview, despite the fact that women are fully capable of adhering to this view. Expressive individualism, on the other hand, was understood as a "soft" or "feminine" view of the world. The expressive vision of the world holds that humans are primarily sensing and feeling creatures, with unique emotional experiences that allow the individual to fuse with others and with nature, to experience a kind of oneness with the cosmos. With its roots in eighteenth- and nineteenth-century Romanticism, expressive individualism offers an image of human beings as joyful and playful—as *Homo ludens*[18]—a being that strives for harmony and unity with the natural world.[19] Ultimately, these competing and seemingly incommensurable notions of instrumental and expressive humanity have proven to be complementary and mutually reinforcing. Some scholars argue that these elements are a permanent feature of modern capitalism, with the expressive dimension providing a safety valve for the excesses of market-driven instrumental rationality.[20]

The Persistence of Calling

The nineteenth-century shift from domestic to factory production, with the emergence of gendered public and private spheres, in many ways provides a mirror image of what one can observe today. While the mid-nineteenth century saw men and women increasingly segregated in public and private spheres, the last quarter of the twentieth century witnessed women entering the paid labor force in ever greater numbers, gradually eroding not only the gender-based segregation of women and men but also transforming the nature of the public and private, commercial and intimate spheres.[21] Simultaneously, an increasingly globalized capitalism demanded new levels of competitiveness and productivity. Downsizing (the layoffs of white-collar and managerial workers who had previously been largely insulated from the recessionary contractions of the economy), outsourcing (the use of outside vendors and consultants for work previously handled by corporate employees), and the use of flexible, contingent temporary workers were some of the strategies employed by companies that were attempting to stay profitable in an increasingly competitive environment.[22] Each of these approaches—characterized as "flexible accumulation strategies"—created increasing uncertainty and insecurity for workers, and placed considerable pressure on the ideal of a single, lifelong occupational calling.

In this context, Cotton Mather's pastoral image of a man rowing to heaven gives way to the tanker ships and luxury liners of multinational capital. On these new, much vaster enterprises, workers must be specialized yet flexible; loyal to their captains yet ever ready to jump ship when new and more lucrative opportunities present themselves, and always ready to man the lifeboats when a particular industry is set adrift, runs aground, or founders on high seas. Nautical courtesies of "women and children first" are replaced with an ethos of every man, woman, and child for themselves, as family structures are increasingly fragmented, and "welfare reform" sinks the last of the lifeboats. While Mather's Christian imagined himself rowing toward heaven, the destination of the contemporary tanker ship seems far less certain. Yet the ideal of paired callings—a general calling focused on some version of salvation and a particular calling in the world of work—has managed to persist, albeit in newly improvised forms.

This is not the first time that the idea of calling has collided with economic circumstances requiring flexibility on the part of workers. The ideology of calling has a long history of adapting in the face of economic and social changes. Take the case of Benjamin Franklin, the quintessential self-made man, for whom "calling" and "occupational specialization" were actually at odds. The "self-making" that was possible for Franklin was the product of significant social and political upheaval. Freed from the tradition of landed aristocracy that had characterized European lives, and empowered by the emergence of literacy as a cultural value, Franklin's pursuit of his own "life course" was an apt exemplar of the new vision of meritocracy.[23] The individual was no longer given an identity by birth; rather, he had the opportunity to create himself anew, aspiring to any occupations and social positions that his energies and abilities could command.[24] Thus, in Franklin's case, his "self-making" was not limited to the pursuit of a single calling. Instead, he made his fortune as a printer; then, at midlife, he left the printing trade as a wealthy man, able to pursue his work as a writer, inventor, diplomat, and statesman unencumbered by the necessity of earning a living. This model is hardly the model of a man pursuing a singular calling. Rather than focusing on service in a single calling, Franklin emphasized "good works," or serving one's community in voluntary associations rather than through a particular occupation. Spiritual progress in a singular calling or profession, the Puritan ethic of serving God as a sign of election, was, for Franklin, secondary to the secular vision of creating sufficient wealth that one might be one's own master and serving the community by leading a life of civic virtue. Building the wealth that freed him from the necessity of earning a living allowed Franklin the opportunity to pursue his interests in science, politics, and community service.

By the mid-nineteenth century, Franklin's model of the self-made gentleman-citizen gave way to the forces of industrialization, as a new model of success emerged in the characters of Horatio Alger's morality tales. The typical hero of an Alger penny novel was a fatherless son whose uncanny good luck (chance meetings with wealthy benefactors or their distressed daughters) resulted in his progress not from rags to riches but from "rags to middle-class respectability."[25] The heroes of Alger's morality tales were as unmoored from the traditions of agrarian communities as were their readers; the figure of the fatherless son helped suggest an inevitable, though nonconfrontational, break with tradition and community.[26] Alger's stories are of particular interest, as they offer a rather strong alternative to the righteous pursuit of a calling. Despite the fact that the name Horatio Alger is used to telegraph the idea of the self-made man, in Alger's universe, the pursuit of a unique individual calling and self-making has a very minimal role in one's success. Instead, his heroes typically pursue a course of upward mobility through marriage to the daughter of a wealthy benefactor rather than through the development of an individual calling or passion. Thus Alger's self-made men were almost entirely "made" by others. While his characters are bound by convention to choose a moral path, success is more a function of good fortune and social opportunism—"luck" and "pluck"—than of a commitment to industry and self-improvement. That popular misconceptions about Alger's heroes would be at such variance with the actual characters and plots of his stories suggests some of the tensions in American fantasies of success. The belief in success through hard work was toggled to narratives that had already begun to eschew it.

Perhaps the ideal of following one's calling might have begun to lose its grip were it not for the emergence in the mid-nineteenth century of Transcendentalism and "self-culture," with its vision of self-realization through the pursuit of one's individual path irrespective of the demands of the increasingly industrialized, specialized, and hierarchical society. Although Transcendentalism was a Romantic reaction against the increasingly mechanized and calculating industrial society and against the specialization required by a new industrialized economic order, in one of the sublime paradoxes of capitalism's advancement, this philosophy served to bolster the ideal of pursuing a calling. Ralph Waldo Emerson, chief among the advocates of self-culture and self-fulfillment, advised the pursuit of one's individual talents regardless of the demands of society or the labor market in his 1841 essay "Self-Reliance":

> Insist on yourself; never imitate. Your own gift you can present
> every moment with the cumulative force of a whole life's cultiva-
> tion; but of the adopted talent of another, you have only an
> extemporaneous, half possession. That which each can do best,
> none but his Maker can teach him. . . . Do that which is assigned
> you, and you cannot hope too much or dare too much.[27]

Yet within the same essay, Emerson admires the occupational resourcefulness of the yeoman who demonstrated the capacity to change professions at any point:

> A sturdy lad from New Hampshire or Vermont, who in turn tries
> all the professions, who *teams it, farms it, peddles*, keeps a school,
> preaches, edits a newspaper, goes to Congress, buys a township,

and so forth, in successive years, and always, like a cat, falls on his feet, is worth a hundred of these city dolls. He walks abreast with his days, and feels no shame in not "studying a profession," for he does not postpone his life, but lives already. He has not one chance, but a hundred chances.[28]

Pursuit of self and the pursuit of a specific occupation are not equivalent. Emerson's endorsement of the generalist who can handle anything that comes his way reflects the values of a preindustrial life that required adaptibility (i.e., self-reliance) from individuals. Yet by 1870, in an essay called "Success," Emerson asserts that specialization, rather than occupational flexibility, is an expression of individuality:

> Each man has an aptitude born with him to do easily some feat impossible to any other. Do your work. I have to say this often, but nature says it oftener. 'T is clownish to insist on doing all with one's own hands, as if every man should build his own clumsy house, forge his hammer, and bake his dough; but he is to dare to do what he can do best; not help others as they would direct him, but as he knows his helpful power to be.[29]

During the thirty-year period between these essays, industrialization accelerated the already rapid erosion of rural and small town life that had characterized the previous century. Finding a calling in an increasingly specialized economy was critical to success, and conflating self-realization (what one might understand as a secularized version of Mather's "general calling") with occupational specialization (or one's particular calling) was one way of shoring up this destabilized construct.

Transcendentalism and the emergence of "self-culture" were by no means the only responses to these structural transformations wrought by industrialization. Religious revivalism, known as the Second Great Awakening (1813–38), was a dominant expressive feature of this social landscape. The historian Mary P. Ryan observes that revivalism provided a discourse for considering the sweeping economic and political changes that were underway without addressing the economic basis and social implications of the changes. While families were fractured by "the corrosive power of commerce," Ryan notes that they were inclined not to "express concerns in economistic terms . . . but rather in the language and central ideological structure of their time, that is, in an essentially religious mode of thought."[30]

Certainly the fundamentalist revivalism of the late twentieth century, though not the focus of this discussion, operates in tandem with self-improvement culture to provide ideological structures for understanding rapid social change.[31]

While religious revivalism helped ease the transition to an industrialized society, the notion of calling continued to adapt to accommodate shifting economic imperatives. In her study of Gilded Age success literature, Judy Hilkey observed how the notion of calling facilitated the transition to a national, corporate economy:

> Insofar as the Puritan notion of a calling evoked a presumably stable and pious albeit idealized past, it suggested that which was comfortably familiar and accepted in rural and small-town America: a view of work characterized by long-standing patterns of father-to-son occupational continuity and self-employment in farming, the trades, and local commerce. On the other hand, the more modern concept of choosing rather than inheriting one's life work opened the doors to a world of new possibilities. . . . Success writers helped to bridge the gap between these two different worlds of work when, by likening the selection of an occupation to a "calling," a Godly summons, they suggested that young men setting forth to find their fortunes were not roaming, drifting, or rejecting the values of the parental household, but rather were making a "choice determined by the prayerful and thoughtful exercise of judgment."[32]

By the turn of the century, the vast agglomerations of wealth that marked the Gilded Age shifted the meaning of success and tested the flexibility of the ideology of following one's calling as a means to success. The historian Richard Weiss notes the increasing equation of wealth with success: he observes that the first definition of success in terms of wealth occurs in the 1891 *New Century Dictionary*, while the first mention of wealth in terms of success occurs in the 1885 *Oxford English Dictionary*.[33] By the late nineteenth century, success became increasingly equated with wealth attained by any means. The consolidation of vast wealth in the hands of a few industrialists, and a burgeoning population of new millionaires, required moral justification. Success literature of the day, best exemplified by two bestselling books, Andrew Carnegie's 1902 *The Empire of Business* and Russell H. Conwell's 1915 *Acres of Diamonds*, proclaimed that creating wealth was a moral obligation. Conwell summarized the links between wealth and godliness: "To make money honestly is to preach the gospel."[34] Wealth was no longer a means of liberating oneself from labor (or from the necessity for instrumental or market-based reasoning). Instead of allowing one the leisure to cultivate one's self and serve one's community, wealth became, in and of itself, a sign of virtue. As Weber observed, the idea that an employer's business activity was itself "a calling," along with a doctrine of "the dignity of all labor," justified an increasingly inequitable situation:

> the whole ascetic literature of almost all denominations is saturated with the idea that faithful labour, even at low wages, on the part of those whom life offers no other opportunities, is highly pleasing to God. In this respect Protestant Asceticism added in itself nothing new. . . . And on the other hand it legalized the exploitation of this specific willingness to work, in that it also interpreted the employer's business activity as a calling. . . . The treatment of labour as a calling became as characteristic of the modern worker as the corresponding attitude toward acquisition of the business man.[35]

During this period of entrepreneurial upward mobility, success was increasingly divorced from any commitment to serving the community and was instead equated with abstract, ethereal flows of revenue. The emergence of New Thought, or a belief in the infinite potential of "mind-power," further justified disparities between the wealthy and the poor. A key proponent of New Thought, Ralph Waldo Trine, wrote a turn-of-the-century bestseller, *In Tune with the Infinite*, that put forward the central tenets of the movement. The book drew on the transcendental optimism of his namesake, Transcendentalism's own Ralph Waldo, and recapitulated Emerson's universe, governed by the Over-Soul and epitomized by individual self-discovery, self-reliance, and self-fulfillment. Success and wealth were signs of alignment with the infinite divinity of the Over-Soul. Although Emerson would have conceded that wealth and property, usually taken as reliable signs of worldly virtue, could be "counterfeited" through theft or inheritance, proponents of New Thought embraced a pragmatic idealism in which wealth and opportunity were characterized as equally available to all through a kind of cosmic abundance.[36] Even though the pursuit of wealth was not considered a useful end in itself among New Thought advocates, wealth was seen as a sign of goodness or attunement with the Infinite, while poverty was equated with sin and vice.

While New Thought may have germinated in the nineteenth-century private sphere—where spiritualism, mesmerism, and mind-cure were the occupations of middle-class women[37]—this was an ideology that quickly jumped the private-public divide as it provided a rhetoric of flows and energy, of an amorphous undifferentiated universe that served the interests of a developing corporate society.[38] Indeed, Trine was a favorite of Henry Ford: the industrialist commended him, noting that Trine's bestseller had sustained him during his efforts to organize his Dearborn factories.[39] The most segmented, rationalized productive spheres relied on a complementary spiritual realm of undifferentiated flows. Such sentiments continue to echo throughout the twentieth century in New Age self-help literature, as well as in such bestselling titles as Napoleon Hill's 1937 *Think and Grow Rich* and, more recently, Suze Orman's 1999 *The Courage to Be Rich*.

As turn-of-the-century fortunes were consolidated—limiting access to both capital and markets—the always tenuous and limited opportunities for advancement by the entrepreneurial route waned, giving way to white-collar corporate approaches to upward mobility.[40] Decreased opportunities for entrepreneurial advancement, coupled with vast new corporate structures, demanded additional adjustments to the ideal of success for American men. The conformity required in an increasingly white-collar corporate milieu called for interpersonal, rather than entrepreneurial, success. By 1956, the sociologist William H. Whyte saw a "decline of the Protestant ethic" and the rise of "the organization man," for whom conformity was prized over initiative.[41] The positive thinking of Emile Coué and Norman Vincent Peale and the corporate conformity and salesmanship featured in Dale Carnegie's 1936 *How to Win Friends and Influence People* met these needs. Dale Carnegie (born Carnegy, but revised in the image of Andrew) described a Hobbesian world in which smiles and good cheer were a kind of currency, with every man and woman able to advance themselves by understanding that all others were only out for themselves.[42] Getting ahead was linked to getting along, with the entrepreneurial aggression of the turn of the century subsumed in an economy of reassuring, if disingenuous, smiles.

The Organization Man and the Feminine Mystique

The midcentury corporate conformist—Whyte's "organization man"—relied to a great extent on his domestic partner, who labored under the social phenomenon that Betty Friedan labeled "the feminine mystique": the ghettoization of large numbers of educated, middle-class women in the role of domestic servants and caregivers.[43] The myth of the self-made man relied, to a very great extent, on the suppression of women's ambitions for the sake of those of their husbands and children. But this phenomenon was hardly new to the 1950s. Traditionally, the mythology of the self-made man had relied on the exploitation of women's labor in their roles of wives, mothers, and sisters, as well as on a pejorative understanding of "the feminine." Often the measure of a man's success was calculated on the basis of his ability to out-earn his wife's capacity for spending, a criterion for success that mirrored the separation of production and consumption, masculine and feminine.[44]

In her consideration of how women helped to "make" the self-made man, Judy Hilkey notes that there were two significant levels. First, at the level of representation, a negative equation of "the feminine" with failure provided an ideological counterpoint to the image of success as vital, virile, and masculine. Within the masculine public sphere, the characteristics associated with femininity—softness, gentleness, and the like—were associated with failure, even if they were sentimentalized in the private sphere. This association of feminine characteristics with failure or weakness continues today in all sorts of contexts. The cultural preference for hard bodies with "cut" and "ripped" muscles rather than soft, voluptuous, well-nourished, and nurturing bodies is one example.[45] Another is the characterization of a presidential candidate as "wishy-washy"—dangerously weak and indecisive when his positions are flexible and responsive to changes of context. And perhaps the most colorful example is California governor Arnold Schwarzenegger's characterization of his Democratic opponents (who were fighting to preserve social services in the midst of a state budget battle) as "girly-men." Softness, responsiveness, and concerns for the weaker and less advantaged members of society are associated with the "feminine" and denigrated. Beyond these metaphorical preferences for characteristics understood as masculine, at a second level—the level of material resources—the actual labor and material sacrifices of mothers and sisters supported sons and brothers in their aspirations to upward mobility.[46] The historian Mary P. Ryan observed that it was not uncommon for nineteenth-century women to pool their resources to support the business or educational efforts of sons, brothers, and sometimes husbands.[47]

Without a trace of irony, the nineteenth-century literature of the self-made man hailed women as the wellspring of male successes, with glowing tributes to the contributions of devoted mothers and helpmate wives in the masculine achievement of success.[48] The contradiction was writ large: what would it say about the myth of the self-made man if it were admitted that a man's wife held the key to her husband's success? The success myth itself required the suppression, if not the repression, of the role of women in male self-making. [49]

Others have contended that newly sequestered middle-class women of the mid-nineteenth century fulfilled their ambitions in spiritualist pursuits, rather than vicariously through the successes of male relatives. For example, the historian Donald B. Meyer argues that as nineteenth-century industrialization increasingly limited the role of middle-class women to home and consumption, the rise of mesmerism, spiritualism, and "mind-cure" answered the needs of middle-class American women for a professional outlet and a sense of personal power. Although more recently historians have begun recovering the all-but-lost history of self-making for women, these amendments to the dominant masculinist history, while important scholarship, ought not be taken to obscure the broader social reality that for the majority of women success was largely vicarious—experienced through husbands and offspring—and that their experiences of individual aims and goals were typically subordinated to the needs of others.[50]

The notion of pursuing an individual calling and the belief in a highly individualistic, self-determining model of human action have been central to the myth of the self-made man. This model of human action, which emphasizes the individual's independence or "agency" over the impact of the social milieu, was a profoundly masculine model. I say this notion was masculine not because only men could subscribe to such a belief system but because it was rooted in the values of a commercial sphere that had heretofore been dominated by men and because the resources and freedoms necessary to embrace such a worldview had been largely limited to men.[51] Women's lives or, more accurately, middle-class women's lives, which had been typically limited to the domestic sphere, followed other patterns, as the sociologist Dorothy Smith has noted:

> Characteristically for women (as also for others in the society
> similarly excluded), the organization of daily experience, the work
> routines and the structuring of our lives through time, has been
> and to a very large extent still is determined and ordered by
> processes external to, and beyond, our everyday world. I think I

would be by no means alone in seeing in my past not so much a career as a series of contingencies, of accidents, so that I seem to have become who I am also by chance. . . . When I read in autobiographies or fiction of the lives of other women, I find these same qualities and the surprises in store for the subject about whom she may become. I do not find them in the same way in the autobiographies of men.[52]

The idea that women ought to pursue success outside the traditional realm of home and family—specifically the popular notion that women ought to work at a career in pursuit of pleasure and self-fulfillment—did not begin to take hold until the early 1960s, with the publication of two germinal books: Helen Gurley Brown's 1962 *Sex and the Single Girl* and Betty Friedan's 1963 *The Feminine Mystique*. Brown's sensational, bestselling advice book made the radical assertion that unmarried women should be pursuing their own pleasure, not necessarily marriage. Work could be a more or less interesting and pleasurable way to pass the time, but, most important, it provided an ideal context in which to meet men:

> Now we're going to turn off men for a while and talk about your job. (Don't worry, we'll get back to them!) What you do from nine to five has everything to do with men anyhow. A job is a way of getting *to* them. It also provides the money with which to dress for them and dress up your apartment for them. . . . Most importantly, a job gives a single woman something to *be*.
>
> A married woman already *is* something. She is the banker's wife, the gangster's wife, the wrangler's wife, the strangler's wife, the conductor's wife (streetcar or symphony). . . .
>
> A single woman is known by what she does rather than by whom she belongs to.[53]

Brown's advice tied work to the pursuit of sexual or marital partners, while Friedan's position—that women ought to have the opportunity to pursue meaningful careers as part of a quest for self-fulfillment—was a relatively conservative position,[54] suggesting a somewhat more disembodied pursuit of self-fulfillment and identity:

> The only way for a woman, as for a man, to find herself, to know herself as person, is by creative work of her own. There is no other way. But a job, any job, is not the answer—in fact, it can be part of

the trap. Women who do not look for jobs equal to their actual capacity, who do not let themselves develop the lifetime interests and goals which require serious education and training, who take a job at twenty or forty to "help out at home" or just to kill extra time, are walking, almost as surely as the ones who stay inside the housewife trap, to a nonexistent future.[55]

While Friedan emphasized that working in a career was essential, Brown stressed that any kind of work to which one properly applied oneself could be satisfying and lead to opportunities. But each advised that taking a job for mere financial reward—out of financial necessity—or pursuing an avocation without professional status was not a route to self-realization.[56] Whether women got the message through Brown's self-help book or through Friedan's more serious scholarship, with these two books the idea that satisfaction in a career was part of a successful life had been extended to women. The implications of this shift, as I will show, have been far-reaching.

From Calling to Self-Actualization: The Therapeutic Turn

While the American mythology of the self-made man pursuing his calling has long served to buoy the hopes of working-class men with visions of entrepreneurial wealth and bootstrapping achievement, the late-twentieth-century doctrine of self-making had to accommodate several major changes in the social and economic landscape: the large-scale entry of women into the paid labor force, the parallel erosion of the division between the public and private spheres, and the emergence of a "flexible accumulation" economy. The shift from an industrial and corporate economy (or Fordist economic structures) to a flexible accumulation (or post-Fordist) model that streamlines profit making with downsizing, outsourcing, and the use of contingent labor has played havoc with the ideal of a lifelong career. In such a context, the belief in finding one's "calling," "mission," "vocation," or "path" ought to have gone the way of the Model T. Nevertheless, these ideas continue to serve as central images in the literature of self-improvement. As William H. Whyte might have anticipated, the decline of corporate structures that emphasized group affiliation has fostered a resurgence in the Protestant ethic, but in its contemporary version this ethic returns as both entrepreneurial and artistic, rational and expressive.

Logic would suggest that an economy that requires flexibility from its labor force would be at odds with an ideology based on finding one's calling or one true path in life. However, the ideology of calling has been in the process of reconstituting itself to accommodate these changing economic conditions. This new-styled version of the traditional calling has been adapted, and at points contorted, to provide exactly the kind of motivation required of a new labor force of women and men faced with temporary positions, downsizing, and non-elective self-employment; in short, to a lifestyle of economic insecurity. The tension between the near impossibility of working in a particular calling or vocation across the course of a lifetime and the ideology that finding one's particular calling is central to achieving salvation (or even this-worldly happiness) is mitigated in two ways: first, an increased emphasis on working on the self, and second, the ideal that one ought to pursue work one loves irrespective of compensation. The pursuit of self-actualization in work—both work on the self and in the labor force—becomes the latter-day equivalent of the Protestant state of grace. As the self-help author Barbara Sher points out, finding "one's own path" is offered as an antidote to the uncertainties that are inevitable in the new economy:

> Once you begin to find your own path, you will have positioned
> yourself at the forefront of a massive historical change. In late
> twentieth-century industrial society, just about everybody—like it or
> not—is going to have to figure out what kind of work and life he
> really wants. . . . Corporations are continuing to downsize, and not
> only because of recent recessions: We're entering a new period in
> economic history. Global competition is forcing companies to make
> themselves lean and mean. Corporations are becoming about a third
> the size they once were, and they'll probably never get big again.
> Middle management is gone. Secretaries are being replaced by
> technology. The top twenty students from every college or business
> school may still get good job offers, but everyone else is on their
> own.[57]

Compare Sher's 1994 advice to the general population faced with corporate restructuring to what Betty Friedan proposed in 1963 for women who wanted to avoid the pitfalls of the feminine mystique:

> Ironically, the only kind of work which permits an able woman to
> realize her abilities fully, to achieve identity in society in a life plan

that can encompass marriage and motherhood, is the kind that was forbidden by the feminine mystique; the lifelong commitment to an art or science, to politics or a profession. Such a commitment is not tied to a specific job or locality. It permits year-to-year variation—a full-time paid job in one community, part-time in another, exercise of the professional skill in serious volunteer work or a period of study during pregnancy or early motherhood when a full-time job is not feasible. It is a continuous thread, kept alive by work and study and contacts in the field, in any part of the country.[58]

The pursuit of one's ostensibly "true" or "genuine" work—one's unique "life plan," that was offered to women in the 1960s as insurance against the contingencies of married life—is revived for everyone in the 1990s as a means of forestalling the contingencies of the economy. One is saved from a life of meaningless contingency and accident by a self-conscious life plan. Work is reimagined, not as a deprivation for which one ought to be compensated but as means of expressing oneself, as a source of identity and personal fulfillment.[59]

This shift in the concept of work is due in no small measure to the influence of humanistic psychologists and psychiatrists in the late fifties and early sixties, among them Abraham H. Maslow, who popularized the use of the term "self-actualizing" to describe individuals who were self-motivating, self-directed, and devoted to some cause or vocation "fully, vividly and selflessly."[60] Identification with one's work was key: "These highly evolved individuals assimilate their work into the identity, into the self, i.e. work actually becomes part of the self, part of the individual's definition of himself."[61] Yet, paradoxically, according to Maslow, such persons are not "self-centered":

> Self-actualizing people are, *without one single exception*, involved in a cause outside their own skin, in something outside of themselves. They are devoted, working at something, something which is very precious to them—*some calling or vocation in the old sense, the priestly sense*. They are working at something which fate has called them to somehow and which they work at and which they love, so that the work-joy dichotomy in them disappears.[62]

Maslow introduced his work on human motivation to industrial managers and laid the groundwork for subsequent management gurus such as Tom

Peters, who would emphasize worker satisfaction and participation. His focus on creative, healthy—even, in his words—"saintly" individuals is also credited with (or incriminated in, depending on your point of view) infusing spirituality into the psychiatric and psychotherapeutic ethos.[63] Indeed, Maslow's work represents a moment where the "triumph of the therapeutic" (over religious structures and spiritual values) that has been posited by the historian Philip Rieff was clearly a victory of assimilation or appropriation rather than obliteration. Psychotherapeutic notions of health and well-being were conflated with spiritual values of saintliness or goodness, while the Protestant religious imperative to pursue a calling was wedded to notions of mental health and psychological well-being.

The importance of pursuing satisfying work was not a new idea, as the earlier review of Cotton Mather's sermon revealed. However, the suggestion that work ought to be pursued primarily for pleasure and self-realization—rather than as a source for sustenance of the individual, service to the community, and social solidarity or affiliation—constitutes a departure from prior values. Even eighteenth-century Puritan thinking asserted that the individual deserved to benefit materially from his or her labor: "*We* expect Benefits from *Humane Society*. It is but equal, that *Humane Society* should Receive Benefits from *Us*."[64] Although Maslow's motivational theories—including his oft-cited pyramid or hierarchy of needs—suggested that workers could only be self-actualizing when their more basic needs (physiological needs, safety, security, and affiliation) were adequately and consistently met, in common usage self-actualizing came to be understood as a characteristic or attribute of an individual personality or character rather than as a possibility for everyone in a society that ensured that all individuals' basic needs were met.

The ideal of a self-actualizing worker, a notion that fused religious and psychological discourses, provided a synthesis wherein self-fulfillment is foregrounded while economic compensation and service to the community recede into the background. Individuals are urged to search their souls to find their proper place in the social division of labor, and if they can't find a spot that suits their desires, they're supposed to search for their true self. Thus the idea of a general calling—though secularized as the pursuit and realization of one's true self—remains central. Work on the self—the quest for a path, the invention of a life, or the search for authenticity—is offered as an antidote to the anxiety-provoking uncertainties of a new economic and social order. It is this newly emerging self—the self perennially at work on itself and the self labored over by the self—that I call the belabored self. But before I turn to a fuller consideration of the belabored self, there is one additional development to consider: the emergence of an aesthetic dimension to augment the spiritual and therapeutic.[65]

From Calling to Composing: The Aesthetic Turn

While the notion of a calling has been newly psychologized as a sign of mental well-being, at the level of metaphor, the idea of calling—understood variously as one's "path," "vocation," and "mission"—has undergone significant transformations as it has been extended to include women. Although these terms are used almost interchangeably in the literature of self-improvement, it is important to tease out some of the distinctions. Calling, despite its secular usage, is a decidedly theistic concept: one responds to divine direction. The same can be said of vocation (from Latin *vocare*, "to call"). The idea of life as a journey, or the pursuit of a path, is rather more secular. The metaphor of the path or journey—in which life is understood in terms of geography, itinerary, crossroads and cul-de-sacs, mapping a course, and getting somewhere—is among the most common figures in the literature of self-improvement. The road is (more or) less traveled. One searches for "a path" or, even better, "a path with heart." One embarks on "*The Artist's Way*."[66] As mentioned earlier, this metaphor of the journey suggests a higher degree of self-direction on the part of the subject, and is arguably a rather masculine metaphor. In a culture where, until recently, women were to stay home and mind the hearth while men ventured forth into the unknown, the image of being on the road or path of life reflects a fundamentally gendered view of personal development. The classical narrative of the *Odyssey*, for example, features Odysseus's heroic quest while Penelope waits at home, each day weaving a funeral shroud that she nightly unravels in order to protect her rights to the *oikos*, the property she controls only as long as her husband remains alive. Some feminist theorists have argued that the metaphor of the journey, when viewed through a psychoanalytic lens, always constitutes the hero as male, while the terrain through which he navigates is inevitably understood as female.[67]

Not only is the idea of a journey masculine, the notion of responding to a calling suggests following the direction of a masculine, Judeo-Christian god. In the early 1990s, the self-improvement literature merged these concepts by adopting the idea of an individual "mission"—a term popularized by Stephen R. Covey's 1989 bestselling book, *The Seven Habits of Highly Effective People*. The idea of a mission combines the notion of a call or direction from a deity (in that *mission* comes from Latin *mittere*, to send) with the idea of a journey. Indeed, the first definition of "mission" in the compact edition of the *Oxford English Dictionary* is "body of persons sent to a foreign country to conduct negotiations."[68] In common usage, "mission" often refers to a military operation, further masculinizing this concept. The idea of mission as "a person's vocation or divinely appointed work in life" is the last definition offered. The notion of "mission" provides both a masculine director and a masculinized actor or agent, a characteristic that has created significant internal contradictions in Covey's advice (as noted earlier in relation to his advice to his daughter and as I will consider more fully in chapters 2 and 3). With the introduction of the notion of the "mission," the responsive, dialogue-based metaphor of the "calling" is fused with the image of the journey, creating a metaphor that is masculine by way of both its theistic tradition and its fundamental narrative structure.

Despite the masculine nature of the metaphors found in traditional self-improvement literature, these texts are most certainly not directed exclusively to men. On the contrary, women are an assumed and central audience, though not, as sometimes is suggested, a majority of readers.[69] However, women reading the ostensibly "unisex," one-size-fits-all literature of self-improvement may find themselves reading with a split consciousness or through a masculine or dominant-culture lens, wherein the experience of men is understood to be the norm—the human—while the experience of women (or any subordinate) group is perceived as the exception, as other.[70] The traditional unisex literature of self-improvement holds rather closely to the masculine models of action—calling, path, journey, mission—while a number of titles written for (and usually by) women begin to propose the notion that one's life be imagined as a work of art.

Of course, the ideal of an aestheticized life is not altogether new. The nineteenth century witnessed the emergence of an aestheticization of everyday life in figures such as the dandy, for whom superior taste and an uncompromising style were the tools that set him apart from the masses, who were held in contempt.[71] But the phenomenon of dandyism was an attempt to rebel against middle-class heterosexual norms and mores, while the contemporary ideal of life as a work of art is offered to the masses as a route out of meaningless, unsatisfying, and insecure work situations (and, not insignificantly, as a spur to consumption.)[72] Mary Catherine Bateson, whose work I will consider in greater depth in chapter 3, was among the first to suggest that the ideal of life as a work of art was a useful antidote to occupational insecurity. In her 1989 bestseller *Composing a Life*, she observed that "the fine old idea of a path and a commitment turns out to be illusory for many people."[73] An aesthetic and improvisatory metaphor, Bateson noted, would be useful as an alternative to both the masculine image of the journey and the phenomenon of increasingly common career detours. The idea of one's life as a work of art, as something to be invented or composed, transforms the occupational insecurity that faces contemporary workers. Instead of foreboding, this literature inspires a sense of possibility.

What exactly would it mean to imagine one's life as a work of art? The literatures of self-improvement that will be considered in greater detail in the coming chapters are somewhat vague regarding this very important point. Bateson suggests that imagining life as a work of art is to value the capacity for improvisation and flexibility, and to pursue goals that are incremental rather than monolithic, cyclic rather than linear. Success, in this model, would be found in attention to balance and proportion rather than in the achievement of a singular goal, however noteworthy. Having a fixed plan—a straightforward itinerary—with predictable benchmarks for success is, she argues, difficult, if not impossible, in the context of late-twentieth-century America. The idea of a life organized around aesthetic, rather than pecuniary or moral, values suggests the possibility of rethinking traditional concepts of achievement. At a time when achieving material success (and even security) became increasingly difficult for a preponderance of Americans, and during a period when traditional moral values were in flux, the idea of life as a work of art, however vaguely defined, offered a sense of creative possibility. Simultaneously, the idea of having a distinctive vision for one's life is consistent with an increasingly visual and media-saturated culture where style is privileged over substance.[74] The metaphor of creating a life eases the burden on the gendered metaphors of calling, path, journey, and mission, while offering an alternative to the increasingly anachronistic ideal of a singular calling.

Max Weber would not have been altogether surprised at this development. Although Weber placed his emphasis on the rational and productive sphere in his development of the Protestant ethic thesis, he was not oblivious to the important role of the expressive and aesthetic dimensions in an increasingly rationalized world. In his 1915 essay "Religious Rejections of the World and Their Direction," he observed a new role for art:

art becomes a cosmos of more and more consciously grasped independent values which exist in their own right. Art takes over the function of a this-worldly salvation. . . . It provides a salvation from the routines of everyday life, and especially from the increasing pressures of theoretical and practical rationalism. . . . [A]rt begins to compete directly with salvation religion.[75]

The aesthetic metaphor increasingly offered an alternative to the religious and theistic, and, within the literature of self-improvement, the emerging ideal of life as a work of art bridges the gap between the secular and the spiritual, while privileging the expressive over the instrumental, or utilitarian, dimension.

Self-help literature does not abandon its traditional terms of missions, paths, roads less traveled, and individual calling. Instead, the literature offers something for everyone. For those who subscribe to a traditional theistic framework, the idea of a general calling—the pursuit of salvation— continues to function as a powerful consolation when the possibility of a personal or particular calling is preempted by the vagaries of the labor market. For those who hold to an agnostic worldview, the increasingly prevalent idea of a life as a work of art, or as one's own invention, serves a similar conciliatory purpose. While Weber imagined that "duty in one's calling prowls about our lives like the ghost of dead religious beliefs," today the ideal of pleasure in one's work—the duty to find pleasure in one's work— prowls around in our lives as the synthesis of the Protestant and Romantic ethics. How these metaphors—of calling and vocation, of mission and path, of works of art and invention—function in the contemporary success and "conduct of life" literatures will be the topic of the next two chapters.

To trace the evolution of the belabored self, this analysis will turn now to a close consideration of the self-help literature itself, focusing on the bestselling literature during the period from 1972 to the turn of the millennium. A careful analysis of the metaphorical structures of the advice literatures of this era reveals a story of continuity and divergence. But, as is the case with most instances of change, continuity and divergence coexist; new notions are bundled inside of old ones, and old ideas can masquerade as revolutionary thinking. For the most part, the literature directed at men, or at a general audience, reflects a strong continuity with its eighteenth- and nineteenth-century antecedents, as well as an inward turn or focus that some social theorists suggest has been underway since the early eighteenth century.[76] Traditional religious and theistic concepts are presented in popular secular language (as in, for example, the work of Stephen R. Covey or M. Scott Peck) and nineteenth-century spiritualism and mind-power is updated with a cybernetic flavor (in, for example, the work of Anthony "Tony" Robbins). The exceptions to this continuity within the literature directed toward men is the emergence of a stark survivalism that, though present in the culture at large as a tendency toward social Darwinism, was unprecedented in advice literatures that had previously couched their recommendations in religious or spiritual terms.

chapter 2

From *Power!* to *Personal Power!*

Survivalism and the Inward Turn

To judge from the rather great discrepancy between the recommen-
dations of the most popular self-help books and the behavior of
Americans as described in the testimony of observers, the primary
function of the self-improvement handbook was not so much to
guide behavior as to explain the dynamic changes of American life
in terms of badly shaken traditional verities.
—John G. Cawelti

T he historian John Cawelti's observation regarding mid-nineteenth-
century advice books might also be applied to more recent self-improvement
literature. Late-twentieth-century and contemporary self-help books attempt
to explain changing social and economic conditions. At the same time, some
of this literature—particularly titles directed toward women—precipitates
aspects of these changes by proposing specific new attitudes, behaviors, and
strategies for coping.

Perhaps the most prominent shift in the social landscape during the last
quarter of the twentieth century has been the large-scale entry of women
into the paid labor force. According to the 2003 *Economic Report of the*
President, the number of women working outside the home between 1970
and 2001 increased by nearly 16 percent, while the number of men declined
by close to 5 percent.[1] Coincidental with this shift, and perhaps at least in
part consequent to it, real wages remained stagnant during all but the last
three years of this period. Simultaneously, increasing globalization has contributed to the demand for a cheaper and more flexible domestic labor
force—flexibility that has been achieved, in part, through the use of contingent or temporary workers.[2] So-called downsizing has made "the organization man" of William H. Whyte's day increasingly anomalous, while

the values of the second wave of feminism have offered middle-class women the opportunity to trade-in Betty Friedan's "problem that has no name" for what Arlie Russell Hochschild has called "the second shift" and, more recently, "the time bind."[3] In the early 1980s, Hochschild observed that women living with husbands, children, and/or dependent elderly parents were working two shifts—one in their places of employment, and the second when they got home from work only to confront the work of maintaining their families. By the end of the 1990s, she observed that both women and men living with families were confronted with a third shift: struggling to manage the multiple demands on their finite time while trying to compensate for the emotional toll that these time shortages exacted from their families.

But despite the fact that recent advice literature serves to help people coping with changing social and economic conditions, it would be a mistake to suggest that this literature is rich in formal and substantive innovation.[4] For the most part, an overview of advice literature of the past thirty years presents a story of more continuity than divergence. Indeed, a close analysis of the literature will demonstrate that most advice books—particularly those titles that are directed toward a general audience rather than targeted to women—draw on figures from previous literatures. Perhaps most important, the unisex or general advice literature reflects an ongoing turn toward interior concerns—an inward turn that, philosophers and social theorists have observed, constitutes a key feature of modernity. Against this backdrop of continuity there are three substantial developments, one in the unisex literature of self-help and the others in the literatures addressed to women. In the literature addressed toward a general audience, a stark survivalism emerges at the beginning of the 1970s, coinciding with the first of the so-called oil shocks and with the beginning of a period of declining wages and increased competition in the labor market. While survivalism, in the form of social Darwinism, had long justified an American belief in the merits of entrepreneurial competition, bald proposals that one ought to "look out for # 1" or "win through intimidation" marked a new ruthlessness in the self-help landscape, a terrain that had previously been marked by its scriptural homilies or appeals to winning friends. In the literatures addressed toward women, a pair of ideas emerged: on the one hand women were urged to apply market principles to their intimate lives—to avoid the newly constructed pathology of "codependence"—and on the other hand they were invited to imagine their lives as creative adventures, as works of art. This chapter will consider the unisex or general audience advice literature of this period, exploring the new survivalism that emerges against the background of a continuing inward turn, while the next chapter will take up the literature addressed to women, with its more substantial innovations.

To track the continuities and divergences in this literature, this analysis will focus on the metaphors that advice authors use to characterize human life. These metaphors include life imagined as a battle, a game, or a sport; a journey or adventure; or a business enterprise. In these cases, individuals are imagined as combatants, contestants, or players; travelers or explorers; and entrepreneurs, salespersons, or managers. For the combatants, contestants, and players, winning is the goal, while power and wealth are typically the prizes. For the traveler or explorer, rewards tend to be experiential, nonmaterial, and spiritual; the traveler is encouraged to "travel light" or "let go of extra baggage." For the entrepreneur, salesperson, or manager, as for the combatant, the goals tend to be material or financial. When life is a business, one is constantly selling or managing oneself. This "enterprising self"—to use the term applied by the social theorist Nikolas Rose[5]—maximizes his or her worldly opportunities through charismatic salesmanship, rational management, or a combination of both. The figure of the artist or visionary for whom life is an aesthetic experience to be imagined and created appears more frequently in the literatures addressed to women, though by the mid-1990s, in response to the staggering volatility of employment markets, the figure of the artist appears frequently in career advice directed to women and men alike. Finally, there is a sixth character: that of the servant ministering to the needs of others. Other metaphors—for example, the self as a computer with mind as software directing body as hardware, or the directional, spatial metaphor of success as "climb to the top"—also operate in the literature. Typically, the most successful authors deploy multiple metaphors for life and success in the interest of creating more compelling images for readers.

While this analysis will focus on the metaphorical constructs invoked in this literature, one might also keep in mind that there are a series of categories or ideal types that can be identified in this literature that coincide with categories observed by others.[6] These types fall roughly along the lines described by Weber: the rational and expressive dimensions. In the rational dimension, one finds a rational-economic man (*Homo economicus*) and a rational-ethical man (following in the tradition of a Kantian ethical imperative),[7] while in the expressive dimension, one finds an antimodernist, mystical type and, with increasing frequency, an aesthetic type. For the rational-economic man, one most frequently finds the metaphors of life as a jungle, a war, a competitive sport, and, of course, a business. In these constructs, the self is understood as an animal, a combatant, a competitor, and either a manager or a salesman or both. The rational-ethical self is most often represented by the figure of the traveler or the humble servant. The rational self—whether governed by economic self-interest or abstract ethics—is also imagined as a cybernetic being that can be programmed for the most effective results. The expressive elements, with metaphors of light, liquidity, and "flows," as well as the ideal of life as work of art, are more typically, but not exclusively, found in the literature addressed toward women. Taken together, these types offer complementary but, not infrequently, contradictory directives to guide the conduct of life.

The Jungle, the Poker Game, and the Survival of the Fittest

Among the most dramatic features in the social and cultural landscape of the 1970s was a renewed sense of scarcity.[8] Middle-class Americans, who had grown accustomed to postwar prosperity, were faced with double-digit inflation, growing unemployment rates, and the first of the oil shocks. A thriving counterculture, made possible in part by the economic affluence of the 1960s, had fostered values of communality that rapidly gave way to what some called "a culture of narcissism" or the "me decade." Against this economic and social backdrop, a new social Darwinism gained credibility; it appeared in the self-improvement literature as metaphors of life as a game and the world as a jungle. Titles such as Robert J. Ringer's 1973 *Winning Through Intimidation* and his 1977 *Looking Out for Number One*, along with Michael Korda's 1975 *Power! How to Get It, How to Use It*, rose to the *New York Times* bestseller list. Ringer, for example, a real estate broker turned libertarian author, describes the working world as a place where "reality confronts a man when he goes out into the business-world jungle and gets clawed and kicked."[9] Michael Korda offers a similar view: "in many offices one can see scenes that remind one of the carnage of the jungle—the stifled shrieks of the victim and the triumphant cry of the successful predator."[10] This is a world where, clearly, it's every man for himself, with winners and losers clearly marked, even if the metaphor of the jungle is softened with the metaphor of the game or the contest, a rhetorical strategy Ringer pursues:

> I thought of the earth as a giant poker table upon which the game of business is played, with only a fixed number of chips on the table. Each player gets to participate for an unknown period of time, and the name of the game is for him to see how many of the chips he can pile onto his stack.[11]

Ringer's own three-part typology of human nature includes:

- Type Number 1, people who are out to get "your chips" and let you know it;
- Type Number 2, people who insist that they want you to get what you deserve, but actually have their eye on your chips all along, and
- Type Number 3, people who genuinely want you to get what you want, but wind up swiping your chips anyway.[12]

In such a world, the self is continuously embattled, though the image of the jungle or the battlefield gives way to the image of the game—in Ringer's case, the image of poker, the quintessential game of opportunity and ruse.

Yet, despite the metaphorical structure of the game or contest, where there is necessarily a clear delineation of winners and losers, no one is ever to see himself or herself as a victim: victims are specifically abhorred. Characterizing oneself as a victim—or, worse still, falling into the role of victim—is anathema. In another bestseller from the same period, the psychologist Wayne W. Dyer asserts: "YOU CAN RARELY BE A VICTIM UNLESS YOU ALLOW IT TO HAPPEN."[13] Dyer devotes the entire first chapter of his 1978 book *Pulling Your Own Strings* to instructing the reader in how to become a "non-victim." Similarly, Korda quotes a successful executive as one who has no patience for explanations about downturns, problems, or failures: "What I want to know is not why you're down, it's 'When are you going to be up?' Give me the how, not the why."[14] Tellingly, Ringer's "Number One"—his self-portrait—is represented throughout his two books by cartoon images of a determined tortoise racing against the superior speed of the hare in the proverbial image of the probable loser transformed into the winner.[15] By deploying this image of life as a journey—albeit a race—any setback can be readily recast as temporary and thus one never falls into that loathed category of "victim."

If identifying oneself as a victim of unfair social circumstances—which had served as a point of departure for collective action throughout the sixties and early seventies—were deemed unacceptable, then involvement in any collective social change would be ridiculed. For example, in *Looking Out for Number One*, Ringer characterizes all collective actions as "crusades" and proceeds to disparage them accordingly:

> There are many reasons why group action is irrational from the individual's standpoint, including the following: 1) The group may never accomplish its intended purpose, in which case the individual might someday feel very bitter over the time and energy wasted—time and energy which could have been supplying fuel needed to better his own life. . . . 2) In many respects, there is weakness in numbers, not strength. . . . 3) Even if the project is "successful," you have no way of knowing that you'll live long enough to enjoy the results.[16]

Ringer goes on to list an array of other "reasons" for avoiding group action and concludes with "the cruelest reality of all . . . *your participation is unlikely to make any difference*. In fact, it probably will retard the cause, since every additional body only adds to the divergence of opinion, the bureaucratic muddling and all the other time-wasting features of group action."[17] In the wake of a decade of social movements for civil rights, and at the outset of the second wave of American feminism, each of these bestselling authors places a premium on isolated individual action on one's own behalf.

The self of this period is embattled and beleaguered: the world it inhabits is a hostile one not unlike that imagined by philosopher Thomas Hobbes. Life, though a game, is emphatically not a team sport. The successful self is the Winner; the chief criterion for evaluating success is the acquisition of power and wealth. While the metaphors of life as a game or battle and the world as a jungle are time-tested images, an unembellished argument for self-interest, shorn of any moral or ethical pretense, is something new in the literature of success, which had hitherto been bolstered with some moral or spiritual justification or constituted in a religious context. Such individualistic self-interest had been advocated in seventeenth- and eighteenth-century European philosophy, where Hobbes had postulated a natural world of constant strife, and Adam Smith advocated the unbridled pursuit of individual self-interest. But even Hobbes saw his contentious natural world regulated by a social contract, while Smith saw individual self-interest guided by "an invisible hand": for Smith, economic self-interest would miraculously prove more beneficial to each and all than charitable intent.[18]

Ringer goes one step beyond even Adam Smith, as he has no concern for the interest of others except insofar as the complete disregard for the needs of another may result in a tarnished reputation:

CONSIDERING THE OTHER GUY'S DESIRES IS IN YOUR LONG-TERM
BEST INTEREST.

   Remember the reality of self-interest. If there's nothing in it for
   the other person, you may get in his pockets once, but in the long
   term you're going to lose a customer, client or business associate and
   will inherit a deserved black mark in the financial community.[19]

The all-but-unmitigated ambition and shameless guile of the Winner as represented in Ringer and Korda suggest that something new is at work in the literature of self-improvement, even if such ideas are not in themselves new to the culture.

By the early 1980s, the reaction to these every-man-for-himself titles emerged with the arrival of two bestsellers focused on the topic of nego-tiating: *Getting to Yes: Negotiating Agreement Without Giving In* and *You Can Negotiate Anything.*[20] While still focused on the idea that one can win, or prevail, in any situation, these advice books also assumed that there were others worthy of honest negotiation, rather than overt manipula-tion or intimidation. Roger Fisher and William Ury, the authors of *Get-ting to Yes*, offer what they call a "principled alternative" to "playing hard or soft ball," to negotiating out of either adversarial or friendly positions.[21] Their negotiation techniques, along with their notion of "principled" reso-lution of a conflict, would reappear at the close of the decade with Stephen R. Covey's emphasis on "principle centered" leadership and "win win" negotiations.[22] Efforts to resolve the tensions between the stark individual self-interest advocated in the survivalist self-help literature of the 1970s and the values of community and equality that had dominated the social landscape in the 1960s would continue to shape the self-improvement literature of the subsequent decades. These efforts emerged in the self-improvement literature in a renewed emphasis on spiritual values recast as a therapeutic theism.

Spiritual Consolation Prizes, or *The Road Less Traveled*

The existence of the winner implies its opposite, the loser. The loser, like the victim, is an unpopular character that is easily banished with another well-worn metaphorical construct: the idea of life as a quest or journey, with an adventurer or traveler encountering a series of tests or obstacles in the pursuit of some goal or destination.[23] While there are countless examples of self-help literature employing the metaphor of the path or journey, the success of M. Scott Peck's 1978 bestseller *The Road Less Traveled* is perhaps the most prominent. Although it took five years for Peck's spiritual Baedeker to make its way to the *New York Times* bestseller list, the paperback edition managed to remain there for a record-breaking 694 weeks, and ultimately sold somewhere between 6 and 7 million copies. As of 1997, Simon and Schuster's publicity department reported that they'd given up keeping track of the sales.[24]

The phenomenal popularity of *The Road Less Traveled* has been the topic of many journalistic investigations that point to the book's Christian themes, which made it a strong seller among Bible Belt readers,[25] as well as to the author's tireless promotion through weekly lectures.[26] Although the book's sales started slowly, an enthusiastic review by Phyllis Theroux in the *Washington Post* made the difference, and Peck's first book climbed the *Post*'s bestseller list.[27] Peck and an assistant sent photocopies of the Theroux review to three hundred newspapers, and eventually the book appeared on the *New York Times* paperback bestseller list, where it remained almost continuously for thirteen years. In *The Road Less Traveled*, Peck, once an agnostic military psychiatrist, recounts his spiritual "journey" from the secular medical realm of psychiatry to a hybrid realm of psychotherapeutic and Christian values. The success of Dr. Peck's therapeutic theism is a prime example of the fusion of psychotherapeutic values with traditional Protestant values.[28] Mental health or well-being is recast as "grace," yet the early Puritan debate about whether grace can be earned through hard work or only freely bestowed by the divine fiat survives throughout Peck's work.

On the one hand, Peck paints a world in which "life is difficult" but where hard work, honesty, and self-discipline can lead to spiritual growth and mental health, which, for Peck, are their own rewards.[29] Peck's alternative to unbridled self-interest is a version of Christianity in which evil is recast as laziness. Whereas the New Testament offers the advice that one should "consider the lilies that neither toil nor weep," Peck describes a world where "original sin does exist; it is our laziness" and where goodness springs from hard work, self-discipline, delayed gratification, and honesty.[30] Growth, spiritual growth, isn't effortless but forced. Perhaps it is no coincidence that Peck's book arrived on the *New York Times* bestseller list in 1983, the year that marked the highest level of unemployment in the postwar period. Life *was* difficult in the extreme for millions of Americans. Peck's *Road Less Traveled* shared the bestseller list with Richard N. Bolles's *What Color Is Your Parachute?*, in which spiritual uplift was augmented with practical job-hunting advice for the millions of unemployed Americans. (I consider the *Parachute* series in greater detail in chapter 4, where I take up the topic of career advice books.)

On the other hand, despite the fact that work—work on the self—is central to Peck's journey, Peck struggles to reconcile the relative merits of work and "grace." Although he insists that grace is something earned, he immediately contradicts himself, asserting that grace is bestowed freely:

> Essentially I have been saying that grace is earned. And I know this to be true.
>
> At the same time, however, I know that that's not the way it is at all. We do not come to grace; grace comes to us. Try as we might to obtain grace, it may yet elude us. We may seek it not, yet it will find us.[31]

Even in the spiritual realm, rewards are uncertain, paralleling the lack of any assurances that hard work will pay off in the material world. Peck's *Road Less Traveled* proposes a spiritual alternative in a world where the likelihood of material success became, for the average American, an increasingly elusive goal. His therapeutic theism served much the same anesthetizing role that had previously been the sole province of religion.

Throughout the period of the 1980s, numerous spiritual consolation books surfaced on the bestseller lists. For example, Robert Schuller's four buck-up books—*Tough Times Never Last, But Tough People Do* (1983), *Tough-Minded Faith for Tender-Hearted People* (1985), *The Be (Happy) Attitudes* (1985), and *Be Happy You Are Loved* (1986)—each attempted to ameliorate the painful realities of life in a contracting economy with home-spun, scripturally derived homilies and with "possibility thinking." Schuller's "possibility thinking" updates the "positive thinking" of his fellow minister in the Reformed Church in America, Norman Vincent Peale. Robert Fulghum's *All I Really Need to Know I Learned in Kindergarten* (1986) and *It Was On Fire When I Lay Down On It* (1988), both of which also enjoyed long runs on the bestseller lists, announced themselves as offering simple advice in simple language in a profoundly complicated time. And from a somewhat different tradition, Rabbi Harold S. Kushner reflects on the nature of suffering and happiness in *When Bad Things Happen to Good People* (1981) and *When All You've Ever Wanted Isn't Enough* (1986). Referencing the isolated individualism that had marked the self-help literature of the prior decade, Kushner offered a chapter entitled "The Loneliness of Looking Out for Number One."[32] The cultivation of a spiritual life and an orientation toward community provided a counterpoint to the unbridled self-interest of the prior decade.

Spiritual consolation prizes are nothing new in the literature of self-improvement. The use of religious messages to sanction business behaviors and buoy those defeated by market values is a long-established practice in self-improvement manuals. Indeed, the history of American success literature is filled with ministers providing moral justification and spiritual boosterism. The nineteenth and early twentieth century saw ministers such as Henry Ward Beech, Lyman Abbott, Russell H. Conwell, and Horatio Alger, Jr., bridging the gap between religious and secular self-help literature and developing new techniques for delivering their messages to mass audiences.[33] Bruce Barton, author of the bestselling *The Man Nobody Knows* (1924), which offered the first representation of Jesus as a businessman, also founded an advertising agency, advocated the use of mass-marketing techniques for selling the religious message, and developed a corporate model for churches. Others of that era, for example, Emmet Fox, the pastor of the Church of the Healing Christ in New York City, and Harry Emerson Fosdick, the pastor of Riverside Church in New York City, also reached out well-beyond the confines of their churches. When Fox outgrew his church, he rented the Hippodrome, Carnegie Hall, and the Manhattan Opera House to preach to growing crowds. His 1934 *Sermon on the Mount* reportedly sold in excess of six hundred thousand copies and was widely read by clergymen, while his 1932 *Power Through Constructive Thinking* sold 250,000 copies and packaged New Thought for a new generation facing not prosperity, but the Depression. Similarly, Harry Emerson Fosdick took his message to the airwaves and through his radio broadcasts became one the most widely known Protestant ministers of his day.[34]

Uplifting without requiring a serious commitment of time or resources, self-help literature offers inspiration by, in the words of the sociologist Wendy Simonds, "shrinking God."[35] Studying readers of self-help literature, another sociologist, Paul Lichterman, observed that self-improvement literature "does not support a deep commitment from readers. Over a period of years, some readers do dive repeatedly into self-help reading, but they discover and rediscover that it is not such a long way from surface to bottom."[36] Less demanding than traditional religious reading and practices—and promising not only spiritual uplift but also worldly success—much popular self-improvement literature, including the most contemporary examples, interpolates spiritual traditions as "natural laws" or "scientific principles." This combination of spiritual traditions with a rhetoric of science is most evident in the work of two bestselling authors, Anthony "Tony" Robbins and Stephen R. Covey.

Charismatic Science and Rational Nature: Anthony "Tony" Robbins and Stephen R. Covey

In the second half of the 1980s and throughout the early part of the 1990s, two self-improvement authors with very different approaches found their way onto the *New York Times* bestseller list with the help of the same Dallas-based book agent, Jan Miller.[37] Anthony "Tony" Robbins and Stephen R. Covey represent two distinct traditions of self-improvement culture: the former privileges emotion and the affective dimension while the latter heralds the superiority of reason, planning, and time management. Yet, paradoxically, Robbins engages in a rhetoric of high-tech science, while Covey engages in a discourse of "timeless natural laws." Robbins fills stadiums, where he puts on charismatic performances of the miracles of mind-power that rival any evangelical revival, while Covey, the president of the FranklinCovey Company, preaches a gospel that is more akin to that of Benjamin Franklin, with whom he shares cobilling in the company's name.[38] Indeed, Robbins is not unaware of his own relationship to evangelical tendencies in the culture. His infomercial coproducer Greg Renker noted that "The infomercial boomed because the televangelists ran into problems. We are the new televangelists."[39] The inheritors of the traditions of Jonathan Edwards and Benjamin Franklin, respectively, Robbins and Covey represent divergent approaches to the pursuit of success, with the former focusing on the tools of sales and the latter employing the tools of management.

In 1978 (the same year that, across the continent, M. Scott Peck was promoting his *Road Less Traveled*) Anthony Robbins, then a twenty-five-year-old nutritional supplements salesman, began offering a $470 "Mind

Revolution" seminar that featured a "firewalk"—a walk across a twelve-foot-long bed of hot coals—as its graduation promenade.[40] The "firewalk" became a Robbins trademark, and within a few years Robbins was earning enough to purchase a Spanish colonial mansion overlooking the Pacific.[41] Robbins's approach owes much of its appeal to his pseudoscientific language. He refers to his methods as "technologies," his business enterprises are organized as a "research institute"—Robbins Research International—and his program relies on a model of a cybernetic self that can be programmed for "maximum personal performance."[42] The basis of the Robbins approach is classic American self-improvement: the power of mind over matter. Hailing back to Mary Baker Eddy's establishment of the Christian Science Church and the nineteenth-century preoccupation with mesmerism, mind-power has long been legitimized by fusing a rhetoric of science with scripture and divine revelation. With the emergence of mind-power came the belief that one is completely responsible for one's own reality: that one creates reality. The belief that Christian Science, rather than medical science, holds the cure to illness ensures that health is increasingly equated with holiness.[43] Thus Robbins's beginnings, as a nutritional supplements salesman, and his emphasis on a particular diet, is fitting: in the doctrine of mind-power, health is the new religion, and one cannot hope for success without it.

By the early 1960s, mind-power—which had continued in the bestsellers of Norman Vincent Peale and Napoleon Hill—was revitalized and reinfused with credibility by the application of a cybernetic model. Maxell Maltz, a New York plastic surgeon turned self-help author, noticed that even after successful plastic surgery many of his patients remained dissatisfied. To remedy this, he suggested that the mind was akin to a computer that simply needed to be properly programmed. His 1960 *Psycho-Cybernetics* became, over time, a bestseller; by 1997 the paperback versions had sold 4 million copies.[44] Some estimates put total worldwide sales of the book, including the five English-language editions and the foreign translations, at in excess of 30 million copies.[45] Mind-power was reinvigorated with a new scientific, cybernetic legitimacy.

Robbins struck on this theme, adapting a little-known and unproven psychotherapeutic technique called "neurolinguistic programming" that had been developed by the linguist John Grinder and the Gestalt therapist and computer programmer Richard Bandler.[46] In a blend of Pavlovian behavior modification and cybernetic language, neurolinguistic programming proposes that desired behaviors and feelings can be "installed": that human emotion and action can be programmed as simply as software is installed in a computer. Imagining that the brain is hardware for which thoughts and feelings are little more than software is an ideology with its roots in the seventeenth-century mechanism of thinkers such as Rene Descartes.[47] Soul or mind is meant to govern body, and one arrives at a theory of mind over matter.

While mind-power was a well-established strain of self-improvement culture, it received an upgrade with the added luster of cybernetic technologies:

> Our brain processes information much the way a computer does. It takes fantastic amounts of data and organizes them into a configuration that makes sense to that person. A computer can't do anything without software, which provides the structure to perform specific tasks. Metaprograms operate much the same way in our brain. They provide the structure that governs what we pay attention to, how we make sense of our experiences, and the directions in which they take us. . . . To communicate with a computer, you have to understand its software. To communicate effectively with a person, you have to understand his metaprograms.[48]

The philosopher Charles Taylor comments that the tendency to imagine the human mind as a computer provides a "self-image [that] is enhanced by the sense of power that goes along with a disengaged instrumental grasp of things."[49] Yet Robbins takes an interesting turn with this metaphor:

> I see our neurological activity as more like a jukebox. What really happens is that human beings keep having experiences that are being recorded. We store them in the brain like records in a jukebox. As with the records in a jukebox, our recordings can be played back at any time if the right stimulus in our environment is triggered, if the right button is pushed.[50]

Combining the metaphors of the computer and the jukebox, Robbins fuses what would otherwise be a rational notion of the self—an idea of disengaged reason—with the expressive dimension of music. In this sense, Robbins moves toward a hybrid of the rational and the expressive. Rather than suggesting, as does Stephen Covey, that self-control should govern the self through the ascendance of mind over body (exercising "character," or, in Covey's metaphor for early rising, "mind over mattress"),[51] Robbins imagines each of us as the disc-jockeys and film directors of our own lives, programming, rather than suppressing, our impulses. In this sense, Robbins leaves behind the Enlightenment notion of the reasonable creature and moves in the direction of a Nietzschean model of "giving style to one's life."[52] Perhaps through his reading of Bandler and others on "neurolinguistic programming," Robbins adopted some of the ideas put forth by more scholarly linguists such as George Lakoff and Mark Johnson, who suggest that metaphors, unconscious and otherwise, shape the individual's worldview. While typically the self-help literature operates with a number of metaphors, Robbins was among the first in the genre to step back and consider the role of metaphors in shaping individual realities.

Given that Robbins uses a rhetoric of science and technology to legitimize his approach, it's not surprising that he was also one of the first of the self-improvement gurus to avail himself of new technologies for distributing his message. Taking advantage of the 1984 Federal Communications Commission's ruling that deregulated television advertising and made way for the infomercial, Robbins has produced one of the most successful infomercials in the short history of the form, reportedly selling $120 million worth of audiotapes in his first five years of broadcasting.[53] His annual sales from seminars and audiotapes are reported to be in the neighborhood of $50 million per year.[54] Robbins also pioneered the use of the internet for self-improvement culture.[55] Robbins's success stems not from anything new or startling in either his message or his understanding of metaphor, but from his effective use of new distribution technologies. Mind-power, a staple of American self-improvement culture, is packaged in handy compact disc and cassette tape format, available today in three easy payments charged to one's credit card. As with Dale Carnegie before him, whose success has been attributed in part to the advent of the pocket book paperback edition,[56] Robbins capitalized on an emerging marketing technique to launch his mind-power empire. In fact, Robbins's sales in the traditional book form are considerably more modest than those of other bestselling self-improvement and motivational speakers. His first bestseller, the 1986 *Unlimited Power*, sold only a quarter of a million copies in its first eight years, and his second, the 1991 *Awaken the Giant Within*, has sold somewhat more than a million copies.[57] While these are better than respectable sales figures for book publishing in general, they are on the low side for bestselling self-help books, and are a fraction of the sales for his audiotapes. *Personal Power II* alone is reported to have sold more than 35 million copies. Rather than relying on print media, Robbins has built his empire on the sales of audiotapes and compact discs and the production of charismatic revival-style spectacles.

Capturing a sense of power and wonder, Robbins's promotional materials are replete with images of nature as a force to be reckoned with: volcanoes, tidal waves, lightning strikes, and other images of natural power that suggest potency and flows. Indeed, Robbins, like the mind-power advocates of the early twentieth century, assures readers that everyone can tap into a universal consciousness or flow:

> many prominent scientists and brain researchers, such as physicist David Bohm and biologist Rupert Sheldrake, believe there is a collective consciousness we all can pull from—and that when we align ourselves through belief, through focus, through optimal physiology, we find a way to dip into this collective consciousness.
>
> Our bodies, our brains, and our states are like a tuning fork in harmony with that higher level of existence.[58]

Recall the language of Ralph Waldo Trine from a century earlier:

> This is the Spirit of Infinite Plenty, the Power that has brought, that is continually bringing, all things into expression in material form. He who lives in the realization of his oneness with this Infinite Power becomes a magnet to attract to himself a continual supply of whatsoever things he desires.
>
> If one hold himself in the thought of poverty, he will be poor, and the chances are that he will remain in poverty. If he hold himself, whatever present conditions may be, continually in the thought of prosperity, he sets into operation forces that will sooner or later bring him into prosperous conditions.[59]

Mind-power replaced an ascetic, self-disciplined work ethic with a vision of natural ease and plentitude, making way for a consumer culture bolstered by fantasies of boundless abundance.[60] The rise of mind-power at the turn of the nineteenth century provided an explanation for the unprecedented accumulations of wealth created by unregulated industrialization and growing disparities between the wealthy and the poor. As mechanization began replacing human labor power, the link between the production of wealth and human labor was becoming less apparent. In the context of late-twentieth-century America, mind-power offered magical explanations for the source of wealth when hard work was clearly no longer a reliable means of securing prosperity.

Central to the idea that one's mind and will control the world is the corollary that failure or misfortune of any kind is due not to external circumstances but to weakness of spirit or to an unconscious desire to fail. In Robbins's world, everyone gets exactly what he or she wants and deserves. The enduring popularity of the mind-power paradigm—and its problematic premise that each individual is solely responsible for his or her own reality—taps the infantile fantasy of omnipotence in the face of what are increasingly complex and unmanageable social and economic circumstances.

While Robbins's mind-power blurs the distinction between opposites—thought and reality, private and public—asserting that the former is wholly constitutive of the latter, Stephen R. Covey's world is a reasoning man's world, where the emphasis is on planning, hard work, and integrity. Covey distinguishes his work from that of others in the self-help industries by noting his emphasis on the development of "character" rather than the cultivation of "personality." Covey observed a phenomenon that other, more scholarly, writers have also noted—that at the middle of the twentieth century, an emphasis on personality gained importance, while the value placed on character diminished.[61] Covey aptly points out: "The Personality Ethic essentially took two paths: one was human and public relations techniques and the other was positive mental attitude."[62] While Covey sees aspects of the Personality Ethic (positive thinking, communication and marketing skills) as necessary for success, he asserts that the "Character Ethic" (his approach) is central. The Character Ethic is based on "the fundamental idea that there are principles that govern human effectiveness—natural laws in the human dimension that are just as real, just as unchanging and unarguably 'there' as laws such as gravity are in the physical dimension."[63] Covey's self is rational but also ethical, following in the tradition of a Kantian ethical subject who subscribes to abstract moral principles—what Covey calls "universal principles" and "natural laws." Character, which is increasingly difficult to sustain under the volatile conditions of advanced capitalism, becomes a form of social capital.[64]

Although Covey deploys a variety of metaphors—for example, the fiscal metaphor of the emotional bank account; the agrarian metaphor of harvesting what one sows; and the computer programming metaphor[65]— his central metaphor is that of life as a path or journey, while his legitimating rhetoric is that of natural laws. Icons—now trademarked—that have

become central to the FranklinCovey Company's enterprise are the impo-
sition of a compass over the image of watch (see, for example, fig. 2.1, a detail
of the cover art for *First Things First*). While one is on a path, one is not to
be guided by a static map but rather by a compass that can keep one on
one's way to "true north," which Covey defines as a reality that is independent of us—abstract moral principles.[66] Managing one's time becomes a
way of staying on one's path, for staying in line with one's "mission" and
with "universal independent principles," irrespective of the particulars of a
given terrain or circumstance.

Developing a personal (as well as a family or organizational) mission
statement is central to Covey's approach. On the basis of one's mission,
one navigates one's course through the changing landscapes of daily life.

Figure 2.1. Detail excerpted from the cover of *First Things First*
(New York: Simon and Schuster, 1994). Used with permission
of FranklinCovey Company. All rights reserved.

The source of the individual's mission in Covey's work is particularly interesting. In an example of the tortured logic that is at the heart of theistic self-improvement literature that attempts to function in a secular context, Covey describes the self as the creator of the self, which he calls "becoming your own first creator," but also posits an a priori self, a transcendent self.[67] One's mission, though self-created, is also preordained: "to be detected rather than invented."[68] Quickly shifting back to a less theistic stance, Covey reverts to the computer metaphor to describe his first two effectiveness habits: "Habit 1 says 'you are the programmer.' Habit 2, then says, 'Write the program.'" Later he'll add Habit 3: "Run the program," "Live the program," [69] in which he introduces time management techniques that are based on distinguishing between urgent and important activities, and on articulating a series of roles that one plays and scheduling goals related to these roles into a weekly calendar (a product marketed by the FranklinCovey Company). The metaphor of the journey or adventure retains some element of fate or destiny—as one can encounter unexpected obstacles or shortcuts—while the metaphor of creating a computer program or script implies an unprecedented level of autonomy.

Indeed, the religious and theological roots of Covey's *Seven Habits of Highly Effective People* can be readily traced back to Cotton Mather's 1710 *Bonafacius, or An Essay to Do Good*. Consider the following two passages, one from Mather and the other from Covey:

> On the *Lords-Day Evening*, we may make this one of our Exercises;
> To Employ most serious and awful Thoughts on that Question;
> *Should I Dy this Week, what have I left Undone, which I should then
> wish I had made more speed in the doing of?* My Friend, Place thy
> self in *Dying* Circumstances; Apprehend and Realize thy Approaching *Death*. Suppose thy Last Hour come; the *Decretory
> Hour*: thy Breath failing, thy Throat rattling, thy Hands with a
> cold Sweat upon them, only the turn of the Tide expected for thy
> Expiration. In this Condition; *What wouldest thou wish to have
> done, more than thou has already done, for thy own Soul, for thy
> Family, or for the People of God?* Think; Don't *Forget* the Result of
> thy Thoughts; Don't *Delay* to do what thou hast Resolved upon.
> How much more Agreeable and Profitable, would such an Exercise
> be on the *Lords-Day Evening*, than those Vanities whereto that
> Evening is too commonly Prostituted, and all the *Good* of the

foregoing *Day* Defeated? And if such an Exercise were often attended, Oh! How much would it Regulate our Lives; how Watchfully, how Fruitfully would it cause us to Live; What an incredible Number of *Good Works* would it produce in the World?[70]

Nearly three centuries later, Covey advises the readers of his *Seven Habits* "to begin with the end in mind":

find a place to read these next few pages where you can be alone and uninterrupted. Clear your mind of everything except what you will read and what I will invite you to do. Don't worry about your schedule, your business, your family, or your friends. Just focus with me and really open your mind.

In your mind's eye, see yourself going to the funeral of a loved one. Picture yourself driving to the funeral parlor or chapel, parking the car, and getting out. As you walk inside the building, you notice the flowers, the soft organ music. You see the faces of friends and family you pass along the way. You feel the shared sorrow of losing, the joy of having known, that radiates from the hearts of the people there. . . .

As you take a seat and wait for the services to begin, you look at the program in your hand. There are to be four speakers. The first is from your family, immediate and also extended—children, brothers, sisters, nephews, nieces, aunts, uncles, cousins, and grandparents who have come from all over the country to attend. The second speaker is one of your friends, someone who can give a sense of what you were as a person. The third speaker is from your work or profession. And the fourth is from your church or some community organization where you've been involved in service.

Now think deeply. What would you like each of these speakers to say about you and your life? What kind of husband, wife, father, or mother would you like their words to reflect? What kind of son or daughter or cousin? What kind of friend? What kind of working associate?[71]

Death-bed reflection or tombstone inscription exercises ("What would you like your tombstone to say?") are a mainstay of self-improvement literature, but even so, the similarity between these two passages is striking. Mather asks "*What wouldest thou wish to have done, more than thou hast already done, for thy own Soul, for thy Family, or for the People of God?*" while Covey asks what family, friends, coworkers, and community members would say about you. Mather and Covey see the self as embedded in the community and refracted through the eyes of others. While Mather calls his congregation to "do good," Covey offers his readers and seminar participants prescriptions for becoming "effective people" and for developing principle-centered leadership. Mather advises his readers to think of their good deeds as stones cast into a pond,[72] generating concentric circles of goodness, while Covey writes of "Circles of Influence," where one focuses only on those things that one can specifically affect in one's immediate sphere, rather than concerning oneself with the wider range of issues beyond one's immediate concerns.[73]

Covey instructs readers to begin at "the very center of our Circle of Influence": in other words, to begin with themselves. But despite the fact that Covey's self is utterly self-centered, that self is refracted through the prism of social roles. Covey's self, embedded in a social world—the self-improvement equivalent of sociologist George Herbert Mead's "me" rather than his "I"—operates from self-centeredness, but as the self is understood in terms of its social relations, the usual notion of I-centeredness is denounced: there is, Covey argues, "little security, guidance, wisdom or power in the limited center of self."[74] Covey argues for a self-centered life mitigated by "universal principles" and facilitated by a sense of roles or participation in the social world through roles; in short, Covey argues for a moral and ethical self.

When faced with a conflict between personal and professional obligations, Covey's approach shifts conflict from external circumstances to internal role conflicts. Unlike, for example, Robert J. Ringer, whose "Number One" saw the world as a battleground and everyone in it as adversaries, Covey's "effective person" is composed of various "roles" competing for the individual's time and priorities. Take the example of a conflict between a work and family commitment. Covey describes a man who is asked by his employer to work late on the same evening that he'd promised to take his wife to a concert, then outlines the various possible responses to the conflict based on differing "priorities." For example, if the priority were one's spouse, the individual would simply decline to work late. If the priority were making money, one would accept the additional assignment. And so on, through a variety of priorities. But Covey concludes that by using "principle-centered" solutions to solve this conflict, "you can communicate to your wife and your boss within the strong networks you've created in your interdependent relationship. Because you are independent, you can be effectively interdependent."[75] Covey glides over conflict with a series of diffusing statements that diminish, and ultimately refuse, the possibility of conflict.

Covey's self is deeply embedded in a social world, always attempting to step outside of the immediate conflict in search of "win-win solutions." This is a self-improvement version of the sociologist Émile Durkheim's functionalism: conflict is ultimately incomprehensible because the faithful performance of one's roles and the execution of one's responsibilities will always come to a harmonious end. The unconscious, and the possibility of unconscious motives, are utterly absent, as are hierarchies, power, injustice, and irrationality. In Covey's universe, there is minimal conflict, as all reasonable people are expected to strive for "win-win" solutions, and the clashes between a profit-driven economic system and the public good are always resolved. Any disagreement or discord—even those caused by notoriously adversarial relationships, such as those between labor and management—can be resolved by drawing on one's "emotional bank account." Even significant downsizing and plant closings aren't a problem in Covey's world. As Covey tells it, mutual trust and teamwork between senior executives and employees transform a plant closing literally into a picnic, "a Kentucky Fried Chicken farewell party."[76]

Although some social theorists have described Covey's conflict-averse system as a sign of a stagnant capitalism that has no purpose other than its own reproduction,[77] one might also read his approach as a way of keeping one's options open. While the disingenuous glad-handler of Dale Carnegie's time could work his way through a hierarchical corporate economy, today's worker has to rely on a network of colleagues and coworkers to keep himself employable. When your assistant last year might be the CEO of a startup next year, "character"—being a decent person, irrespective of organizational hierarchies—gains renewed currency. "Managing" one's life and career requires ongoing business and social relationships, not a backstabbing climb up a corporate ladder. Covey and his colleagues describe a collapse of public and private spheres where "All Public Behavior is Ultimately Private Behavior."[78] Public policy is private morality writ large: "Ultimately there's no such thing as 'organizational behavior'; it's all behavior of the people in the organization."[79]

This collapse of public and private, work and leisure, echoes the characteristics of what social theorist John Sabel has called the "open labor market," where workers are increasingly required to maintain dense social networks through work and leisure time to ensure their ongoing employability:

> Workers under these circumstances must acquire skills, including the ability to cooperate in particular settings in order to be employable, yet cannot rely on long-term relations with any single employer. . . . In order to move from job to job in an economy in which boundaries between firms and between firms and society are blurring, they must join various networks that cross company lines and reach from the economy into social and family life. I will call this situation an open labor market. [80]

Sabel goes on to observe that work in the restructured economy reduces the employee's freedom or autonomy because individuals are urged to consider their entire private life as a series of social networks meant to ensure their continuous employability. He notes: "Only those who participate in . . . multiple, loosely connected networks are likely to know when their current jobs are in danger, where new opportunities lie, and what skills are required in order to seize these opportunities."[81] In the process, he observes, it becomes more difficult to say when one is working and when one is at rest. Working on one's employability becomes an ever expanding task, while distinctions among work, leisure, and family life are blurred. In a world where personal and public are merged, "character," though increasingly difficult to maintain, regains some of its currency where "personality" might previously have been able to prevail.

New Age Apostles of Amorphous Abundance

While Stephen Covey merges self and other by imagining all conflict as internal—between one's various roles in life rather than between persons and institutions—and Anthony Robbins dispels the distance between self and other through his "empathetic technology" and the mind-power belief that reality is little more than wishes, the New Age inheritors of New Thought posit a world in which there is ultimately no distinction between self and other, matter and energy, reality and imagination. In such a world, anything one does on one's own behalf ultimately benefits everyone. This worldview ventures far beyond Adam Smith's assertion that an invisible hand will guide self-interest toward the highest good of the community.

This is a mystical world without need of morality or ethics: since self and other are indistinguishable, self-interest and other's interests are identical.

Deepak Chopra, a central figure in the promotion of this mystical approach, first found a spot on the *New York Times* bestseller list in 1993 with his *Ageless Body, Timeless Mind*, which promised a version of immortality through mind-body medicine. A physician who established himself in Western medicine, rising to the rank of chief of staff at New England Memorial Hospital in Stoneham, Massachusetts, Chopra went on to found centers for Ayurvedic medicine in Lancaster, Massachusetts, and La Jolla, California. By 1995, Chopra was back on the bestseller list with his *Seven Spiritual Laws of Success*, a rewrite of his earlier *Creating Affluence: Wealth Consciousness in the Field of All Possibilities*. *Creating Affluence* had been organized as an alphabetical primer: "'A' stands for all possibilities, absolute, affluence, and abundance. . . . 'B' stands for better and best," and so on.[82] When the alphabetical schema failed to land the book on the bestseller list, its content was repackaged as *Seven Spiritual Laws of Success*. Numbers— seven habits, twelve steps, and so on—suggest good fortune, and seemingly provided it for Chopra. Rewritten, restructured, numbered, and repackaged, *Seven Laws* garnered seventy-one weeks on the *New York Times* bestseller list.

What is interesting about Chopra's 1994 success book is that while it annuls the boundaries between self and other, it also insists on the critical importance of discovering one's special talents or one's purpose in life:

> *The Law of Pure Potentiality* could also be called the *Law of Unity*, because underlying the infinite diversity of life is the *unity* of one all-pervasive spirit. There is no separation between you and this field of energy. The field of pure potentiality is your own Self. And the more you experience your true nature, the closer you are to the field of pure potentiality.[83]

Like Emerson's "Over-Soul" and Trine's "Infinite," this is another (or an ongoing) theory of abundance without boundaries. But to tap into this abundance, one has to first discover one's true Self; second, express one's unique talents; and third, find a way to provide a service for humanity by asking "How can I help?"[84] Yet all this is expected to happen without effort, as it is subject to "The Law of Least Effort." Following the law of least effort requires unconditional acceptance of existing conditions: "This means that I will know that this moment is as it should be, because the whole universe is as it should be."[85] The second component of the law of least effort is "responsibility," which Chopra defines as "not blaming anyone or anything for your situation, including yourself."[86] This notion of responsibility suspends the literal meaning, ensuring that no one is actually accountable for anything.

Chopra's mysticism proposes a path of self-discovery and service while representing the path as effortless, a characteristic of his work that I will consider in more detail in chapter 5. In Chopra's universe, where distinctions between self and other, matter and energy, past and present are blurred, the self at work on the self isn't really at work on the self: everything is effortless, everything is as it should be, and everything can be just what you want it to be, too. While it is difficult to engage such a worldview in a rational argument, it is easy to see that such a belief system offers an expressive and antimodernist antidote to the rational planning and instrumental thinking that predominates in the self-help literature.

Within the New Age literatures, one finds that concerns about money are deflected with precisely the sort of language used by early twentieth-century New Thought authors. For example, the bestselling New Age author Shakti Gawain writes in her 1986 *Living in the Light*:

> Because the creative energy of the universe in all of us is limitless and readily available, so, potentially, is money. The more willing and able we are to open to the universe, the more money we will have in our lives. A lack of money merely mirrors the energy blocks within ourselves. . . . The stronger and more open your channel is, the more will flow through it.[87]

She continues, advising readers that when "you learn how to listen to the universe and act on it, then money increasingly comes into your life. It flows in an easy, effortless, and joyful way because there is no sacrifice involved."[88]

Similarly, health, well-being, and emotional happiness are attributed to finding one's place in the "flow."[89] The movement toward a language of liquidity isn't new: the early twentieth-century New Thought author Ralph Waldo Trine wrote: "the Infinite Spirit that is manifest in the life of each must be identical in quality with that Source, the same as a drop of water taken from the ocean is, in nature, in characteristics, identical with the sea, its source.[90] And Karl Marx and Friedrich Engels had, of course, observed that in the nascent industrial capitalism "all that is solid melts into air."[91] This liquefaction continues in what the social theorist Zygmunt Bauman has called "liquid modernity." While industrial capitalism had melted away much of the structures of social life (traditional loyalties, customary rights, and obligations), advanced capitalism has, in Bauman's view, melted any relationship between individual actions and those of political collectivities.[92] The language of New Age literature renders this liquefaction as not only harmless but also beneficent.

The Self-Help Menagerie: Sharks, Mice, and a Kinder, Gentler Survivalism

Despite the emergence of a language of flows and infinite possibilities, the brutal social Darwinism that marked the beginning of the 1970s never completely vanished. Rather, it reemerged in a tempered version that included animal villains and heroes from sharks to mice. Harvey B. Mackay's 1988 *Swim with the Sharks Without Being Eaten Alive* and Spencer Johnson's 1998 *Who Moved My Cheese?* each made their way to the *New York Times* bestseller list and revived a survivalist mentality that had never quite vanished. Mackay's story of up-from-under is one of salesmanship and management prowess and illustrates the shift from the "kill the competition" mentality that emerged in the early 1970s to the "serving your customer" rhetoric that came to dominate success literature, while Johnson, who had coauthored the enormously successful *The One Minute Manager* with the management consultant Kenneth Blanchard, prescribes flexibility as the only possibility not only for success but also for survival.

Unlike so many self-improvement authors who made their personal fortunes within the self-improvement industry, Harvey B. Mackay made his fortune in manufacturing. His success story unfolds as follows. At the age of twenty-six he purchased a failing envelope company in the Twin Cities and built it into a $35 million industry leader. He describes himself as the volunteer leader who catalyzed the community effort that culminated in the building of the $75 million Hubert H. Humphrey Metrodome in Minneapolis.[93] Representing himself as not only a successful businessman but also a businessman-citizen-volunteer, Mackay tempers his individualism with a rhetoric of service. Selling your product is a service to your customers. While one may be swimming with the sharks, one is not oneself a predatory creature. And while other business people may prey on their competition and customers, in Mackay's world, customers are coddled. Mackay offers one of his "secrets": the "Mackay 66"—a sixty-six-question customer profile form that each salesperson in his company was required to complete about any prospect.[94] The form included spaces for extensive personal information, from medical history to hobbies and vacation habits. Much of sales is impression management, and the customer information profile is an important tool in the salesperson's repertoire. Mackay suggests that keeping the profiles on hand was pivotal to keeping business when particular sales staff left his company. With the profile on hand, one can appear attentive and personally engaged with people one has only just met. The merging of personal and private is entirely part of the game of sales, and Mackay makes no secret of this. Knowing your customer—recast as maintaining your marketing database—is central to success.

Other kinds of seemingly benign guile are encouraged. Mackay recommends that when you don't have access to a private club where you can entertain your clients, you should "make the best restaurant in town your own private club," and then offers specifics about how to turn a business lunch or dinner into a display of status.[95] Conversely, he advises readers on how to not be pulled in by such displays. In a chapter called "Never Buy Anything in a Room with a Chandelier," Mackay advises against being taken in by grand surroundings or glamorous trappings.[96] Status displays matter; just don't be suckered by them yourself. And social networking is central. "Short notes," Mackay writes, "yield long results."[97] Mackay's advice bridges the world of a Dale Carnegie, where guile is foremost, with the negotiation techniques of *Looking Out for Number One*. Mackay may be looking out for Number One, but he's not telling you that's what he's doing. Instead, Mackay is simply avoiding being "eaten alive"—for which no one could fault him—while providing a service for customers.

At the end of the 1990s, the decade that witnessed the emergence of the term "downsizing," Spencer Johnson's *Who Moved My Cheese?* compares four characters—two mice and two "little people"—and finds that when it comes to adapting to change, the mice (Sniff and Scurry) far outpace the people. The "little people" of his story (Hem and Haw) find themselves attached to beliefs, expectations, and traditions. Rather than remaining ready to move at a moment's notice, they built lives, traditions, and communities around their initially bountiful "cheese station." Instead of swiftly responding to a change in resources, as the rodents did, the humans are dismayed, angry, troubled, and profoundly resistant to change. Rather than operating as nomadic cheese-seekers, the humans suffer when "things change." Eventually one of the little people, Haw, sets out in search of new cheese, leaving guideposts for his tradition-bound friend Hem, with pointers such as "If you do not change, you can become extinct."[98] Finally Haw catches up with the rodents, finds "New Cheese," and enjoys his new abundant life, while remaining ever vigilant about anticipating the next change before he's left hungry again.

The maze parable is interesting in that the context is not natural, as was the jungle landscape conjured in earlier survivalist self-help. Rather, the maze is manmade—a product of civilization. Although the changes that occur are not natural they are deemed to be inevitable. Invisible masters move the cheese, and mice and men alike are meant to scurry in search of some new means of sustenance. This new survivalism admits that this radical repositioning of life's rewards is not solely a function of the natural world, but it is no less inevitable for that. One of the signposts reads "Be Ready to Quickly Change Again and Again—They Keep Moving the Cheese." The invisible and seemingly omnipotent "They" are never discovered or uncovered.[99]

Johnson's parable is positioned within another story—that of a school reunion where former classmates compare the changes in their lives, and their responses after hearing the "A-Mazing" story of the mice, the men, and the missing cheese, allowing for an ongoing commentary on the conditions the mice and the "little people" face. One of the school reunion characters compares his children with Hem:

> My children seem to think that nothing in their lives should ever
> change. I guess they're acting like Hem—they're angry. They're
> probably afraid of what the future holds. Maybe I haven't painted
> a realistic enough picture of "New Cheese" for them. Probably
> because I don't see it myself.[100]

As human beings require a prolonged period of nurturance—especially when compared with rodent litters—the requirement of displacing and uprooting children is obviously at odds with the search for "new cheese." Indeed, parenting books urge parents to provide a sense of tradition, continuity, and stability for the health of their children, not perpetual motion and relocation.[101] The "little people" of Johnson's maze aren't people with families, though "finding Cheese" meant "having a loving family *someday*" (emphasis added).[102] Instead, they are individuals who can drop their families, backgrounds, traditions, geographical location, habits of thinking, and beliefs in the interest of finding some cheese. Johnson's parable offers a defense of what social theorists call "detraditionalization"—the tendency of advancing capitalism to disrupt the cultures and traditions that may stand in the way of the accumulation of profit.[103] The little people of Johnson's maze are not self-actualizing individuals acting on their beliefs and realizing their dreams in some expressive New Age narrative; rather they are beleaguered individuals scrambling to feed themselves; they are not even stable enough to have families. These characters—deemed less resourceful than mice—are reduced to their animal needs, to hunger and despair, rather than elevated in their human capacities. Survivalism returns, not with the predatory violence of the jungle, but in the faceless violence of a rational capitalism where humans are deemed less able than lab rats.

From *Power!* to *Personal Power!*

As the last quarter of the twentieth century began, the dominant self-improvement literature focused on impression management: manipulating symbols and wielding power in the world. Robert J. Ringer and Michael Korda were not advocating work on the self or improving the self; they were offering advice on the uses of trickery and deception—essentially combat, or poker table strategy—to advance one's position financially or within existing power hierarchies. But just twenty years later, Korda's *Power!* was supplanted by Robbins's *Personal Power!*. Robbins offered individuals instructions on mastering their inner experience—what he calls their "state"— as a means of mastering the external environment, while Stephen R. Covey recommended the pursuit of "private victories" as the route to public ones. New Age cosmologies in the work of Deepak Chopra and Shakti Gawain represented the world as amorphous—without significant differentiation between self and other, cause and effect (or anything else, for that matter). Even when survivalist themes reemerged in the literature of self-improvement, they were treated with a more personal emphasis: tempered with calls to service and focused on adjusting one's attitude rather than sharpening one's claws.

With the exception of Harvey B. Mackay, who incorporates some of the impression management techniques of the earlier literature, the top-selling literatures of self-improvement culture had, by the early 1990s, registered a shift toward understanding the external world as internal. This "inward turn" is not in itself something new. The move toward a greater sense of interiority and a focus on the self has been a tendency of modernity, tied to the development of print culture, and linked to the tendency of advancing capitalism to transform and attenuate community ties.[104] In the twentieth century, the emergence of a focus on psychology and psychiatry intensified this shift, leading to the concern with a development of what some and others called a hedonistic or narcissistic personality.[105] The generic literature of self-help during the last quarter of the twentieth century signaled an intensification of tendencies in American culture that had been evident, in some cases, since the nation's founding. Thus this unisex literature represents, on the whole, the continuity in this genre, with the last quarter of the twentieth century demonstrating a further spiral in the overall inward turn that has marked the development of modernity. We will need to look at the literature of self-improvement directed primarily toward women to observe what appear to be the newer—if not altogether new—cultural developments.

chapter 3

From *Having It All* to *Simple Abundance*

Gender and the Logic of Diminished Expectations

When a woman decides to have it all as is, nothing changes.
Except the woman's expectations, her standards for herself, and the
demands upon her already depleted energy. But the burden is on
her . . . *institutions are undisturbed.*
—Letty Cottin Pogrebin

Among the most striking features of the "unisex" literature of self-improvement is the poverty of the solutions offered to women in their quests for self-made success. Although mainstream self-improvement authors suggest that their advice is applicable irrespective of gender or race, the picture is considerably more complicated. Without dwelling on making the case that the "one-size-fits-all" literature falls seriously short, consider the following examples of advice from Robert J. Ringer, M. Scott Peck, and Stephen R. Covey. Ringer denies the possibility of gender inequities, declaring: "There is no male/female distinction in my philosophy. Therefore, where a specific gender is used, you may assume that the opposite gender is automatically interchangeable." However, in the more than 320 pages of the hardcover version of *Looking Out for Number One*, there are few instances where women are described as anything other than objects of male desire or overbearing, cheating wives.[1] With the exception of references to his hero, the libertarian novelist Ayn Rand, the only instance where professional women are mentioned in Ringer's book is when, in keeping with his aversion to any kind of social solidarity, he denounces the women's movement:

A woman actively engaged in making things happen for herself doesn't have time to get bogged down by cumbersome women's movements. In becoming part of such a "cause," she detracts from her own unique abilities. In the book industry, for example, a great many of the most prominent positions are held by women, many of whom I am personally acquainted with. All seem far too preoccupied with their careers to have time for carrying signs or marching on courthouses.[2]

Perhaps more important than the omission of stories reflecting women's experiences is Ringer's assertion that human interactions have to be understood in terms of the "Screwor-Screwee Theory," in which every individual imagines him or herself the "screwee" but never acknowledges that they might be the "screwor."[3] One would be hard pressed to find a more explicit example of the phallocentrism of Ringer's world.

Peck's journey along the road less traveled doesn't offer much deviation from traditional gender roles either, except as a way of warding off dependency, a most dreaded condition in a culture that prizes individual self-sufficiency:

> In marriage there is normally a differentiation of the roles of the two spouses, a normally efficient division of labor between them. The woman usually does the cooking, housecleaning and shopping and cares for the children; the man usually maintains employment, handles the finances, mows the lawn and makes repairs. Healthy couples instinctively will switch roles from time to time. The man may cook a meal now and then, spend one day a week with the children, clean the house to surprise his wife; the woman may get a part-time job, mow the lawn on her husband's birthday, or take over the checking account and bill-paying for a year. The couple may often think of this role switching as a kind of play that adds spice and variety to their marriage. It is this, but perhaps more important (even if it is done unconsciously), it is a process that diminishes their mutual dependency. In a sense, each spouse is training himself or herself for survival in the event of the loss of the other.[4]

Stephen R. Covey, whose daughter's dilemma marked the point of departure for this inquiry, suggests a world in which women caring for children ought to simply drop their self-definition and time management systems in order to be able to attend to that which is most "needful"—the care of infants.[5] Covey's books, particularly the 1994 *First Things First*, coauthored with the husband-and-wife team of A. Roger Merrill and Rebecca R. Merrill, suggest that the subordination of women's need for self-fulfillment to the larger needs of family are necessary and "effective." Throughout *First Things First*, Rebecca Merrill's first-person accounts of her struggles with putting aside her personal needs for those of her family are offered as an exemplar of effective behavior. She describes her envy of another woman who had written a book and her longing to do this kind of meaningful work, her desire to go back to school to finish the college degree she had abandoned when she married and her difficult decision not to, and countless other cases of putting the needs of others before her own.[6] Unlike most women who make the kinds of sacrifices Merrill describes, she managed to find a way to write at least part of a bestselling book, albeit as the third-listed author. Advocating strategic subordination, a topic I will consider further in the upcoming examination of Helen Gurley Brown's *Having It All*, is a time-honored technique for acquiring secondary access to power.

While the bestselling "one-size-fits-all" unisex literature of self-improvement was unable to comfortably fit new self-actualizing women within its framework, the self-help literature written by and for women began to accommodate the changing roles of women and the diminished distinction between personal and public life. In the process, new concepts, frameworks, and metaphors emerged or were appropriated, and old concepts were adapted or refined. This gendered split in the self-improvement literature at the outset of the 1980s reflects the growing impact of the women's movement: women were entering the labor force in increasing numbers and asserting the self-interested individuality that had once been primarily the prerogative of men.

Women's increased participation in the paid labor force during the last quarter of the century was dramatic, but the trend was most accelerated during the period of 1973 through 1983, when, according to the 2003 *Economic Report of the President*, the percentage of women employed in the civilian labor force increased from 44.7 percent in 1973 to 52.9 percent in 1983, nearly an 8 percent increase. During the same decade male labor force participation declined by nearly 2.5 percent (from 78.8 percent to 76.4 percent). While women's participation in the labor market had been steadily increasing since 1950, the 8 percent increase over ten years was nearly double the rate of increase for the prior two decades. (In the twenty-year period between 1950 and 1970, labor force participation for women increased by 10 percent, while in the ten-year period between 1973 and 1983 it increased by 8 percent: the rate at which women were entering the labor force was almost doubled.) By 2002, the percentage shifts were even greater; male labor force participation had declined to 73.9 percent, while women's participation rose to 59.9 percent.

Paradoxically, it was during this period—when women were being told that they could "have it all"—that women and children began to dominate the poverty statistics. According to the sociologist Ruth Sidel, the trend toward the feminization of poverty began in the early 1970s: the result of the convergence of several social and economic factors, including "the rapid growth of female-headed families; the continuing existence of a dual-labor market that actively discriminates against female workers . . . and the time-consuming yet unpaid domestic responsibilities of women, including child care."[7] By entering the waged labor force without guaranteed affordable childcare and pay parity, women have been, arguably, "working their way to the bottom."[8] Far from "having it all," women, in particular women with children, found they had less and less.[9] Simply put, movements for gender equity, including increased labor force participation and weaker family life, had inadvertently resulted in increased poverty. In what the sociologist Arlie Russell Hochschild calls a "stalled revolution," an unintended (and hope-fully temporary) consequence of the women's movement was increasing poverty for women.[10] Feminists had not intended that entry into the labor market would impoverish women; on the contrary, work outside the home was seen as a path to personal and economic enrichment. Nonetheless, in the aggregate, the harder women worked at "having it all," the greater their losses were becoming.

The literature of self-improvement directed specifically toward these in-creasingly belabored women offered a series of "solutions": the application of market values to every corner of one's experience, in the image of "win-ning women" who defined their lives as business transactions and worked to avoid "codependence"; a Romantic alternative in the form of the idea of one's life as a work of art or one's life as part of a revolutionary transformation; and finally, the traditional solution to these diminished expectations, in the form of a retreat to domesticity and appeals to simplicity.

Winning Women: From Game to Business

While the bestselling books of the early and mid-1980s featured numerous books of spiritual consolation written by men for a general audience, of which *The Road Less Traveled* is only the most prominent example, the bestsellers written by and for women during this period pushed for a heavy dose of individual, material self-interest. These titles urged women to be, do, and get whatever they wanted. Most famously, Helen Gurley Brown's 1982 *Having It All* suggested to women readers: "you can have whatever I have and probably much, much *more* . . . if you want to."[11] Similarly, Irene C. Kassorla,[12] whose bestselling 1980 *Nice Girls Do!* urged young women to pursue sexual satisfaction in their relationships, extended her approach to all areas of life—love, family, wealth, and career—in her 1984 *Go For It!* The metaphor of life as a game figures prominently for Kassorla, whose book section titles include "Winning Beats Losing," "Winners Get Going," "Winners Are Positive," "Winners Are Real," "Winners Communicate," and "Winners Face Their Fears."[13] This "winning" self-improvement literature addressed to women was groundbreaking, even revolutionary, in that it suggested that women had the right to self-fulfillment—and should "win"—not only in work (as Betty Friedan had suggested in her 1963 *Feminine Mystique*) but also in expressing their sexuality. Yet this literature was simultaneously reactionary, in that the vision of self-fulfillment proposed was modeled on traditional masculine versions of an isolated individual pursuing his or her own insular self-interest in the ostensible free market of opportunities.

The stark competition of the kinds of "winning," best exemplified in the harsh survivalist images used by Robert J. Ringer and Michael Korda, were not automatically applicable across gender lines. With the application of the notion of "winning" to women, the idea of what constituted the self—and what constituted a "win"—was subtly altered. *Having It All* represents a transition from "winning" as a game played against another to winning as a game against one's own best game:

> Competition may be bad for *lazy* people or dumbbells, but all "competing" *really* is is being "your best self."
> Does anyone *really* say to herself, "Aha! I will make this sale because it will just *kill* old Ralph, or I will design this great dress

because Daphne, my rival, will be furious!" You sell and design because it's what you *do* in life and you do it the best you can; you're not even *thinking* about anybody else most of the time when you work. You are simply "getting on with it."[14]

This is not the self against the other, but rather the self continuously outdoing itself, the self rising above its own best. For the women of Brown's generation, overt competition with others may have suggested uncomfortable breaches of gendered propriety. This inward turn—from competition with external figures to competition against one's own personal best—suggests how the self-improvement literature for women may have contributed to the inward turn observed in the general self-improvement literature. While Brown champions competition, this is not the "Screwor-Screwee" game advocated by Ringer,[15] but the beginning of the movement toward the "private victories" of self-control and personal bests that Stephen R. Covey advocates.[16]

Although Helen Gurley Brown's *Having It All* presents an image of success, of "winning," other metaphors figure prominently, specifically the image of "rising to the top" and the belief that one's life is a business enterprise. Along with the suggestion that competition is against one's personal best, a dominant metaphor in Brown's writing is the one of vertical motion, of upward mobility, of getting up from under. In her second chapter, she explains "How to 'Mouseburger' Your Way to the Top."[17] "Mouseburgering" is Brown's neologism for playing the role of subordinate so effectively that one arrives in the role of master. Essentially Brown advocates a Hegelian (and Sadean) reversal where the slave, by virtue of her obedience, controls—and ultimately becomes—the master. Subordination as an avenue to power is embodied in the nonsensical neologism of "mouseburgering." While it is difficult to imagine how Brown arrived at this term except to say that mice are timid and burgers are common, it captures the idea of success for the common woman, who lacks extraordinary beauty or intelligence: "people who are not prepossessing, not pretty, don't have a particularly high I.Q., a decent education, good family background or other noticeable assets—can come a long way in life if they apply themselves."[18]

Brown writes of moving to another "plateau" and of the problems of life as "the yeast that leavens bread," about the time when you "Get to the Top" and of "Phase IV: At the Top. . . . And now you're at the pinnacle."[19] She even comments on her own preoccupation with stories set in airplanes:

"I seem to write a lot about airplanes, but things *happen* to me there."[20] The metaphor of climbing a ladder or rising to the top is a far-from-new phenomenon in the literature of success. Think of Horatio Alger, Jr.'s *Struggling Upward or Luke Larkin's Luck* and any number of other images of social ascent.

The image of life as a competition or game to be won and the idea of life as an uphill climb through a hierarchical social order are hardly new. What is new in Brown's language is her unabashed use of business metaphors for personal life: In chapter 10, on the topic of friendship, she calls for "Reciprocal Trade" and asserts that "Everything costs something": "And so you may be a friend who gives selflessly, endlessly—money and gifts as well as counsel and cheer, without wanting a thing in return—but hold on a minute—you should want something in return. You hold that person's marker."[21] Brown recommends keeping tabs on one's emotional investments and balances five years in advance of Stephen R. Covey's introduction of the idea of an "emotional bank account." While one is supposed to keep careful track of one's emotional investments, particularly in friendships, one ought to be generous and giving in a professional context:

> Being too niggardly and selective about what assignments you'll accept—"but I'm not getting *paid* to do that!"—is like being too skimpy with how much *love* you are going to give out in life: it may be better to *over* invest. It may seem that people are "using you" but actually it's the other way around—you are using *them*. Do get *credit* if you can—no use coming in on Saturday to straighten the files if no one ever knows you were *there*. Just don't be too stingy with your "free labor" for bosses or co-workers (emphasis in original).[22]

The selflessness once reserved for the intimate sphere is harnessed in the workplace as a means to professional advancement. Indeed, in Brown's professional world, one is expected to give generously of all one's resources. In an assertion for which Brown has become notorious, she advised women victims of sexual harassment that if they were uncomfortable with such behavior they should simply look for a new job.[23] Brown confides: "With the exception of my present job at *Cosmo*, may I say I have never worked *anywhere*—and I've worked a lot of anywheres—without being sexually involved with *somebody* in the office."[24] Sexuality in the workplace is to be fostered:

one could accuse you of "using sex" in business when you gaze straight into his eyes. That's okay. The sexual you is part of the *whole* you and doesn't snap off—God, we *hope* not, anyway!—between nine and six. At any rate, you can *think* sex and still do business—I've done it for *years*! The *garbage* one reads about keeping sex out of your work! [25]

Not surprisingly, Brown's most recent book, a memoir, reveals that in the earliest days of her career, when she worked as a secretary to support her mother and disabled sister, that she was a paid companion to an older man.[26] Brown describes herself as learning from an early age that one "tried to do whatever you needed to do to survive."[27]

In keeping with this blurring of boundaries between public and private, professional and personal, Brown's feminine version of survivalist advice includes everything from diet to wardrobe hints, exercise to makeup tips. Four full chapters out of twelve are devoted to these topics. If there is no distinction between personal and public life, then the maintenance of one's body—one aspect of one's "human capital," to use the words of economistic social science—is vital for success. While the historian Jeffrey Louis Decker attributes the new emphasis on physique and personal appearance in the literature of success to the rise of a visually mediated celebrity culture, the emphasis on fitness can also be attributed to the fact that in a world of increased competition and attenuated community, one can't afford fatigue or illness.[28] The image of the toned, muscular (and masculinized) body is equated with vigor, the antithesis of "moral flabbiness."[29] While presenting an image of muscular vitality matters, fitness matters more fundamentally as a source of the boundless energy and drive that the enterprising, entrepreneurial self relies upon.[30] Consider Brown on exercise and "drive":

> "*You have drive.* You *look* tame, but there is this fierceness, the never quite giving *up* on a project, the willingness to put more *in*. Physically you are not stronger than other people. Your drive comes from your brain. You sometimes hear people who *aren't* making it say they don't have the physical strength to be driven, but "physical" isn't where drive comes from. If you eat properly, sleep enough and exercise, you have the energy.[31]

With the language of "tame" and "fierce," one can almost imagine the jungle survival scenarios that Ringer and Korda evoked. And although Brown asserts that "drive" is an emotional state unaffected by physical phenomena, her chapter on exercise emphasizes the energetic benefits of fitness: "Any regular exerciser will tell you his/her body feels different (better) with than without. You have more energy, get sick less."[32]

Still, Brown is careful to note that there are subtle differences between a professional and personal life, particularly when it comes to letting people know about your successes, where she advises careful impression management:

I think you keep two sets of books. In one set, you record the
truth—how well you are really doing. This is the secret set—just
for you and your loved ones. In the other set are more modest
entries and statements, and these are for public consumption!
That's just the opposite of how you might think the game would
be played.[33]

Life is a business where one keeps books, not double-entry ledgers, but double sets of ledgers, to guard against envious others. Life is part game, part climb, and all business. In the business of life, Brown is clear that children are a liability in the pursuit of success, even if the "all" in "having it all" necessarily includes children for many of her readers:

When I was a copywriter . . . my six male co-workers used to growl
when they saw me curved over my typewriter at 5:30 p.m. when
they went home to Pasadena, Altadena, and Alhambra to spend the
evening with their families. One of them even complained to our
boss that I was taking advantage of the rest of them because I
wasn't married and didn't have to go home.[34]

Sixteen pages later, she assures readers that they can, without any question, successfully raise children and hold a big job. The "secret" is to hire someone to care for them.[35] Apparently those persons hired to care for one's children are not in the business of "having it all" for themselves. Winning, for women, was contingent on avoiding the costly and time-consuming demands of childrearing. Caring for others constitutes a significant problem for the entrepreneurial bottom line unless one is willing to imagine the home as part of one's market calculations, factored into one's personal profit-and-loss statement. As a woman, Brown had to navigate the conflicts between professional and personal life rather differently from the way a man of her generation would have; accordingly, she represents an advance guard position in the elimination of boundaries between professional and public life. In Brown's world, labor in childcare had to be minimized to ensure that one could give freely and generously in the workplace.

Loving Too Much and the Culture of Codependency

The idea of "winning" or "having it all" was extended from the public to the private sphere with the mid-1980s books aimed at "women who love too much" and the emergence of the concept of codependence. With the concept of codependence, the public logic of commercial exchange was proposed as the solution to the private dynamics of personal relationships. Giving to another, viewed as an entry on a ledger sheet, had to be balanced. If one gave with no regard for return, one fell into the trap of codependency. Women who gave too much or "loved too much" could never "have it all." Instead, their generosity—previously a characteristic particularly valued in women— set them up for a negative balance sheet and a life without fulfillment.

The emergence of a new term or concept often serves as a marker of significant social change. As the social theorist Norbert Elias pointed out in his discussion of the rise of the word *civility*, "the more or less sudden emergence of words within languages nearly always points to changes in the lives of people themselves."[36] While it remains to be seen whether "codependence" will persist in the English language as "civility" has, a 2001 draft version of a definition for the term is posted in the *Oxford English Dictionary Online*, suggesting that the term has a strong potential for a similar longevity.

Some feminists have argued that the rise of a literature focused on women's ostensible neediness was part of an orchestrated backlash against women's increased power and prominence in the labor force.[37] In the literature of "loving too much," the portrait presented was one of women who were achieving success in the professional world but whose personal lives (perhaps as a result) were a shambles. Others have argued that the concept of codependency is little more than the pathologization of a culture of caring that has traditionally been associated with women.[38] Clearly the development of the concept of codependency was determined by multiple factors and underscores the tensions created by the increased emphasis on labor force participation for women. Even as Helen Gurley Brown portrayed a world in which a woman could have both a successful, usually glamorous, career and a fulfilling (if childless) personal life, an extensive literature—including Robin Norwood's 1985 *Women Who Love Too Much: When You Keep Wishing and Hoping He'll Change*, Susan Forward and Joan Torre's 1986 *Men Who Hate Women and the Women Who Love Them*, among others[39]—suggested that women's personal lives were in disarray. Norwood's book was particularly important in promoting the concept of "love addiction," or what was then called "co-alcoholism," even including a chart graphing the similarities between alcohol addiction and "love addiction." Before long, adult children of alcoholics and other "codependents" were well represented in the bestseller list with books on dysfunctional families, toxic parents, and the resulting "codependency" that was said to be at the root of all interpersonal problems, but especially those of otherwise successful women. While the 1983 publication of Janet Geringer Woititz's bestselling *Adult Children of Alcoholics* had pushed the concept of codependency into the mainstream, between 1988 and 1991 the bestseller list was dominated by titles that reflected the new language of codependence and family dysfunction.[40]

The social theorist John Steadman Rice argues that the concept of "codependency" fused the divergent values of liberation psychotherapy (with its distrust of social institutions and identification of society as the source of emotional pathologies) and the Christian morality and small-group dynamics of the Alcoholics Anonymous tradition. The hybridization of these two worldviews constructed a compelling, if contradictory, new interpersonal paradigm: social institutions were suspect, yet recovery could only occur in the social context of the freely chosen group. The institution most maligned in the codependency literature was the already beleaguered nuclear family.[41] Dubbed "dysfunctional," the family was identified as the source of all interpersonal and social problems. The new self-constructed "family" of the support group provided a substitute family and a self-selected social world.[42]

Given that the culture of self-improvement had so ostracized the position of victim, there was but one place left where being a victim was permissible: children (even "adult children") were exempted from the victim-hating diatribes of self-improvement culture. As "victims" of allegedly "dysfunctional" families, the role of victim had gained a new legitimacy. After all, who would be willing to say that children could not be victimized by their parents? But while identifying as victims of racial, ethnic, gender, or sexual oppression had allowed other groups to forge political identities, the culture of codependence used the notion of childhood victimization to create a group solidarity that was thoroughly insulated from any political potential. By identifying themselves as "adult children," participants in recovery groups represent and experience themselves as victims—not of present-day situations that might be redressed with political action—but instead as utterly helpless in the past (as children) and completelyresponsible for in the present, where they are victims of nothing more than their own willingness to be victimized.[43] Thus within the discourse of recovery, the family, set aside and sequestered as though it operated independently of the larger frameworks of society, is located as the source of one's oppression (in the past) and one's problems (now personalized and depoliticized in the present). The possibility of redress through political channels has been effectively eliminated: the victimized child grows up, throws off the shackles of family and liberates himself completely except from his membership in a depoliticized recovery group.

Codependency's conservative political efficacy located the family as the source of all social and interpersonal problems and identified the liberated, self-interested individual as the source of all solutions. Further, the emergence of the concept of codependency offered additional evidence that market values were being transferred to the private sphere: it was not only Helen Gurley Brown who was keeping an emotional ledger book. Arlie Russell Hochschild argues that the development of the concept of codependency is similar to the rise of the Protestant ethic: that much as "religious ideas jumped the churchyard fence to land in the marketplace" in the sixteenth and seventeenth centuries, a similar phenomenon is at work today as feminism escapes from a social movement and begins "to buttress a commercial spirit of intimate life."[44] Feminism, Hochschild writes, has been "abducted" to legitimate the encroachment of a market logic on the private sphere. The concept of codependency, which characterized caring without keeping an eye on the emotional balance sheet as a pathology, was little more than the application of market values to intimate life. Hochschild notes that "the authors of advice books act as emotional investment counselors. They do readings of broad social conditions and recommend to readers of various types, how, how much and in whom to 'invest' emotional attention."[45] She observes: "The ascetic self-discipline which the early capitalist applied to his bank account, the late twentieth-century woman applies to her appetite, her body, her love. The devotion to a 'calling' which the early capitalist applied to earning money, the latter day woman applies to 'having it all.'"[46] Under the guise of feminism, women were being encouraged "to assimilate to male rules of love": to delay falling in love until after consolidating a career, to separate love from sex, and to generally engage in a "cooler" attitude toward their relationships with men.[47]

Life as a Work of Art: Invention and Improvisation

One alternative to the problem of envisioning one's life as a business—of organizing one's life around emotional and fiscal cost-benefit analyses—has been the move toward imagining one's life as a work of art. A private arena of aesthetics and sentiment, usually understood as feminine or effeminate, has provided a counterpoint to, and a respite from, profit-driven, masculinized, rational economic systems. Artists don't need to "have it all" or to keep balance sheets to avoid "codependency." Instead, they succeed by improvising their way out of any difficulty and creating their own novel solutions. The emergence of the popular belief that one might benefit from imagining life as a work of art also owes a debt to both the nineteenth-century aestheticism most frequently associated with Friedrich Nietzsche,[48] and the increasing popularity of psychoanalytic and psychotherapeutic discourses. With the 1900 publication of *The Interpretation of Dreams* and the 1901 publication of *The Psychopathology of Everyday Life*, Freud demonstrated how each and every individual might come to understand the minor events of daily life—from slips of tongue to physical illnesses—as metaphorical utterances. "Freud's account of unconscious fantasy," the political philosopher Richard Rorty observes, "shows us how to see every human life as a poem."[49] With the increased participation of women in the paid labor force, this Romantic vision of living the creative life has been newly emphasized and expanded through the admonition that each individual can and should imagine her life as a work of art.

By 1979 the metaphor of life as a work of art was pronounced enough to be detected by social science surveys. In a survey of three thousand Americans working either full- or part-time, Yankelovich, Skelly, and White observed that 17 percent of the population placed personal self-fulfillment above all other concerns, including the conventional, traditional values of wealth and power.[50] Yankelovich noted that these Americans are "squarely in the mainstream of the traditional American pursuit of self-improvement," with one exception:

Only when it comes to the *object* [emphasis in original] of self-improvement do they veer sharply from tradition. In the past the purpose of self-improvement was to better oneself in the tangible, visible ways associated with worldly or familial success. But for these strong formers [Yankelovich's term for trendsetters] the object of their creative energies is . . . themselves. Self-improvement is pursued more for its own sake than for external rewards. "*I am my own success story and my own work of art* [emphasis added]. I lavish on myself the riches of Western civilization and the accumulated affluence built up by earlier generations of Americans," they seem to say. [51]

Perhaps because those who emphasize self-fulfillment as a value constitute less than a fifth of the working population, the metaphor of life as a work of art or as something to be crafted remained, for quite some time, just below the radar of conventional measures such as the *New York Times* bestseller list. For example, Barbara Sher's 1979 *Wishcraft: How to Get What You Really Want*, which suggests that one's life should be crafted as a work of art, has remained in print—backlisted for more than twenty years—and has sold more than a million copies, without ever breaking through the bestseller-list ceiling. Similarly, Shakti Gawain's bestselling 1979 New Age *Creative Visualization*, which announces on its final pages that "Your Life Is Your Work of Art," has also remained in print since its publication and has sold 3 million copies to date in North America alone without ever appearing on a single bestseller list.[52] Gawain was one of the earliest self-help authors to propose that life is a work of art:

> I like to think of myself as an artist, and my life is my greatest work
> of art. Every moment is a moment of creation, and each moment
> of creation contains infinite possibilities. . . . What a wonderful
> game we are all playing, and what a magnificent art form.[53]

Only in 1989, with the arrival of the cultural anthropologist Mary Catherine Bateson's book *Composing a Life* on the *New York Times* bestseller list, did the concept of "one's life as a work of art" gain a more prominent place in the popular landscape. Though not, strictly speaking, a self-help book, *Composing a Life* warrants attention nonetheless, as Bateson offers advice to her readers in the form of stories of ordinary women's lives as exemplars. Bateson defined her project as follows: "This is a book about life as an improvisatory art, about the ways we combine familiar and unfamiliar components in response to new situations, following an underlying grammar and an evolving aesthetic."[54] The image of one's life as a work of art has gained increasing credibility, in part, I have argued earlier, because the metaphor of life as a path or journey was simply too gendered in its origins to continue to function effectively in a world where women as well as men were increasingly encouraged (or compelled) to develop themselves. Although Bateson's choice of women's lives for the subject of her book underscores this, her introduction contends that it is as much economic changes—changes in the job market rather than changes in the composition of the labor pool—that require this new metaphor:

Much biography of exceptional people is built around the image of a quest, a journey through a timeless landscape toward an end that is specific, even though it is not fully known. The pursuit of a quest is a pilgrim's progress in which it is essential to resist the transitory contentment of attractive way stations and side roads, in which obstacles are overcome because the goal is visible on the horizon, onward and upward. The end is already apparent in the beginning. The model of an ordinary successful life that is held up for young people is one of early decision and commitment, often to an educational preparation that launches a single rising trajectory. Ambition, we imply, should be focused, and young people worry about whether they are defining their goals and making the right decisions early enough to get on track. . . . Graduation is supposed to be followed by the first real job, representing a step on an ascending ladder. . . .

These assumptions have not been valid for many of history's most creative people, and they are increasingly inappropriate today. The landscape through which we move is in constant flux. Children cannot even know the names of the jobs and careers that will be open to them; they must build their fantasies around temporary surrogates. Goals too clearly defined can become blinkers [sic]. Just as it is less and less possible to replicate the career of a parent, so it will become less and less possible to go on doing the same thing through a lifetime. . . .

Many of society's casualties are men and women who assumed they had chosen a path in life and found that it disappeared in the underbrush.[55]

The metaphor of life as a work of art to be woven, composed, or improvised is one that accommodates both changing occupational opportunities and the need for a new model of success that can encompass the complexities of women's lives, with their need to juggle children, parents, spouses, and employment. Life as a work of art provides a ready alternative to the older metaphor of life as a journey with a singular trajectory.

Without the masculine construct of the path, and without the theistic idea of a calling from a masculine god, the idea of the life as a work of art infuses self-invention with the type of spirituality that Max Weber suggested would supplant theism: the substitution of aesthetic judgments for moral ones.[56] Weber observed that aesthetic values would come to stand in for traditional ethical values during times of increasing intellectualism and among intellectuals, so the fact that the idea of one's life as a work of art would be popularized by the daughter of two of the twentieth century's most preeminent anthropologists, Margaret Mead and Gregory Bateson, seems only fitting.

But Bateson was not the first intellectual to introduce the idea of one's life as a work of art into the public's imagination. No less prominent a thinker than philosopher Michel Foucault discusses much the same idea in a 1983 interview published in *Vanity Fair*, where he suggests: "From the idea that the self is not given to us, I think that there is only one practical consequence: we have to create ourselves as a work of art."[57] Foucault takes pains to distance himself from what he calls "the Californian cult of the self" in which, he notes, one is "supposed to discover the true self, to separate it from that which might obscure or alienate it, to decipher its truth thanks to psychology or psychoanalytic science."[58] Foucault's distinction between his version of "life as a work of art" and popular versions thereof hinges on his renunciation of the figure of a singular, unified authentic self that can discover itself in favor of an ideal of mastering oneself. Much as his intellectual forebear Friedrich Nietzsche had suggested, Foucault asserts that it is possible to "become what one is" not by discovery, contemplation, or self-knowledge but by asserting a certain style of life, by creating one's life, or coming into one's own. For Nietzsche, self-creation was a matter of embracing the multiplicity of one's possible selves. Of himself he said that he was "happy to harbour . . . not 'one immortal soul', but *many mortal souls* within."[59] Self-discovery is, for Nietzsche, pointless, even counterproductive. "To become what one is," he writes, one must not have the faintest notion *what* one is. From this point of view even the blunders of life have their own meaning and value, the occasional side roads and wrong roads, the delays, the 'modesties,' seriousness wasted on tasks that are remote from *the* task. All this can express a great prudence, even the supreme prudence: where *nosce te ipsum* [know yourself] would be the recipe for ruin, forgetting oneself, *misunderstanding* oneself, making oneself smaller, narrower, mediocre, becomes reason itself.[60]

This distinction between self-discovery and self-creation, this rupture with the Socratic tradition of "the examined life," prefigures the shift from the metaphor of one's life as journey to that of one's life as a work of art. Rather than "finding oneself," one is meant to create or invent one's self. While Foucault distinguished his rarified self-creation from the popular "California" versions of self-discovery, and Nietzsche offered pursuit of one's life as a work of art as a way to distinguish oneself from the common man or the horde, increasingly the ideal of life as a work of art is offered to the masses.

Despite Foucault's dismissal of the vernacular self-improvement culture of self-discovery and authenticity, there are surprising similarities between some non-Socratic Greek ethical practices circa 380 B.C. that Foucault seems to advocate and the practices proposed by contemporary self-help culture. The Greek citizen, according to Foucault, invented his own life through exercises such as journal writing, reflection, and reading.[61] Such practices provided a way of training oneself out of a variety of perceived defects such as anger, envy, gossip, and flattery and are startlingly similar to those found in the contemporary literature of self-improvement culture. Consider the following excerpts from meditations in Sarah Ban Breathnach's 1995 book *Simple Abundance: A Daybook of Comfort and Joy*, which enjoyed nearly two years on the bestseller list. If Bateson and Foucault have provided the theory, Breathnach has provided the guidebook for practice:

FEBRUARY 7: AN ARTIST IS SOMEONE WHO CREATES

Today, take a real risk that can change your life: start thinking of yourself as an artist and your life as a work-in-progress. Works-in-progress are never perfect. But changes can be made to the rough draft during rewrites. Another color can be added to the canvas.

The film can be tightened during editing. Art evolves. So does life. Art is never stagnant. Neither is life. The beautiful, authentic life you are creating for yourself and those you love is your art. It's the highest art.

FEBRUARY 8: YOU ARE AN ARTIST

. . . each of us is an artist. An artist is merely someone with good listening skills who accesses the creative energy of the Universe to bring forth something on the material plane that wasn't here before. . . .

So it is with creating an authentic life. With every choice, every day, you are creating a unique work of art. . . .

Today, accept that you are creating a work of art by making big and little choices between playing it safe and risking.[62]

FEBRUARY 9: A FRESH CANVAS EVERY TWENTY-FOUR HOURS

. . . Preparatory steps are necessary in all the arts. They are also necessary in life if we want to live authentically. Every twenty-four hours we are given a fresh canvas to prime, to make ready for the vision. Quieting our minds in meditation, carving out time to dream and express ourselves with our daily dialogue and illustrated discovery journal, becoming aware of our true preferences, slowing down to concentrate on completing one task at a time.

With its cover art of a woodcut of an oak tree, bordered in pink, *Simple Abundance* announced itself as a repository of wisdom for women. The idea that one ought to consider one's life as a work of art was finding fertile ground among dissatisfied women, who were being encouraged to retreat into domesticity.

Revolution from Within: Another Inward Turn?

Within the Romantic ethos, the myth of the artist operating outside the market represents one line of resistance; the revolutionary represents another. In 1992, Gloria Steinem tapped into this Romantic mythology with her *Revolution from Within: A Book of Self-Esteem*. Widely viewed as a retreat from politics,

Steinem's entrée into the self-help book market was generally greeted with jeers from critics and intellectuals who found Steinem's characterization of herself as lacking in self-esteem hardly credible. Many critics perceived the self-help book as yet another symptom of the psychologizing of the political, the inversion of the notion that the personal is political.[63] If one considers self-help books as purely repressive ideology (and disregards the idea of self-improvement books as a sign of social dissatisfaction or prepolitical protest), then Steinem's book, with its full embrace of the self-help genre (complete with meditation guide for inner healing and a chapter on embracing and nurturing one's inner child) looks like reactionary backsliding. But I think it's important to consider Steinem's foray into self-improvement discourse in its larger social context. In 1992, the same year that Tom Peters's *Liberation Management* provided corporations with the tools for managing the self-actualizing worker, Steinem was attempting to provide social justice movements with the tools for mobilizing the self-actualizing masses. Steinem was asking critical questions: How do you organize people who are opposed to organizations? How do you mobilize people who are suspicious of groups?

Describing herself as "codependent with the world," Steinem embarked on the project of reconciling social activism and self-improvement culture.[64] Perhaps, she noted, an increasingly popular recovery movement offered something vital that was lacking in social change movements. The popularity of Twelve-Step groups and the rise of the "recovery movement" suggested that a large portion of the population had embraced a "liberation psychotherapy" notion of the individual as sullied during the socialization process—in need of liberation from the strictures of society so as to "recover" a lost self.[65] The isolation engendered by a worldview that attributed all of one's problems to the very processes of socialization and to the individuals (specifically parents and other family members) who had contributed to one's development reinforced a widespread sense of anomie. Although the tenets of liberation psychotherapy had become entrenched, they had not led to stable social relationships, institutions, or identities. Individuals began to search for and create solutions to this social isolation; Twelve-Step recovery groups were one context in which individuals sought a sense of community.[66] Steinem sought to tap the dynamism of Twelve-Step groups to restore the social context to "self-help":

we seem to have come into a time of polarization, with self-explorers refusing to vote and activists refusing to restore themselves; with

New Agers who put off action for so long that, like women restricted to the house who develop agoraphobia, they've come to fear it; and with activists who criticize self-realization or recovery movements without ever asking what they are offering that social justice movements are not.[67]

And, perhaps more important, from a strategic point of view, in her 1993 afterword to *Revolution from Within*, Steinem asked the difficult question: what are self-help and Twelve-Step groups offering people that feminism, the Left, and the labor movement have failed to provide?

While the self-help genre and title of Steinem's book implied that she was arguing that political change was not possible without personal change, her text actually suggests the inverse: that self-esteem isn't possible for oppressed groups without social and political change. The examples she offers suggest that her "self-esteem" rose not from self-reflection but from confronting social injustice in the world: from action in the world à la Nietzsche's "becoming what one is." However, her form or genre—a self-improvement manual—suggested the opposite. Steinem offers numerous examples of personal change forged in the context of collective political action. Taking herself as an example, she described her own increased sense of well-being after she challenged the manager of New York City's Plaza Hotel, who had previously expelled her from the hotel lobby in accordance with the late 1960s rules that unescorted females were not permitted. What motivated her challenge to his authority and the hotel's policy? The fact that a group of feminists—of which she had chosen not to be a part—had recently picketed the Plaza's restaurant because of its exclusionary policy. Steinem describes this as "catching the contagious spirit of those women who had picketed the Oak Room."[68]

Steinem's viral contagion model of political mobilization is in keeping with her organic view of social systems. Just as every cell in the body contains the blueprint for the entire body, argues Steinem, so every cell must demand to see itself represented in the social body:

> Look at it this way: if each cell within our bodies is a whole and
> indivisible version of those bodies, and each of us is a whole and
> indivisible cell of the body politic, then each of us has an organic
> need to be part of a group in which we can be our whole and
> indivisible selves.[69]

The metaphor of society as an organism is by no means new. One need only look at Hobbes's 1651 *Leviathan* to see a corporeal metaphor providing a rationale for the privileging of the "head of state." Organic metaphors, metaphors of growth, permeate the literature of self-improvement. But what is interesting in Steinem's organicism is its post-Cartesian, post-Watson-Crick-and-Franklin formulation.[70] Steinem's organicism doesn't privilege the mind or brain over the rest of the body. Hers is a decentralized view organized at the cellular level. As each cell in the body is said to contain the DNA "blueprint" for the entire organism, Steinem's individual is called upon to realize itself in the whole.[71] In such a model, individual change would inevitably lead to social transformations, as long as the individual led a life of self-expression rather than conformity.

Steinem was hardly the first person to suggest that pursuing one's "authentic self" would inevitably result in social change. *The Greening of America*, Charles Reich's influential 1970 book, had argued that the quests for personal authenticity launched in the 1960s would inevitably transform American society for the better. In a more scholarly context, the historian Marshall Berman put forth a similar thesis: that the demand for individual authenticity would necessitate egalitarian social transformations.[72] And more recently, arguments are being advanced that a new class of "cultural creatives" are changing America for the better by pursuing fulfilling private lives governed by values of creativity and sustainability.[73] But the pursuit of individual self-actualization that characterized the 1970s didn't lead automatically and inevitably to progressive social change, as is easily demonstrated by the 1980s, a decade of unbridled greed and the consolidation of wealth in the hands of a few. This idea of self-fulfillment as the route to progressive social transformation failed to recognize that the pursuit of self-fulfillment by those who already possess the greatest share of wealth and opportunities could have precisely the opposite effect: it could instead maintain the status quo. The optimistic contagion theory of social change fails to recognize the malignancy at the economic base of the social body: an economic system that not only privileges profit over any other value but that was, during the last part of the twentieth century, restructured to foster ever greater economic inequality. Beyond this fundamental problem, the contagion theory of social change has other shortcomings. Crowds are purportedly irrational and easily swayed: contagions are neither rational nor predictable and easily mobilized for less-than-egalitarian purposes.[74] In a culture driven by public relations, contagions are all too likely to be more akin to ideological germ warfare than a spontaneous effluence of emancipatory fervor.[75]

The pursuit of self-fulfillment could only lead to progressive social change if the self were to be imagined as relational and embedded: individuals would have to be understood as members of a society comprising more than just voluntary, self-selected groups.[76] This relational self would need to constitute itself relative to others of all social and economic positions, which is what Steinem envisions when she argues that social justice must necessarily be part of the agenda:

> So, as a result of what I've learned from readers of this book, here is a suggestion for a goal by the year 2000: *A national honey-comb of diverse, small, personal/political groups that are committed to each member's welfare through both inner and outer change, self-realization and social justice.* It doesn't matter whether we call them testifying or soul sessions as in the civil rights movement; consciousness-raising or rap groups as in early feminism; covens, quilting bees, or women's circles as in women's history; or revolutionary cells, men's groups, councils of grandmothers, or "speaking bitterness" groups as in various movements and cultures. Perhaps they will have an entirely new name, since combining the elements of diverse communities will make them different from all of them. I think of them just as "revolutionary groups," for a revolution is also a full circle. The important thing is that they are free, diverse, no bigger than an extended family—and everywhere.[77]

Then Steinem throws out the "dare" to her readers: "This isn't as large an order as it sounds. If two white male alcoholics could start a national network of meetings that are free, leaderless, and accessible, so can we."[78] Steinem's self-selected groups can only be effective if they include people from all walks of life, and, more important, find the means to institutionalize the changes they desire. The hitch is that this relational self creating social change could only be effective if it were global, extending not only to one's own quilting bee or reading group but organized to be inclusive of everyone. Precisely how such groups could and would confront institutionalized and moneyed power is left to one's imagination, a concern that I will consider further in the final chapter.

More Spiritual Consolations: The Simple Life and the Retreat to Domesticity

For those who are disinterested in revolution and unwilling to engage in the soulless pursuit of economic self-interest, self-improvement culture for women offers another spiritual consolation in the form of the domestic retreat. Just as "the road less traveled" offered an alternative to the dog-eat-dog world represented by writers such as Robert J. Ringer, the idea of "simple abundance" offers aesthetic and domestic consolation prizes to women who are not yet ready to embrace market values in every area of their lives. A series of authors emerged to offer spiritual consolation to women, encouraging them to relish their roles as domestic goddesses. The most successful of these has clearly been Martha Stewart, whose fetishized domesticity captured the American imagination. But as Stewart's books fall outside the self-improvement genre—she takes as her object of improvement the domestic environment as an extension of the self rather than the self itself—I will focus on Sarah Ban Breathnach's 1995 *Simple Abundance*. Consider an excerpt from a meditation included at the very beginning of the daybook:

> January 11: Is It Recession or Depression?
>
> . . . Perhaps the recession has personally affected you and yours.
> . . . Millions of women are scaling down their expectations of what constitutes the good life, redefining their values, reordering their priorities, and accepting the challenge of making a virtue out of necessity. But it's very easy to surrender to an emotional depression when a financial one occurs. It's easy to be pessimistic about tomorrow when today seems so bleak.[79]

Breathnach doesn't conceal the fact that "simple abundance" is offered as an antidote to economic contraction; however, she does claim that "scarcity" is imaginary. Consider the meditation from the next day in the series, which begins with a quotation from a 1932 *Ladies' Home Journal*:

> January 12: There Is No Scarcity
>
> *When money is plenty this is a man's world. When money is scarce it is a woman's world. When all else seems to have failed, the women's instinct comes in. She gets the job. That is a reason*

why, in spite of all that happens, we continue to have a world.
Ladies' Home Journal, October 1932 . . . .

If you are worried about money today, take heart. You have the power to change your lifestyle and move from a feeling of lack and deprivation to a feeling of abundance and fulfillment. . . . The simpler we make our lives, the more abundant they become.

There is no scarcity except in our souls.[80]

The feeling of abundance is substituted for the reality of economic insecurity—a substitution that is hardly new in American popular culture. Marjorie Roulston Hillis's 1937 *Orchids on Your Budget* was a Depression-era bestseller.[81] More recently, Catherine Ponder's 1965 *The Dynamic Laws of Prosperity* has been reissued. Ponder—who has been called "the Norman Vincent Peale among lady ministers"[82]—draws up a table of contents for her book that illustrates how persistent the belief in infinite abundance, or God as Supply, can be:

Poverty Is a Sin
Prosperity is Your Divine Heritage
Success Is Divinely Ordained
The Bible Is a Prosperity Textbook
Why Poverty Is Not Spiritual
Right Attitudes Will Pay Your Bills[83]

At a time when a woman's chances of poverty have actually increased along with women's increased labor market participation, books such as Breathnach's encourage a retreat from the difficulties of the labor market into an idealized domestic sphere. But despite the appeal to simplicity, the book offers a mixed message: while money doesn't matter, consumerism is central to Breathnach's advice. She writes:

when some women hear of Simple Abundance they mistakenly
believe the path is part of the new and much-heralded frugality
movement. This is not true because the frugality movement of the
1990s is based on fear, and fear repels abundance rather than
attracting it. . . . Simple Abundance is not about deprivation. . . .
One of the ways in which we can start to experience more affluence
in our daily lives is through pampering ourselves with affordable
luxuries.[84]

Directives to consume are peppered throughout her other advice:

"Rent *Out of Africa* from the video store."[85]

"Treat your authentic self to the most fetching straw hat you can find."[86]

"Get a yard of fisherman's netting in a shell shop or five-and-dime."[87]

"Call for the J. Peterman Company mail-order catalogs."[88]

One attains Breathnach's version of simple abundance in large measure by shopping. Other examples of this "simplify by shopping" approach are themselves abundant: the 1999 debut of the mass market magazines *Real Simple* and *Simplicity*; a series of books organized around the concept of "simple chic"; and other self-help books aimed at helping women, and sometimes men, "simplify their lives."[89] While there are anticonsumerist voluntary simplicity tracts, such as Duane Elgin's *Voluntary Simplicity*, these titles are not multiweek bestsellers, and Breathnach's daybook doesn't fall within that alternative category.[90] Instead, her recasting of mind-power—with its focus on abundance provided by a mysterious universal Supply (which in this context might be called consumer credit)—reflects a time-worn American infatuation with simplicity as an antidote to anxieties about abundance and excess.[91]

The Time Bind and *Take Time for Your Life*

At the close of the twentieth century, as Americans, particularly American women, struggled to balance the demands of full-time jobs and full-time responsibilities as parents, two books appeared: one a work of qualitative sociology, Arlie Russell Hochschild's 1997 *The Time Bind*, and the other a self-help book, Cheryl Richardson's 1999 *Take Time for Your Life*. Time, or more accurately, the lack of it in the face of increased demands on women, was foregrounded as an issue in its own right. In Hochschild's analysis, the interpenetration of public- and private-sphere values had generated a situation in which the workplace came to feel like a refuge and haven for beleaguered parents, in particular mothers, much as the home had been a "haven in a heartless world" for the previous generations of male workers. Overworked mothers were seeking refuge in their workplaces from what Hochschild calls the "third shift"—managing the emotional repercussions of their time-starved personal lives. Parents, she observed, increasingly turned to self-help books that encouraged children to engage in "self-care" rather than make demands on their exhausted parents.[92] Recalling the label "narcissistic" that Christopher Lasch had attributed to Americans, Hochschild observes:

> For many working parents in the 1990s, however, "narcissism" has taken an odd turn. Adapting to the rigors of timebound lives, they steel themselves against both the need to care for others and the need to be cared for. Emotional asceticism, then is one defense against having to acknowledge the human costs of lost time at home. If we can't see a need as a need, how can we imagine we need time to meet it?[93]

Hochschild's study concluded by making the case for a time movement—a political movement organized around limiting labor force work hours in the interest of maintaining time for personal and family life.[94]

Shortly after the 1997 publication of *The Time Bind*, Cheryl Richardson's book *Take Time for Your Life* appeared. Richardson, a leader in the then-nascent field of personal coaching, developed and popularized the idea of "extreme self-care," a concept originated by Thomas Leonard, the founder of Coach University.[95] The suppressed need for care that Hochschild identified had already begun resounding through the popular culture of self-improvement. The theory behind the idea of "extreme self-care" is that when one's needs are met and exceeded, one has "reserves," and thus others will find one attractive and appealing and one will have a relatively simple time continuing to meet, and exceed, one's own needs. Not surprisingly, both Richardson and Leonard began their coaching careers as personal financial counselors who found that their clients needed considerably more than financial planning advice. In an era when the average working family's income remained static or dropped while costs for basics such as healthcare, housing, and education skyrocketed, financial planning took on a new, interpersonal dimension. The financial self-help author Suze Orman wrote: "Like most Certified Financial Planner® professionals, I started my practice to help other people with their money, but as time went on, I realized that it was far more than their money (or lack of it) that needed attention."[96] As rational economistic principles were being applied to the private sphere, financial counselors were particularly well-positioned to meet the need for personal coaching.[97] Orman again: "It's as if the language of money has pervaded out culture in a new way and is imploring us to listen."[98] The encroachment of market economics into every corner of the world, into every sphere, contributed to the fusion of psychological and financial counseling.

Richardson's work was catapulted into the public spotlight when she led a team of "lifestyle makeover" experts for the *Oprah Winfrey Show*. The first of these programs aired on May 29, 2000, and the series continued more or less every other week for a year. The shows were described as "a revolution of the spirit," with Winfrey exhorting her audience: "Join the revolution. Live your best life." The use of the word "revolution" in the series is instructive. In one interview, Tracey, an exhausted mother who conducted a business from home while parenting her child and managing her household, needed to organize a way to get some time for herself without "breaking the bank." Tracey's solution: organize a babysitting co-op. Richardson commends Tracey's action:

> Tracey was courageous to walk her neighborhood and put these flyers in the mailboxes. That's revolutionary. . . . You've got to get that kind of revolutionary spirit and energy behind the fact that you are reclaiming your life and you'll do whatever it takes to make it happen.[99]

Malcolm X's imperative—"by any means necessary"—returns as an invocation on self-help television. And thinking outside a market economy—not hiring a sitter but organizing a co-op—might indeed be somewhat revolutionary, though women have been exhaustively instructed on how to operate outside the economy. Yet when the question of economic concerns arises in another interview, its importance is minimized. Amy, a mother of four young boys, explains that it is not only time that causes her stress:

> Money has been a huge strain between my husband and I. We are drowning in bills and the four boys, they are very expensive. My family needs my salary to make ends meet. I work full-time as a labor and delivery registered nurse on the night shift. I know I have to go to work, but I really want to be home for my kids. I feel really guilty. There are times when I'm driving to work and I'm just in tears. . . . I feel like I've lost myself because I'm so busy doing my other roles: mother, wife, nurse. I don't know what I would do if I had an hour to myself.[100]

Richardson breaks in and says "Amy is a good example of a lot of women in this country who are sleepwalking through life." When Winfrey asks Richardson how our mothers' generation managed—"Were they sleepwalking, too?"— Richardson attributes the stress and strain not to Amy's financial situation but rather to the proliferation of telecommunications technologies— answering machines, e-mail, and cell phones:

> Back then, we didn't have answering machines. We didn't have fax machines. We didn't have e-mail. We didn't have pagers and cell phones. Today because of technology there are so many ways for people to get at us. We are faced with way so much more than our mothers—you know what I'm talking about. And yet we still internally think we can be our mothers. It's like our inner operating system hasn't caught up to the outer operating system . . . of a new very fast-paced world.[101]

A number of prominent social scientists and social critics would agree with Richardson about the impact of communication technologies,[102] but what is remarkable as the exchange continues is the absolute avoidance of any discussion of the declining real wages of families over the prior thirty years. The beleaguered mother of four continues, "I would like to go to the grocery store and not have to count every penny. I would like to go into the store and get them what they needed without using the credit card. I don't want it to be about money."

When Richardson proposes that "Amy needs to create space and time for herself" Winfrey, to her credit, interjects:

> You know, if I was watching this—it's very easy for me to say sitting in a chair with my rich self . . . I'm thinking if I'm worrying—counting pennies when I go to the grocery store, you telling me to take a little time for myself would only be *ir-ri-tating* me. Because I'm thinking I can take all the time I want, but I'm still going to have to get to the grocery store and wonder how am I going to pay for all of this.[103]

In response, Richardson recommends downscaling one's life, as well as taking a "revolutionary" step:

> I think that that's the most challenging piece is—if you do have to work full-time. And you have to look at things like is there a way to

down—cut back in your life, to downscale. I know you've been—Amy's been—looking at that. I mean, if you're in a situation where you're can't—you're—you're barely—barely putting food on the table and you're already cut back, then that's the time—*the revolutionary thing to*—thing to do is to reach out and ask for help.[104]

The moment is instructive as the usually well-spoken Richardson finds herself struggling, even stammering, to come up with language to address the problem. The work of avoiding politics is hard work.[105] In the context of self-help television, this labor of displacement is accomplished by adopting the notion of revolution to the most depoliticized possibilities: revolution is alive and well just as long as it's a revolution from within that stays within: as long as it's a revolution of the spirit, or a plea for help. Political discourse is held at bay: this context provides no opportunity to discuss the social, political, and economic realities that have contributed to these women's shortage of time and money. Some of America's most successful women, Winfrey and Richardson among them, find themselves avoiding a discussion of what self-help authors would call the elephant in the living room: the changing economic realities in American life that have led to the phenomenon of middle-class poverty.[106]

To further contain the discussion, Winfrey introduces a segment from an upcoming show in which the "money expert" Suze Orman reassures viewers:

> True wealth lies within each and every one of us. That's where true fortunes are found. I'll say it over and over again, you have to go within in order to never do without. You want to find the true pot of gold, look within, bring it out. Show the world who you really are. And when you can stand up in truth with self-effort and grace, money will start to come your way. But please remember, it's also going to take self-effort as well. Your thoughts create your destiny, your self-effort creates your destiny. Grace, however, is there for every one of us all the time.[107]

When Time = Money, Money = Life

While Suze Orman's 1997 book *Nine Steps to Financial Freedom* is technically not a book directed solely at women, let's consider it here, in the context of the time and money binds experienced by women in the last quarter of the twentieth century. Offering "practical and spiritual steps so you can stop worrying," Orman writes:

> I don't know if I have discovered the meaning of life, but I have learned a great deal about what money can and cannot do. . . . I have come to think that money is very much like a person, and it will respond when you treat it as you would a cherished friend— never fearing it, pushing it away, pretending it doesn't exist, or turning away from its needs, never clutching it so hard that it hurts. Sometimes it's fatter, sometimes it's skinnier, sometimes it doesn't feel so good and needs special nurturing. But if you tend it like the living entity it is, then it will flourish, grow, take care of you for as long as you need it, and look after the loved ones you leave behind.[108]

In Orman's calculus, all prior economistic metaphors are collapsed: life is not just a business. Rather, money is alive—a life force in itself.[109] Although Orman is quick to note in her "First Law of Financial Freedom" that people come first, before money, she has so thoroughly anthropomorphized money that the distinction is all but moot. Offering an explanation of why rich people get richer, Orman explains:

> Money is a living entity and it responds to energy exactly the same way you do. It is drawn to those who welcome it, those who respect it. Wouldn't you rather be with people who respect you and who don't want you to be something you're not? Your money feels the same way. This is one of the reasons why the rich get richer.[110]

To a certain extent, Orman is correct: while money isn't alive, or a life force, or "feeling offended" at one's disrespect, a significant number of economists would agree that money is "congealed human labor." Human labor and, therefore, life are frozen in this abstract form. When Orman talks about investing one's money so that "it will work for you," she is describing the way in which interest and dividend income are derived from the expansion of the economy, which is, of course, dependent on the productivity of working people. Thus when an investor's money is "working" for that investor, somewhere, someone is working and taking home less than the value of what he or she has produced in his or her day's work. Or, more aptly, everywhere, almost everyone is working, producing increments of value for which they are not compensated. The only way out of this conundrum—in Orman's view—is for working people to scrimp and save so as to become investors themselves and recoup something of what has been appropriated from them.

What is missing in Orman's equation is the degree to which people would need to scrimp and save simply to stay in the same place. The decline in real wages during the last quarter of the twentieth century is well documented. Let's consider just one reliable measure: the *Economic Report of the President* for 2003 reports that average weekly paychecks (in private nonagricultural industries) dropped from a high of $315.38 in 1972 to a low of 254.87 in 1993, only slowly climbing back to $277.50 in 2002. During roughly the same period, the real gross domestic product nearly tripled, rising from 3.6 trillion dollars in 1970 to 9.2 trillion in 2001. Americans were productive—very productive—but most weren't sharing in the wealth they were producing. While the economy had formerly enjoyed the unwaged labor of women at home, it now enjoyed the discounted wages of women in the labor market, as well as the disappearance of what had once been called "the family wage." To justify these discounted wages, the market would soon appeal to the myth of the impoverished artist who works for the simple satisfaction that work brings, as I will show in the coming chapter.

From *Having It All* to *Simple Abundance*

For the women who were managing households, raising children, and holding down jobs, the appeal of having it all had led most unexpectedly to the reality of having less and less. Yet self-improvement literature urged them onward, alternating between the free market feminism of a Helen Gurley Brown and the domestic oblivion of Sarah Ban Breathnach's simple abundance. Seizing upon the possibility of inventing their lives outside the traditional roles of wives and mothers, women in the last quarter of the twentieth century amplified both the rational and expressive cultural tendencies that have resonated through Western cultural life since the early nineteenth century. For Helen Gurley Brown, the idea that one's life is a business extended into the personal and intimate sphere, laying the groundwork for the entrepreneurialization of personal life.[111] Concurrently, the concept of codependency came into widespread use, and the assertion that "women were loving too much" popularized the idea that women ought to be applying a rational cost-benefit analysis to their intimate relationships.

While the rational business model was expanded into the personal sphere, the notion that one's life is a work of art, a concept implicit in the Romantic tradition, was also elaborated and more clearly enunciated (and, as I will show in the coming chapter, extended into the workplace). Having been democratized through the popularization of psychoanalytic thinking and then bolstered in the cultural arena, the idea that everyone is an artist—the creator of his or her own life artwork—was further popularized when Mary Catherine Bateson challenged the traditional masculine metaphor of life as a journey. Another Romantic notion, that personal transformation will inevitably result in political change, was suggested by Gloria Steinem's *Revolution from Within*. Finally, for women who could not stomach the pecuniary vision of "having it all," of calculating each emotional investment, and for whom revolution was either taking too long or of little interest, domestic retreats to "a simple life" were offered as an alternative.

Thus the extension of the ideal of self-realization to women—the proposal that all people are entitled to and responsible to "be all they can be"—accelerated tendencies that were already apparent in the cultures of capitalism. Indeed, if one imagines these two threads in capitalist culture—instrumental/rational and expressive/affective—as the strands in a rope twisted tighter and tighter, then the rope began to double up and curl back onto itself as rational calculations were proposed for the intimate sphere and, as I will show, expressive and affective approaches were proposed in the arena of work and career. This doubling back, so evident in the advice literature directed toward women, was also apparent in the popular literature of occupational satisfaction. In that literature, the newly popularized ideal that one's life is a work of art finds its corollary: the artist as the ideal worker.

chapter 4

The Self at Work

From Job-Hunters to Artist-Entrepreneurs

"I am not a businessman, I am an artist."
—*Warren Buffett*

At the end of the twentieth century, wealth—whether earned, inherited, or otherwise acquired—continued to serve as a sign of divine favor, as it had since the late nineteenth century. However, in a culture where a psychotherapeutic ethos had augmented, and, in some cases, supplanted religious beliefs and spiritual traditions, wealth, in and of itself, was no longer sufficient. Self-realization through work was also required as a sign of salvation, whether here or in the hereafter. The journalist David Brooks describes this as the emergence of a new class: "bobos," or bourgeois bohemians, a group for whom wealth earned through some self-fulfilling quest constituted the highest level of achievement.[1] While there is some merit to Brooks's observation—that satisfaction in one's work combined with wealth had formed a new couplet signifying success—obtaining the latter became increasingly difficult as real wages declined in the last quarter of the twentieth century (excluding, of course, the speculative bubble of the late 1990s).

As the gap between the wealthy and the poor grew during this period, so did the notion that self-fulfillment might serve as a genuine sign of one's secular salvation. While even the Puritans hoped to link individuals with work that was "agreeable" to each, the late-twentieth-century emphasis on a fulfilling career as the right—and responsibility—of each and every individual, irrespective of gender, race, or ethnicity, served to motivate a workforce that experienced shattered job security, frequent unemployment, declining real wages, and, when employed, greatly increased work time and productivity expectations.[2] Simultaneously, linking work to self-realization channeled the counterculture value of self-fulfillment back into the productive sphere —back into the workplace. Pleasure in work offered an antidote to ambivalence about pleasure for its own sake. And, perhaps most important, for an economic system that requires the ongoing reduction of production costs, an emerging ideology of creative self-fulfillment in work, even without compensation, emerged as more and more women entered the labor force. If women were no longer willing to work without compensation, who would? Artists, who have been notoriously willing to work for little or nothing, and the idea of working as an artist works, stepped in to fill the gap.

Advice to Job Hunters: Where Necessity Meets the Market

The career advice manual, the job seeker's guide, is an unusual commodity, in that it exists at a critical juncture positioned between the individual's needs (for food, shelter, medical care, etc.) and the exigencies of the labor market. The job seeker's guide offers strategies to workers selling their labor, and in that process reveals the values associated with work, career, and vocation. While the workplace itself may present problems to be managed and negotiated, the absence of gainful employment, unless mitigated by other financial means, constitutes a personal crisis for which career self-help books offer solace and practical advice. The all-time bestselling book in this category is Richard Nelson Bolles's *What Color Is Your Parachute? A Practical Manual for Job Hunters and Career Changers*, which is revised annually. With more than 8 million copies in print and translations in twelve languages, *Parachute* has come to be called the "the job hunter's Bible."[3] The comparison to the Bible turns out to be much more than simply a figure of speech. Bolles's blockbuster was initially self-published in 1970 as part of his counseling work for the Protestant United Ministries in Education. Working as an Episcopalian minister on a college campus, Bolles had observed that a number of the individuals he counseled had difficulty keeping their jobs. He set out to help them by creating a booklet of job-hunting tips. Bolles mailed the 162–page spiral-bound photocopied manuscript to members of the clergy and placed ads for the booklet. The story goes that before long he was receiving orders from across the country: not only from churches but from schools, colleges, corporations, and the career counseling community.[4]

By 1972, Bolles's booklet was picked up by Ten Speed Press, a publisher whose only other title was a bicycle repair manual. Sales of the book were slow at first but, buoyed by the rising unemployment of the early 1970s and by a new emphasis on career education at the U.S. Office of Education, built steadily until 1979, when the book landed on the *New York Times* trade paperback bestseller list. It remained on the bestseller list almost continuously for four years, until the beginning of 1984. The success of the job hunter's manual resulted in a 1975 decision to publish the book as an annual, updated and revised each year.[5] These annual editions are valuable artifacts in tracing the evolution of the job hunter.

For Bolles, the timing of the publication of *Parachute* could not have been more fortuitous: from 1955 until around 1974, the annual unemployment rate was relatively low, hovering between 3 and 6 percent. Then it began to rise, reaching a peak of nearly 10 percent in 1983. Only at the end of the century (in 1997) did the unemployment rate again drop to below 5 percent.[6] *Parachute* also benefited from a change in educational policy: the book appeared just as the newly minted term "career education" (replacing the more plebian "vocational education") became a highly visible influence at the U.S. Office of Education. Beginning in the early 1970s, the Office of Education called for a "revitalized" K–12 education using a curriculum based on the career education theme.[7]

Perhaps the most obvious changes in *Parachute* across its three decades of revisions are the various transformations of the book's physical appearance. Over the course of twenty-five years, the volume has swelled from 201 pages in 1972 to 525 pages (divided between 228 pages of text and 297 pages of appendices) in 1997.[8] As sections gained in importance, they were often revised and expanded as appendices. For example, the topic "job-hunting while on the job" is mentioned in the 1981 edition but by 1987 grew into a detailed appendix, where the preponderance of the advice offered is to utilize every moment of one's leisure time—evenings, weekends, lunch breaks, and vacation time—in search of one's next position.[9] Work at remaining employed overflows into every moment of life.

Cover art for the book changes only gradually: an etching of an airborne team transported by a parachute/balloon hybrid served as the cover illustration for fifteen years, from 1972 through 1987 (see fig. 4.1). By 1987, the etching

Figure 4.1. Book cover changes for Richard Bolles's *What Color Is Your Parachute?* 1972, 1987, 1989, 1992, 1997, 2000, 2001, and 2002. Reprinted with permission from *What Color Is Your Parachute?* 1972, 1987, 1989, 1992, 1997, 2000, 2001, 2002 by Richard Nelson Bolles. Copyright 1972, 1987, 1989, 1992, 1997, 2000, 2001, 2002 by Richard Nelson Bolles, Ten Speed Press, Berkeley, CA. www.tenspeed.com, www.jobhuntersbible.com.

remains, but the background has been upgraded to include a gestural water-color wash. Two years later, the image is revamped: the parachute/balloon airship is pictured gliding above a brightly colored tropical landscape. Then, in 1992, perhaps reflecting the sobering situation for job hunters, the tropical paradise is replaced by a somber Arcadian image dominated by dark blues. The balloon image appears only as a minor icon, receding into the distance of a dark landscape. By 1996 the airborne parachute/balloon, in rainbow col-ors, has returned as the central image on the cover art, and remains in this location until 2002. The edition for that year, produced after the turn-of-the-century collapse of the stock markets, features a gloomy cover with a black and grey background and a small iconic parachute/balloon. While conventional wisdom suggests that one ought not judge a book by its cover, book buyers tend to, and the changes in the tone of the job hunter's Bible provide a curious barometer of employment outlooks.

Parachute offers specific exercises and activities to assist the unemployed in finding a match between themselves and the labor market. Self-assessment exercises designed to help the "job hunter" identify his or her skills and interests, along with advice on where to find "the person who has the power to hire you" are served up with zany images that lighten what otherwise might seem a grim topic (see fig. 4.2). Inventories of skills, along with story-writing exercises about one's past accomplishments, charts, graphs, and tables are designed to help the job hunter identify his or her "transferable skills," that is, his or her skilled labor power that can be sold to a variety of possible employers in a changing labor market. Self-knowledge is offered

Figure 4.2. Detail from board game in Richard Nelson Bolles's *What Color Is Your Parachute?*, 1972 edition, pp. viii–ix. Reprinted with permission from *What Color Is Your Parachute?* by Richard Nelson Bolles. Copyright 1972, 1987, 1989, 1992, 1997, 2000, 2001, 2002 by Richard Nelson Bolles, Ten Speed Press, Berkeley, CA. www.tenspeed.com, www.jobhuntersbible.com.

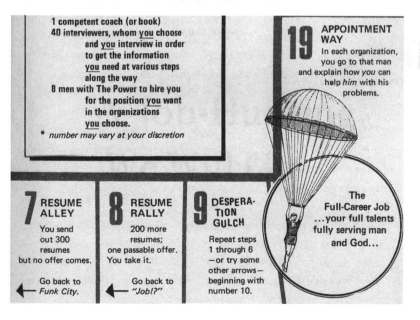

as a central component of career success, but knowledge of the labor market is of equal importance. Yet even this emphasis on skills and employability would soon be changing, giving way to the idea of pursuing "one's passion."

Carriages, Parachutes, and Other Means of Conveyance: Metaphors of Path, Sport, and War

We know what a job hunter is: someone whose life necessities have driven him or her into the labor market in pursuit of a wage or salary. But what is a "career changer"? Who is the other group of persons to whom *Parachute* is marketed? Webster's *Third New International Dictionary* offers a definition of career as "a profession for which one undergoes special training and which is undertaken as a permanent calling; an occupation or profession engaged in as a lifework." The *Oxford English Dictionary* (OED) records the equestrian roots of the word. "Career" originates in the French word "carriere" for race course, the Spanish "carrera" for road, and "carraria" for carriage road. In its early usage, "career" was used to denote the ground on which a race is run, or the course over which any person or thing passes; a road, path, or way. It was also used to indicate the "short gallop of a horse at full speed, as in a tournament or battle." Only in the early nineteenth century (1803) was the term used to indicate, in the OED's words, "a person's course or progress through life (or a distinct portion of life), esp. when publicly conspicuous, or abounding in remarkable incidents." Thus "career" combines the idea of a journey or path with that of a game or sport, the tournament. The "career," with its jousting for position, has its roots in the medieval tournament, a game that tested the battle skills of its men in short, fast, and violent runs. And, as the cultural historian Raymond Williams points out, the notion of career suggests being nearly out of control, linked as it is etymologically to "career."[10] Career merges the notion of path with the idea of the race course, evoking not only speed but also sport or game. In short, the idea of career brings the metaphor of "a path in life" together with the idea of "life as a game."

Bolles's invocation of parachuting in his title links an image of skydiving with the notion of aerial disaster: the pilot's escape or paratrooper's descent. The title *What Color Is Your Parachute?* was, Bolles reported, a response to the expression "I'm bailing out of this job."[11] The book's publisher, Phil Wood, noted that Bolles's title, which conjures the image of the lone parachuter, complete with the narrow escape from the downed plan(e), the exhilaration of skydiving, the notion of an aerial view, and the promise of escape or safe landing, was key to the book's success: "If this book had died, it would have been the title that killed it. Now that it lives, it's the title that saved it."[12] Yet despite the reference to parachuting, the cover of *What Color Is Your Parachute?* never pictures a lone parachuter. Instead the image is a hybrid: part airborne balloon, part parachute silk. While the language of "parachuting" bridges both war and sport, the image of the balloon foregrounds pleasure and adventure. Bolles merges the idea of a sport or recreational pursuit with language that evokes the image of aerial battle and impending doom. Rather than following the linear paths of the earthbound carriage driver or cyclist, the parachuter/balloonist can take shortcuts and land in unexpected locales. The skydiver, paratrooper, or balloonist enjoys an aerial perspective, a God's-eye view of the world, and sees the "roads less traveled" and earthbound paths as mere landmarks. The perils and promise inherent in the technology of flight, one of industrial capitalism's most remarkable achievements, are evoked in Bolles's title. The fact that the book found its home at the publisher of a bicycle repair manual seems somehow overdetermined: although the technology of cycling persists despite the prevalence of the automobile, bicycling continues, in the U.S. context, mostly as a sport or fitness pastime. In short, what was once an important means of transportation has become a recreational activity, much as the work that once filled vital needs (e.g., weaving and sewing, gardening, fishing and hunting) reappear as hobbies, as activities of leisure, as labors of love.

One's Calling and Mission: Traditional Christianity in Bolles

Although Bolles evokes a powerful image of twentieth-century technological advances, the undercurrent of his rhetoric ensures continuity with the Puritan principle of finding and pursuing one's "particular calling" only after one has pursued the "general calling"—only after one "knows God." Consider this passage from the 1988 edition of *Parachute*:

> Your first Mission here on Earth is one which you share with the rest of the human race, but it is no less your individual Mission for the fact that it is shared: and that it is, **to seek out and find, in**

daily—even hourly—communication, the One from whom your Mission is derived. *The Missioner before the Mission*, is the rule. In religious language, your Mission here is: *to know God, and enjoy Him forever, and to see His hand in all His works.*[13]

No doubt the eighteenth-century Massachusetts Bay Colony clergyman Cotton Mather would be pleased to see the influence of his 1710 pronouncement. Consider this passage from his *Bonafacius or An Essay to Do Good*:

> Indeed, no *Good Works* can be done by any man until he be *Justified.* Until a Man be United unto the Glorious CHRIST, who is *our Life*, he is a *Dead Man.* And, I Pray, what *Good Works* to be Expected from Such a Man? They will all be *Dead Works.*[14]

As a skillful rhetorician, Bolles is aware of his audience and responsive to their limits. Indeed, his rhetoric with respect to "calling" and "mission" changes significantly across the years, varying with the tenor of the times. In the very earliest editions of *Parachute*, Bolles makes numerous theological references posed playfully or in passing, without any passages that are as directly theistic as those found in the 1988 edition. For example, the 1972 edition includes a board game, "Operation Parachute," where the winning square is "The Full Career Job . . . Your Full Talents Fully Serving Man and God" (see fig. 4.2). The same year, and for many years thereafter, Bolles advocates the pursuit of a suitable calling in pious terms: "God's world already has more than enough people who can't wait for five o'clock to come so that they can now go and do what they want to do."[15] But by 1987, Bolles has made a subtle shift; "God's world" disappears:

> There is a vast world of work out there, where 111 million people are employed in this country alone—*many of whom* are bored out of their minds. All day long. Not for nothing is their motto TGIF—"Thank God It's Friday." They *live* for the weekends, when they can go do what they really want to do.[16]

Subtle, perhaps inconsequential, and arguably an improvement in style, the shift to a more vernacular usage—from the pious "God's world" to "TGIF" —is consistent with other changes in the book.

The indexes of the various editions of *Parachute* also offer some changes that suggest uncertainty about how to locate the book's religious antecedents. While the term "calling" appears in the indexes of the 1972 and 1977 editions of *Parachute*, by 1982 the word vanishes. One could argue that the entire book is about finding one's calling, thus indexing this concept would be impossible, but similar peculiarities of the indexing suggest that there was some concern about limiting the book's religious references for its growing secular audience. On close examination, inconsistencies between the index and the book's text emerge. While interpreting such errors is a risky business—perhaps overreaching—let's consider just one. In 1982 edition of *Parachute*, the index includes, "talents, parable of the."[17] However, there is no actual discussion of the biblical parable of the talents (Matthew 25:14–30) in the body of Bolles's book. While the word "talent" is used (for example on page 142: "the more you enjoy what you are doing and where you are doing it, the better you are going to use the talents which God gave you"), no actual explanation or explication of the biblical parable of the talents appears in the text. Whoever prepared the index could have imagined the biblical association of the parable of the talents and included it in the index, despite the fact that there is no reference to the parable in the book's text—or perhaps the parable had been included in the text and was subsequently deleted. Whatever led to the curious indexing error, by 1987 the anomaly had been eliminated, and references to "calling" had also vanished.

Throughout the 1970s and mid-1980s, *Parachute* became increasingly secularized, despite its genesis in a Protestant ministry. Then, in 1988, at a point when Christian fundamentalism had grown increasingly powerful in national political life, Bolles reemphasizes the Christian premises of his work with an appendix entitled "Religion and Job-Hunting: How to Find Your Mission in Life." Bolles writes that he developed the new section after readers had requested it and claims that it was the most popular addition he'd made to the book in eighteen revisions over the previous twenty years' time.[18]

The mission appendix lays out Bolles's own version of the Christian concept of mission in three parts, reminiscent of Cotton Mather's 1701 sermon "A Christian at His Calling." Parts 1 and 2 of Bolles's version of one's mission correspond to Mather's "General Calling," in that this mission is said to be shared by all. Everyone is required to "know God" and to "make the world a better place." And the third aspect of Bolles's version of mission corresponds closely with Mather's idea of a "personal calling," as the reader is asked:

(a) to exercise that Talent which you particularly came to Earth to use—your greatest gift, which you most delight to use,

(b) in the place(s) or setting(s) which God has caused to appeal to you the most,

(c) and for those purposes which God most needs to have done in the world.[19]

Bolles's decision to reintroduce and emphasize the Christian content of *Parachute* during the height of Christian fundamentalism of the late 1980s offers an example of how responsive the advice literature is to cultural trends, yet it also demonstrates the persistence of the traditional idea of calling or mission across two centuries. The seemingly secular literatures of calling and vocation are grounded in longstanding Christian thinking regarding work as a reflection of God's will.

From Livelihood to Identity: Downsizing and Depression

Despite the continuities with traditional Christian values, there were other subtle changes within the text of *Parachute*—and greater changes within the job search literature as a whole—as the recession of 1990 swept through the ranks of the employed in the form of the then newly minted term "downsizing." Take, for example, the appearance of the topic "depression" in the index of the 1992 edition. Although Bolles discusses the emotional strain of job hunting using the term "rejection shock" throughout the series, it was not until 1992 that the word "depression" appeared in this context.[20] By 1996, the single-line index entry of "depression" had evolved into an entire chapter devoted to the topic and acquired thirteen subheadings, including "unemployment as cause." While the appearance of depression in the index of *Parachute* may be as much a result of increased public awareness of mental illness and the wide availability of antidepressant medications, there is no doubt that the "downsizing" of the early 1990s—a term that makes it into the *Parachute* index in 1994[21]—contributed to depression in numerous individuals.

There was a time, the historian Karl Polanyi reminds us, when the "problem" of unemployment for the laborer was not so much a problem of lack of work as lack of wages.[22] Today this reality is obscured: lack of work— unemployment—constitutes an acute psychological crisis. The loss of occupational identity has been socially constituted as at least as significant, if not more significant, than the loss of livelihood. Bolles offers an extensive series of common-sense coping strategies for the depressed job seeker, such as getting adequate sleep and exercise, eating well, and some mental exercises, including making a list of things that you enjoy and writing stories about your life.[23] Indeed, by 1996 Bolles has even downplayed the thought of death. Rather than asking readers to complete the sentence "Before I die I want to . . ." (as he had done in prior editions), Bolles's 1996 edition of *Parachute* offers a less morbid approach to life planning. Under the heading "Your Biography As You Would Like It to Read, Someday," Bolles proposes:

> There are various way to approach this. Some people sit down and write what they would like their imaginary obituary to say, after they die. Other find this approach too morbid for words, so they like to pretend that they someday get into *Who's Who*; and they write what they would like that entry to say about them. Others prefer to consider all their heroines or heroes, write what it is they like about them, and then circle those things which they would like to be true about themselves.[24]

Parallel to this shift toward more uplifting language, consider the change in the conclusion of the chapter entitled "Where Do You Want to Use Your Skills?" In 1992, the chapter wrapped up with a metaphor of reciprocity:

> Job-hunting is a two-way street. For the time being, whether the places you visit during your research happen to have a vacancy, or happen to *want* you, is premature and irrelevant. In this dance of life, you get first choice: you get to decide first of all whether or not you want them. Only after you have decided that you do want them, is it appropriate to ask if they also want you.[25]

By 1996, the chapter concluded not with a metaphor of job hunting as a two-way street, but rather with an ode to the possibilities for individual fulfillment through the pursuit of one's dreams:

> It is amazing how often people do get their dreams, whether in stages or directly. The more you don't *cut* the dream down, because of what you *think* you know about *the real world*, the more likely you are to find what you are looking for.

Most people don't find their heart's desire, because they decide to pursue just half their dream—and consequently they hunt for it with only *half a heart*.

If you want to pursue your whole dream, your best dream, the one you die to do, I guarantee you that you will hunt for it *with all your heart*. It is this *passion* which often is the difference between successful career-changers, and unsuccessful ones.[26]

In Bolles's more recent narratives of the job search, passion about what one does and effort in managing one's career path emerge as the central components of one's success. Getting a job is no longer sufficient, since today's job is tomorrow's pink slip. Although occupational satisfaction had always been central to Bolles's approach, the balance of the demands of the market (accommodating oneself to the market and "playing the game") and the desires of the job seeker (realizing one's "authentic path") has been tipped markedly toward the desires of the individual job seeker. And how could it be otherwise? When the market is utterly unpredictable, one can't plan on accommodating oneself to market demand. Instead, the emphasis is on individual pleasure, an idea that emerges full blown in another unexpected career advice bestseller, Marsha Sinetar's 1987 *Do What You Love, The Money Will Follow.*

New Age Advice to Job Seekers: *Do What You Love, The Money Will Follow*

In 1987 Paulist Press, a small publishing house in New Jersey whose primary books had been religious texts, published a title that would, like *Parachute*, become a surprise bestseller. Marsha Sinetar's book *Do What You Love, The Money Will Follow* sold so well that in 1989 the title was reissued by Dell.[27] According to *Publishers Weekly*, the trade journal of the publishing industry, Sinetar's book rode the wave of unemployment and downsizing that swept the United States during the recession of 1990–92, with more than one million copies in print by 1995.[28] Sinetar described the epiphany that provided her with the concept and title for her most successful book to date:

> as I drove along beautiful Wilshire Boulevard in Los Angeles, on a smogless, sunny California morning, a startling thought entered my head. It was as clear a thought as if someone was speaking to

me: "Do what you love, the money will follow." At that very moment, I knew I had to, and would, take a leap of faith. I knew I had to, and would, step out, cut myself loose from all those things that seemed to bind me. I knew I would start doing what I most enjoyed: writing, working with industry (instead of public education) and living in the country instead of in the city.[29]

Her story is reminiscent of the New Testament description of the conversion of Paul, in transit, thrown from his horse by a great flash of light.[30] Although Sinetar is clearly located in the Christian tradition of thinking of life as a spiritual journey, she takes pains to distance herself from the image of a joyless work ethic, offering her own vision as the corrective to the Puritan notion of work:

> Perhaps [the idea that work is drudgery] evolved out of the Puritan ethic, which kept people's noses to the grindstone, grimly slaving away from sunrise till sunset. A respite was needed—not so much from the work, as from the attitudes behind the work, which were based on a deep antipathy to joy and playfulness. The Western concept of controlling nature, our love and fascination with "progress," our admiration of material success and victory over obstacles have helped us equate work with those tasks and activities by which we shape and control external things: nature, time and the enemies of life—poverty, blight, a ferocious landscape, illness, the limitations of geographic distance and space. It would be natural to want to rest after channeling one's anger and anxieties toward work projects such as these. Viewed in this way, work becomes something cut off from the self, a survival vehicle and an avenue of activity that can make a person bitter, tired or cynical. Work then fragments and splits the personality, instead of integrating it.[31]

Along with a revisited and revised Protestant ethic, Sinetar evokes a hybridized—and not altogether accurate—version of the Buddhist concept of "right livelihood." Rather than research and represent the Buddhist doctrine of right livelihood, Sinetar makes up her own definition and uses appeals to a natural order as her rhetorical strategy:

> Right Livelihood is an idea about work which is linked to the natural order of things. It is doing our best at what we do best. . . . There is no way we can fail. Biology points out the logic of Right

Livelihood. Every species in the natural world has a place and function that is specifically suited to its capabilities. This is true for people too. Some of us are uniquely equipped for physical work, athletics, or dance; some of us have special intellectual gifts . . . some of us have aesthetic abilities. . . . Examples are numerous of nature's way of directing us to the path that will support us economically and emotionally; this is the path that we are meant to travel.[32]

Despite her shifting register—from species to individual—Sinetar's examples, for the average reader, establish her claims within a natural order and within the comfortable time-worn metaphor of the path. Then, to establish some level of theological legitimacy for her use of the term, Sinetar hedges her bets about the authenticity of her use of the concept of "right livelihood," noting that "the original concept of Right Livelihood *apparently* comes from the teachings of the Buddha, who described it as work consciously chosen, done with full awareness and care, and leading to enlightenment."[33]

The Buddhist notion of right livelihood is a somewhat more nuanced concept, encouraging the seeker to make her or his living "only in ways that avoid deceit, treachery, trickery, and usury. Five occupations are specifically condemned: trading in arms, living beings, flesh, intoxicants, and poison."[34] Claude Whitmyer, who also promotes the ideal of right livelihood through his Center for Good Work, observes:

As the concept of right livelihood has been absorbed by twentieth century Western culture, its meaning has expanded beyond the Buddhist idea of doing no harm, to include the ideas that work should make a difference in the world, benefit the community, and be personally fulfilling.[35]

Although the Western use of the concept of right livelihood can be viewed as an expanded one—fused with the Protestant ethic—Sinetar limits her use of "right livelihood" to the idea that work be personally fulfilling and all but excludes the original precepts. Specifically, she advises readers that they ought to dispense with succumbing to societal demands and imperatives and seek to fulfill their inner dreams and ambitions. Like Bolles, Sinetar offers her readers self-assessment exercises in the form of questions: for example, "What makes me happy? . . . What memories fill me with joy? . . .

Which of my traits or characteristics, when expressed, make me happy to be me?" to discover what their personal path might be.[36] But, unlike Bolles, who suggests that job seekers adapt their skills to the demands of the labor market, Sinetar offers no advice on how to connect one's inner ambitions with remunerative work. Instead, she advises that following one's passion will always lead to a happy ending. And if it doesn't, she offers a plan B, in the form of the dignity-of-all-labor doctrine.[37] Blending the Buddhist idea of mindfulness with the humanistic psychology concept of self-actualization, Sinetar writes:

> the actualizing person . . . sees work as a joyful exercise, a calling that is almost effortless. For him, work becomes a way in which to understand life around him, a resolver of paradoxes and a path for personal development. For him, work is a creative, graceful, present-moment experience. This is in line with the Buddhist perspective, which uses simple, daily routines as way to grow, as a way to maintain an elegant concentrated connection with the world, and as way to see the self as having a place in the scheme of things. . . .
>
> No matter how impersonal, dull or tedious the job might seem to others, for the individual whose work is like play, daily life is expressed as a lucky or blessed experience. . . .
>
> Any job—telephone operator, bank clerk, office administrator, librarian, carpenter, physician, auto mechanic, sales—is enlivened when performed by an actualizing adult. This individual, working at what he or she really enjoys—even when working at something unappealing on a short-term basis—has a different inward posture.[38]

And where Bolles offers advice on how to negotiate a salary and advises job hunters to consider the level of compensation that they need when evaluating where they'd like to work,[39] Sinetar suggests that individuals cultivate "inner affluence": in her words, "the quality of being that enriches us in all the really important, life-affirming ways."[40] In this model, financial compensation doesn't just take a back seat to self-fulfillment; it has no seat at all. Work as worship supplants work as livelihood. The idea that one ought to work without any assurances of compensation—that one should wait hopefully "for the money to follow"—is consistent with an economy that is moving toward the artist as one of two models of the ideal worker.

The Artist's Way: Self-Subsidy and the Artist
as the Exemplar for a Postindustrial Workforce

Artists continue to be among the most poorly compensated professionals and are often compelled to subsidize their own labor. No other occupational group is as renowned for pursuing their work irrespective of compensation. Self-subsidy is a foregone conclusion for most working artists. A 1997 report entitled "Creative America," prepared by the President's Committee on the Arts and the Humanities, describes the economic hurdles that American artists encounter:

> A good case can be made that our cultural life is underwritten
> by the undercompensated labor of artists and scholars. Despite
> the highly publicized—and deeply misleading—examples of
> musicians, opera singers, or authors who earn millions of dollars,
> the average working artist usually finds only intermittent work
> and must often supplement his or her profession with a second
> job.
>   An extensive survey of 12,000 craft artists, actors and painters
> found that the vast majority earned less than $20,000 per year
> from their work. Only 28% of Actors Equity members sampled in
> the survey made more than $20,000 per year. Over 90% of the
> painters earned less than $20,000 and nearly three-fourths made
> only $7,000 or less a year from sales of their work.[41]

Uncompensated or undercompensated labor makes the arts, as we know them in the U.S. context, possible. Although some cultural critics have even argued that art work can only be produced when shielded from the demands of the marketplace, operating in a sequestered "gift economy," such an approach begs the question of how artists are to continue subsidizing and sequestering their work when fewer and fewer jobs offer the possibility of adequate compensation to pursue such a dual path.[42]

It was within this context, and in the midst of the height of the recovery movement, that the self-described recovering alcoholic Julia Cameron created and self-published *The Artist's Way*. Subtitled *A Spiritual Path to Higher Creativity* and supertitled *A Course in Discovering and Recovering Your Creative Self*, the book was subsequently published in 1992 by Putnam/Jeremy Tarcher as a $12.95 trade paperback. According to the book's publisher, sales to date are in excess of 1.5 million copies and multiple sequels include *The Vein of Gold* (1996) and *The Artist's Way at Work* (1998).

To understand the magnitude of Cameron's sales, compare its success with that of M. Scott Peck's *Road Less Traveled*. Recall that Peck's book, which enjoyed a record-breaking 694 weeks on the *New York Times* bestseller list and was marketed to the widest possible readership as a generic self-help book, is reported to have sold between 6 and 7 million copies.[43] Cameron's roadmap, on the other hand, never appeared on the *New York Times* bestseller list and was targeted to a significantly smaller segment of the self-help market in the "creativity" subgenre of the literature. When these facts are considered, Cameron's sales are record-breaking in their own right.

The Artist's Way relies on techniques designed to cultivate an "authentic self": chief among them the "morning pages" and the "artist's date." The former is the practice of writing three pages in longhand immediately after waking up in the morning every day. This writing is not to be thought of as writing, but rather as a kind of fodder for creative production and a place for uncensored reflection.[44] "Morning pages," writes Cameron, "are a meditation, a practice that bring [*sic*] you to your creative and to your creator God."[45] The second tool or technique, the "artist's date," is defined as

a block of time, perhaps two hours weekly, especially set aside and committed to nurturing your creative consciousness, your inner artist . . . an excursion, a play date that you preplan and defend against all interlopers. You do not take anyone on this artist date but you and your inner artist, a.k.a. your creative child.[46]

The daily routine of the morning pages recalls the daily prayer of religious practices, while the weekly two-hour "artist's date" mirrors the time structures typically allotted for religious services. Artists are also instructed to create "an artist's altar" and to devise rituals to "become spiritually centered."[47] Creativity, like sobriety, is conceived of as a natural state that has been disrupted by the civilizing process.[48] A God or Higher Power, in this case often appropriately enough referred to as a "creator," is assumed to guide one's creative recovery. And one is to attend or care for one's "inner artist" or "creative child." In every aspect of its language, *The Artist's Way* reflects the formulations that were popularized by the literature of the recovery movement: "recovering" one's "inner child" is revamped as "discovering" one's "creative child" or "inner artist."

Journalistic accounts of the success of *The Artist's Way* report that creativity self-help programs based on the book have been offered by corporate human relations departments, university extension programs, and in a host of holistic health and therapeutic contexts, as well as in less formal groups of friends and colleagues.[49] Some claim that millions of individuals have met in *Artist's Way* support groups.[50] In addition, numerous online discussion groups have been predicated on principles from *The Artist's Way*.[51]

In 1998 Cameron and collaborator Mark Bryan tapped into the career self-help market with *The Artist's Way at Work.* The first line of the book focuses on the central premise and the shift in the workplace: "Intellectual capital—ideas as money, money as ideas—is today the real currency of the business world."[52] Indeed, the new book adapted their techniques for fostering creativity as a means to spiritual fulfillment for the workplace and crystallized a trend that had been developing in the culture: the idea of the artist as an exemplar for the postindustrial worker.

The evidence of this phenomenon-in-the-making had been mounting. A 1992 career advice book by Laurence G. Boldt called *Zen and the Art of Making a Living* expressly argued that shaping one's work life ought to be conceived of as art.[53] Meanwhile, corporate workers were being urged to be more creative, artful, and poetic. In the mid-1990s, the performance artist Martha Wilson, who had founded Franklin Furnace, a New York City alternative artists' space, began offering creativity workshops to corporate clients. Similarly, the poet David Whyte, who had published a book entitled *The Heart Aroused: Poetry and the Preservation of the Soul in Corporate America,* had begun providing poetry workshops for discouraged and disheartened corporate workers who had survived the winnowing of the workforces in their offices only to be saddled with handling the work of their former colleagues.[54] Around the same time, a cartoon appeared in the *New Yorker* that suggested the parallels between the lifestyles of artists and those of the postindustrial labor force (see fig. 4.3).

In the mid-1990s, the artistic mentalité provided an ideal vehicle for motivating a demoralized, downsized, and otherwise dissatisfied labor force.[55] And artists provided the ideal work model for this new postindustrial labor force, as they

- Are trained to work with symbolic forms, so they offer an ideal model for the newly christened "knowledge workers"

"Workaholic? Brokers and salesmen are workaholics. Artists are obsessed. There's a difference."

Figure 4.3. *New Yorker* cartoon by Edward Sorel published April 24, 1995. © The New Yorker Collection 1995 Edward Sorel from cartoonbank.com. All rights reserved.

- Have been engaged in a pursuit of excellence for its own sake well in advance of Tom Peters's 1982 "search"
- Are accustomed to working without supervision
- Find ways of motivating themselves even in the absence of compensation
- Typically work out of their own workspace, thus shifting costs of overhead (space, office equipment, software, etc.) to the worker (and thereby reducing fixed capital costs for corporations)
- Blur the distinction between work and pleasure. This ensures that workers who think like artists won't be watching the clock or looking for overtime

Finally, last and best of all:

- They work for free. Artists notoriously engage in their creative work for little, or even no, financial compensation.

What finer characteristics could a system like capitalism seek in a worker? The cultural critic Andrew Ross points out that this new model of artists/workers—unlike Marx's "industrial reserve army" of the unemployed, always available to keep the cost of labor low—creates a reserve *volunteer* army of people who will work for fun.[56] Here, Ross asserts, we have not just a *low-wage* reserve industrial labor force, but a *no-wage* labor force.

The Romantic myth of the artist toiling over his work alone in his garret[57]—sequestered from the demands and rewards of the marketplace and foregoing the pleasures and demands of childrearing—has, to some extent, persisted through the twentieth century. This ethos, which encourages the pursuit of one's work out of love of the work or craft without sullying oneself with concerns about marketplace viability, and without exhausting oneself with the demands of childrearing, provides an ideal rationale for encouraging labor without compensation.

In 1956 the sociologist William H. Whyte aptly described "the organization man," whose characteristics—conformity, limited initiative, and a loathing of genius or excellence—were best suited to work in a hierarchical corporate context. The energetic entrepreneurial spirit of the Protestant ethic was in decline, Whyte asserted, as group solidarity and company loyalty were increasingly critical for individual advancement. But with the so-called reengineering of corporations in the 1980s, "the search for excellence," and the rise of knowledge-based industries, work styles and human resource management models have necessarily adapted, and a new form of the Protestant ethic emerges where individual work satisfaction substitutes for "grace."

The quest for occupational satisfaction is an understandable, individual attempt to solve the problems of alienation, boredom, and rage in hierarchical work settings. But because the problem is framed as an individual problem, any solution is necessarily partial, contingent, and temporary. As long as the satisfaction of human needs is subject to a social division of labor with inequitable distribution of resources and opportunities, and organized to privilege profit-taking over meeting human needs, any version of occupational satisfaction is double-edged, with the desire for vocational happiness serving as a powerful means of social control.

One of the central lessons of Weber's Protestant ethic thesis is that when it comes to social action, intentions are not what matters. Sixteenth- and seventeenth-century Puritans did not set out to create the conditions for the development of industrial capitalism; they merely attempted to find a solution to the devastating psychological implications of the doctrine of predestination. Nineteenth- and twentieth-century artists have not set out to provide the ideal model for the postindustrial worker; they have simply attempted to find some means to happiness in their work—some way to avoid the stifling alienation borne of the industrialized division of labor and the conformist requirements of corporate cultures. But one unintended consequence of these choices is the development of an ideal of work as the central, even sole, source of self-fulfillment.

The ideal that everyone ought to work purely for the intrinsic rewards of his or her work—for his or her own amusement and delight—would be an appealing notion if only the extrinsic necessities of life were assured. Even Abraham Maslow had called for the satisfaction of primary physiological, emotional, and social needs before the satisfaction of "higher needs," such as his ideal of self-actualization, would be possible.[58] Thus this move toward separating work from compensation could be a radically progressive one, were it coupled with a call for a new definition of rights in terms of human needs. Rather than a "right to work," one would speak of a right to all the basic necessities of life: food and shelter, healthcare and retirement benefits, access to education, and an environment protected from wanton pollution. These material rights would serve not as a means of re-creating oneself as labor power but as a means of realizing oneself and enjoying one's life, which is, after all, the ostensible goal of all of this self-improvement literature. In the absence of this possibility, the primary way individuals seem to imagine achieving any measure of safety and security is by identifying with capital—by imagining themselves as entrepreneurs, as the "CEOs of Me, Inc.".

Tom Peters: From Managing the Self-Actualizing Worker to the CEO of Me, Inc.

Motivating workers in a climate of decreased compensation levels and heightened insecurity about employment poses a particular challenge for managers. By the early 1980s, U.S. unemployment rates had reached nearly their highest point since the depression of the 1930s, with official unemployment figures showing 9.6 percent of the population out of work, and nearly 20 percent of the African-American population unemployed.[59] At the same time, median real wages had dropped to the lowest point since 1970.[60] It was into this setting that Thomas J. Peters and Robert H. Waterman, Jr., introduced the concept that would be used, in lieu of wage increases and job security, to motivate an increasingly anxious and demoralized workforce. "Excellence" became the watchword of the 1980s, and occupational satisfaction in the pursuit of this abstraction was offered as employee motivation. The title of Peters and Waterman's book, *In Search of Excellence,* became the management mantra of the 1980s, and managers were advised to offer employees greater control over their work and increased input into decision-making. Such management strategies, imported from the quality circles of Japanese corporations, offered a sense of engagement and participation when the traditional rewards of job security, salary increases, and promotions were unlikely. Indeed, by 1987, Peters (who was now writing under the friendlier, less academic "Tom" rather than "Thomas") is offering a seven-point strategy for enhancing business performance, drawn in large measure from Japanese management principles:

> (1) "Kaizen, the never-ending quest for perfection"; (2) "the development of full human potential"; (3) "Jidoka, the pursuit of superior quality"; (4) "build mutual trust"; (5) "develop team performance"; (6) "every employee as manager"; and (7) "provide a stable livelihood for all employees." These seven features, supported by simple systems, extensive training, and a host of other devices, have resulted in startling performance improvement in short order.[61]

Second only to "the never-ending pursuit of perfection," the development of human potential is seen as pivotal for developing productivity, as Peters asks managers to examine their own beliefs: "Do you genuinely believe that there are no limits to what the average person can accomplish, if well trained, well supported, and well paid for performance? Such a belief is the #1 spur to achievement."[62]

Along with training, support, and adequate compensation, Peters asserts that maintaining an effective workforce requires some measure of job security: *"only some guarantee of security will enable firms to induce employees to (1) constantly take risks (improve things, add new skills) and (2) be flexible enough to deal with constant change."*[63] To maintain this ideal workforce, which is well paid (at least in Peters's estimation) and enjoys a secure livelihood, Peters advocates that managers "develop a plan for using temporaries, subcontractors, and overtime in conjunction with staffing at 85 to 90 percent of normal demand requirements."[64] In exchange for this putative security, employees are asked to "accept inconveniences, such as mandatory overtime," and "agree to perform tasks outside their normal job definition."[65]

The trouble with Peters's formulations is that the increased use of temps and subcontractors to ensure the job security of regular workers creates the ever present specter of unemployment, poor compensation, and lack of benefits among as many as seven out of every fifty workers (simply using his recommended percentage of maintaining permanent staffing at 85 to 90 percent of normal demand).[66] Peters advocates the elimination of all middle management and invokes the management consulting firm McKinsey & Company, where he had been employed when writing *In Search of Excellence:* "The first step in accomplishing successful plant floor implementation of new manufacturing approaches is the clearing out of *all* the middle managers and support service layers that clog the wheels of change".[67] Peters continues with his reflections on what came to be called "reengineering":

> What do we do, as a firm or nation, with the huge excess of middle
> managers? There's no easy answer here either. Many can be
> devolved to the field, but many will not survive the transition.
> Extensive retraining is a minimum. . . . But a whole generation
> who did their jobs well and a new generation of women and
> minorities finally making it into management's lower and middle
> ranks have been cast adrift. . . . [A]djustment assistance . . . is
> needed as a matter of policy; but most proposals, mine and others',
> still don't deal adequately with the immensity of this problem. . . .
> Demotions back to nonsupervisorial status seldom work out.[68]

Although Peters recognizes the need for job security as a prerequisite for a motivated and flexible workforce, he asserts that to remain competitive, businesses must cut their costs by eliminating employees. The contradiction between management's need for a secure (and therefore) productive workforce is confounded by the conflicting need to cut staffing. How to maintain a secure yet expendable workforce becomes an intractable management problem.

What is required, then, is some means of making employees feel secure even when they know they're not. One solution to this is to place the onus of employment security on the individual worker by making each and every worker responsible for his or her own "career." If the idea of "Kaizen," or the constant quest for perfection, is transferred from the product to the worker, then the responsibility of maintaining financial security is shifted to the worker. Work on the self becomes an integral part of the worker's new work, as I will explore in greater detail in the next chapter.

Although Peters began his career writing management books—that is, self-help books for organizations—the 1994 publication of *The Pursuit of Wow* marked a shift in his focus and target audience: he moved from advising organizations to advising individual entrepreneurs. Case studies in *Wow* focus not on corporate successes or failures but on individual successes, sometimes noting an organization that the individual founded or leads. Peters suggests that he is attempting to provide viable solutions for "the immensity of the problem" of unemployed managers that he identified in his 1987 *Thriving on Chaos*. In August 1997, Peters published an article— "The Brand Called You"—that summed up his recommendations for individuals:

> It's time for me—and you—to take a lesson from the big brands, a lesson that's true for anyone who's interested in what it takes to stand out and prosper in the new world of work.
>
> Regardless of age, regardless of position, regardless of the business we happen to be in, all of us need to understand the importance of branding. We are CEOs of our own companies: Me Inc. To be in business today, our most important job is to be head marketer for the brand called You.
>
> Start right now: as of this moment you're going to think of yourself differently! You're not an "employee" of General Motors, you're not a "staffer" at General Mills, you're not a "worker" at General Electric or a "human resource" at General Dynamics (ooops, it's gone!). Forget the Generals! You don't "belong to" any company for life, and your chief affiliation isn't to any particular "function." You're not defined by your job title and you're not confined by your job description.
>
> Starting today you are a brand.[69]

Specifically, Peters now advises individuals to market themselves using a variety of techniques for fostering word of mouth, each of which involves additional work for the new CEO of Me, Inc.:

> Try moonlighting! Sign up for an extra project inside your organization, just to introduce yourself to new colleagues and showcase your skills—or work on new ones. Or, if you can carve out the time, take on a freelance project that gets you in touch with a totally novel group of people. If you can get them singing your

praises, they'll help spread the word about what a remarkable contributor you are. . . .

[T]ry teaching a class at a community college, in an adult education program, or in your own company. You get credit for being an expert, you increase your standing as a professional, and you increase the likelihood that people will come back to you with more requests and more opportunities to stand out from the crowd. . . .

If you're a better writer than you are a teacher, try contributing a column or an opinion piece to your local newspaper.

. . . And if you're a better talker than you are teacher or writer, try to get yourself on a panel discussion at a conference or sign up to make a presentation at a workshop.[70]

In 1999, Peters consolidated his observations about how to transform oneself into the CEO of Me, Inc., with the publication of *The Brand You Fifty*, subtitled *Fifty Ways to Transform Yourself from an "Employee" into a Brand That Shouts Distinction, Commitment, and Passion!*

Peters's advice wouldn't seem all that new to any reader of Helen Gurley Brown, who nearly two decades earlier offered a similar success strategy. In a section of *Having It All* called *"Always* Be Working Out," Brown advocates continuous work.[71] Although Brown puns on the expression for working on one's physique, what she's actually advising is precisely what Peters suggests: work without compensation. She writes: "Although I've suggested you do just about anything that keeps your motor tuned, work-oriented or not, the working out is best applied to your job, and gradually you will begin to undertake little projects that contribute to it."[72] Brown goes on to share some examples of her "little projects"—providing free ad copy to a beauty salon and developing and implementing a direct mail marketing campaign for a weight reduction salon. Brown reports that the beneficiaries of the direct mail campaign "never really thanked me, not even with a free ride on one of their motorized couches," but the hair salon came through for her, with a single free hairdo.[73] Brown concludes: "My advice is to volunteer like crazy and also turn in work that nobody asked for—*but make it easy and comfortable for your boss to ignore that extra work or say No to your requests. Don't be irritating.*"[74] Let's say that again: "Make it easy for your boss to ignore that extra work." The road to success, for Brown and for Peters, is paved with uncompensated labor. Perhaps because women have long been accustomed to working for free, putting in hours of unwaged labor in the home, the thought of working for free was not altogether alien. Women got to the idea of working for free sooner since they've been doing it all along. Transferring that unwaged work to the workplace at least offered some opportunity for advancement, or a free haircut. Unfortunately for those women who were also mothers (as well as for their partners committed to coparenting), saying yes to that extra project at the office, teaching that uncompensated course at the local college as a way of promoting one's business, or working on that self-promotional project would be likely to lead to child neglect, additional childcare costs, or both. While the "family man" was once the standard of the reliable employee (as he was assisted by the labors of a homemaking spouse yet held captive to his employer by the raw vulnerability of his dependents' needs), the situation had changed. Parents were caught between the demand that they devote all of their time to the demands of their careers—using all their evenings, weekends, and vacations to catch up on work projects or seek out new employment opportunities—and the demand of caring for their families. The CEO of Me, the lone artist and the singular entrepreneur, signaled a new model for the ideal worker free of the baggage of dependents.

Artist and Entrepreneur: Redoubling the Metaphors

While the artist-worker is expected to work without compensation purely for love of his or her work, the entrepreneur is expected to work on spec, for possible rewards to be reaped down the line. The artist and the entrepreneur differ in their motivation—the former operates from an intrinsic motivation while the latter operates from an announced profit motive—but both work without any immediate sign of compensation. Ironically, the desire for unalienated labor, for engagement in one's work, results in giving away the store (the artist's way) or working countless hours of overtime in order to "brand" and "market" one's self. What were once discrete categories—artist and entrepreneur—have collapsed, even as the artist has been enrolled as an exemplar for the labor force. If Benjamin Franklin was "an avant-garde of one" for the eighteenth century,[75] Andy Warhol serves something of the same role for the late twentieth century:

> Business art is the step that comes after Art. I started as a commercial artist, and I want to finish as a business artist. After I did the

thing called "art" . . . I went into business art. . . . Being good in business is the most fascinating kind of art. During the hippie era people put down the idea of business—they'd say, "Money is bad," and "Working is bad," but making money is art and working is art and good business is the best art.[76]

With Warhol's pop art synthesis, the model of the artist-entrepreneur has begun to bridge the distinctions between labor and capital, workers and owners. Once again, a cartoonist illustrates the synthesis (see fig. 4.4). The older models for work and workers, of contestants, combatants, trailblazers, and adventurers, will linger. However, the newer models of workers as

Figure 4.4. Cartoon by Frank Cotham for cartoonbank.com.
© 2004 Frank Cotham from cartoonbank.com. All rights reserved.

"I like to think of myself as an artist, and money is the medium in which I work best."

entrepreneurs and artists, as artist-entrepreneurs, are ideally suited to the new forms of capitalism. While work for free and work on spec under the appealing banner of unalienated labor is a central feature of the new ideal in the labor market, in the next chapter I'll show how work on the self—investing in one's own human capital—becomes a central preoccupation. Although the self-help literature of occupational satisfaction idealizes engaged and unalienated labor, work on the self, which arguably can only be an alienated form of labor, is required to maintain employability. Next I want to explore the various ways that readers of self-improvement literature are urged to work on themselves. Behind the happy and engaged image of the resourceful and self-sufficient artist-entrepreneur is the shadow—some might say Janus-face—of this new figure: a beleaguered and belabored self.

chapter 5

At Work on the Self

The Making of the Belabored Self

What strikes me is the fact that in our society, art has become something which is related only to objects and not to individuals, or to life. That art is something which is specialized or which is done by experts who are artists. But couldn't everyone's life become a work of art? Why should the lamp or the house be an art object, but not our life?
—*Michel Foucault*

When philosopher Michel Foucault proposed an aesthetics of everyday life, he traced this ideal to the ancient Greeks, for whom the cultivation of the self was a responsibility and privilege of the citizen. Just as participation in the *polis*—the political life of the city—was reserved for citizens who did not engage in productive labor, so the cultivation of the self was a value reserved for propertied men who did not have to engage in the labors of daily life. Women and enslaved persons were not expected to cultivate themselves. Indeed, to extend the ideal of self-mastery to persons who were so obviously subject to the will of their husbands and masters would have been preposterous.

Arguably, the contemporary extension of the ideal of an aesthetic life to each and all could be a democratic move: each person would occupy the role of citizen-artist, governing, cultivating, and enhancing his or her own existence. The advice that one work on oneself to produce one's life as a work of art offers what might seem an appealing alternative to other metaphors. Certainly the aesthetic ideal seems less abrasive than the image of life as a game of survival, or of life as a business proposition where all relationships are reduced to a cost-benefit analysis. But extending the notion of "self-creation" to each and all has not been without its own paradoxes and contradictions, particularly when the vast majority of people are subjects of a capricious and increasingly competitive labor market. The trouble arises when these citizen-artists are also working people, persons who rely on their own labor power to sustain themselves and their families. While working people are not subject to the demands of a particular husband/head of household or individual master, they are subject to the whims of the labor market and the demands and expectations of employers competing in a globalized economy. While the Greeks realized that the idea of a slave or wife as master of his or her own life was absurd, contemporary self-improvement literature proposes that each and every individual, wage-slave or not, pursue self-mastery.

Part of the problem arises from our culture's conflation of the terms *labor* and *work*. The philosopher Hannah Arendt offered a distinction between labor and work that may illuminate the problems in the ideal of life as a work of art. Arendt points out that the words *work* and *labor*, though they are used almost interchangeably in our culture, are actually quite etymologically distinct and retain distinctive usage, despite the modern tendency to blur them. Classical Greek distinguishes between *ponein* and *ergazesthai*, Latin between *laborare* and *facere* or *fabricari*, French between *travailler* and *oeuvrer*, and German between *arbeiten* and *werken*.[1] The word *labor*, Arendt points out, when used as a noun, never designates the finished product, the result of the laboring, and in most European languages is associated with the physical exertion of childbirth. Quite the opposite is the case for the word *work*. *Work* is used to describe both the process of producing something and the product produced. And, Arendt notes, "it is also interesting that the nouns "work," *oeuvre*, *Werk*, show an increasing tendency to be used for works of art in all three languages. "[2]

For Arendt, the work-labor distinction rests on whether the products of the activity will be rapidly consumed and incorporated into the flow of life—whether the labor involved is used merely to meet the survival needs of human beings—and whether the product of the work will become more permanent, a part of our fabricated existence. Labor is the work that sustains and reproduces the body and is readily absorbed into the flow of life without leaving much of a trace (except insofar as the species continues). Labor, Arendt argues, reduces man to his animal nature, or *animal laborans*. Work, on the other hand, is the product of *Homo faber*, man the fabricator, and leaves with it a sense of purpose, permanence, and something outside of ourselves, something that lasts beyond the lifespan of our bodies. Labor is tied to life, to the continuation of life, while work is tied to fabrication and the creation of something more permanent than transitory human lives. However, Arendt points out, even work that might leave its mark was denigrated when it was pursued under the necessity of sustaining one's life:

> all ancient estimates of human activities . . . rest on the conviction that the labor of our body which is necessitated by its needs is slavish. Hence occupations which did not consist in laboring, yet were undertaken not for their own sake but in order to provide for the necessities of life, were assimilated to the status of labor."[3]

To insulate one's activities from this degraded status, ancient physicians, navigators, and architects (among others) would engage in an "art of earning money" (*technē mistharnētikē*) as a practice separate and distinct from the pursuit of their professional work. Arendt notes that, "This additional art is by no means understood as the element of labor in the otherwise free arts, but on the contrary, the one art through which the 'artist,' the professional worker, as we would say, keeps himself free from the necessity to labor."[4] The very fact of human necessity—the fact of human bodily needs —provided the basis for the debased category of "labor."

In our own historical period, labor is, according to Arendt, erroneously equated with work. This conflation has its genesis in the work of the Western philosophers John Locke, Adam Smith, and Karl Marx, who described labor variously as the source of all property and all wealth and, in the case of Marx, as the source of all productivity and the very expression of man's humanity.[5] Yet Marx, as with many of his elaborators, maintains a contradictory view of labor. While labor is the source of man's very humanity, the revolution, for Marx, would not simply amount to emancipating the laboring classes but would also emancipate man from labor itself. Only when labor is abolished can the "realm of freedom" supplant the "realm of necessity."[6] While many contemporary theorists follow the Western tendency to eschew any distinctions between work and labor,[7] Arendt's distinction between work and labor should be kept in mind as I consider the various ways in which contemporary readers of self-improvement literature are urged to work on themselves.

Work without End and No Work at All

In describing the nature of work on the self, the literatures of self-improvement offer two distinct options: the path of endless effort and the path of absolute effortlessness. These correspond to the modernist/antimodernist, rational/expressive pairs encountered before. Those experts who are committed to rational self-mastery (for example, Stephen R. Covey, Anthony Robbins, Helen Gurley Brown) propose the effortful life, while those who focus on the expressive dimension (for example, Deepak Chopra, Julia Cameron, Richard Carlson, and Eckhart Tolle) emphasize self-acceptance through a mystical oneness. Despite their apparent opposition, both approaches represent an effort to come to terms with the problem of contingency and vulnerability in both the labor force and life itself.

For the rationalists, one of the cardinal characteristics of the work that the individual is instructed to perform on himself or herself is that it is unending. With the exception of the terminus of death, work on the self is work without end. In this respect, this work on the self is consistent with Arendt's notion that labor is in fact not more nor less than life itself, what Marx calls "man's metabolism with nature."[8] In the rationalist self-help literature, continuous and never-ending work on the self is offered as a road not only to success but also to a kind of secular salvation. The pain of feeling alienated from one's self in the present is offered as a sacrifice for the vision of what may come in the future. Consider Anthony Robbins's recommendation that everyone commit themselves to what he calls CANI!:

> When you set a goal, you've committed to **CANI! You've acknowledged the need that all human beings have for constant, never-ending improvement.** There is power in the pressure of dissatisfaction, in the tension of temporary discomfort. This is the kind of pain you *want* in your life, the kind of pain that you immediately transform into positive new actions.[9]

Indeed, Robbins is so committed to this notion that he has trademarked the phrase "Constant And Never-ending Improvement." While Robbins acknowledges the discomfort of focusing on goals—those things that one has yet to attain, those characteristics or experiences that one lacks—he asserts that this is a necessary part of the process of attaining what one desires.

Similarly, Stephen R. Covey and his coauthors, A. Roger Merrill and Rebecca R. Merrill, advocate for constant improvement in their bestselling book *First Things First*. In order to gain someone's trust, Covey and company argue that it is not enough to be good and honest; one also has to stay current in one's profession. They tell of a CEO who can't figure out why he doesn't trust an honest vendor until it dawns on him: "I realize now it's because they're not competent. They haven't stayed current in their profession. They're obsolete. . . . They don't have the *spirit of continuous improvement*."[10] Endless mindfulness is also proposed by M. Scott Peck in his spiritual roadmap:

> The third thing that a life of total dedication to the truth means, therefore, is a life of total honesty. It means **a continuous and never-ending process of self-monitoring** to assure that our communications—not only the words that we say but also the way we say them—invariably reflect as accurately as humanly possible the truth or reality as we know it. . . . Such honesty does not come painlessly.[11]

The ideal of constant improvement and renewal is inscribed in Covey's *Seven Habits* as habit number 7, which he calls "Sharpening the Saw"—renewing one's resources on a ongoing basis. Instead of describing this renewal as rest or relaxation, Covey represents this as effortful exercise that will "preserve and enhance our capacity to work and adapt and enjoy."[12] This work on the self is characterized as an "investment": "This is the single most powerful investment we can ever make in life—investment in ourselves, in the only instrument we have with which to deal with life and to contribute."[13] Similarly, Helen Gurley Brown admonishes her readers:

> You want it all and you are "willing to pay the price." You want material blessings as well as deep emotional satisfaction. You want life to be rich and thick rather than thin and watery, but—and this separates you from the dreamers and rationalizers—you simply do not kid yourself that what you want is "inexpensive," let alone free. You know the price for the kind of life you want is work—hard work![14]

The notable exceptions to the admonitions to pursue painful "work without end" can be found in the New Age or metaphysical self-improvement literatures, which suggest that attaining one's goals can be accomplished with a minimum of effort—that the realization of the self is "natural." Deepak Chopra suggests that an individual's success is supposed to take place subject to the "Law of Least Effort":

> Nature's intelligence functions effortlessly, frictionlessly, spontaneously. It is nonlinear; it is intuitive, holistic, and nourishing. And when you are in harmony with nature, when you are established in the knowledge of your true Self, you can make use of the Law of Least Effort.[15]

To arrive at this effortless state, one is instructed to "make a commitment to follow the path of least effort," which requires that one follow a series of three steps: practicing "acceptance," "responsibility," and "defenselessness."[16] And immediately after mastering these steps, one is instructed in the mastery of the "Law of Intention and Desire," for which Chopra advises readers to make lists of their desires and then "release [them] . . . trusting that when things don't seem to go my way, there is a reason, and that the cosmic plan has designs for me much grander than even those that I have conceived."[17] Similarly, in his 1997 book *Don't Sweat the Small Stuff, and It's All Small Stuff*, Richard Carlson advises readers to "Remind Yourself That When You Die Your In-Basket Won't Be Empty." Carlson continues:

> we convince ourselves that our obsession with our "to do" list is only temporary—that once we get through the list, we'll be calm, relaxed, and happy. But in reality this rarely happens. As items are checked off, new ones simply replace them.
>
> The nature of your "in basket" is that it's meant to have items to be completed in it—it's not meant to be empty. There will always be phone calls that need to be made, projects to complete, work to be done.[18]

A focus on the present moment to the exclusion of all else is offered as the path to peace of mind:

> To a large degree, the measure of our peace of mind is determined by how much we are able to live in the present moment. Irrespective of what happened yesterday or last year, and what may or may not happen tomorrow, the present moment is where you are—always![19]

Similarly, Eckhart Tolle's 1999 bestselling spiritual guide, *The Power of Now*, suggests that one focus so intently on the present that the past and future are moot:

> Have you ever experienced, done, thought, or felt anything outside the Now? Do you think you ever will? Is it possible for anything to happen or be outside the Now? The answer is obvious, is it not?
>
> Nothing ever happened in the past; it happened in the Now.
>
> Nothing will ever happen in the future; it will happen in the Now.[20]

The key, writes Tolle, is to:

> End the delusion of time. Time and mind are inseparable. Remove time from the mind and it stops—unless you choose to use it.
>
> To be identified with your mind is to be trapped in time: the compulsion to live almost exclusively through memory and anticipation. . . .
>
> Time isn't precious at all, because it is an illusion. What you perceive as precious is not time but the one point that is out of time: the Now. That is precious indeed. The more you are focused on time—past and future—the more you miss the Now, the most precious thing there is.[21]

The seeming futility and effortfulness of endlessly repetitive labor is eliminated when time is imagined as illusory. By focusing on the present, by suspending one's belief in temporality, one is absolved of the endless labor of living and the necessity of leaving a legacy through a "life's work." As in other mystical traditions (for example, in the writings of the thirteenth- and fourteenth-century Christian mystic Meister Eckhart, Tolle's namesake), embracing this metaphysical present serves to absent the reader from the ceaselessness and futility of laboring.

While the rhetoric of effortless realization offers a respite from the relentless pursuit of perfection, it is not itself so effortless as it claims to be. Even as these authors advocate effortlessness, they propose a series of activities (meditations, creative visualization exercises, and other practices) to achieve this state. This metaphysical literature, with its obliteration of any distinction between self and other, cause and effect, and any and all terms of discrimination, offers effortless effort, passive activity, and endless work imagined as effortless, exertion.

The Gratitude Antidote

If the prescription of endless work requires an antidote in the form of effortless effort, the discomfort of continual dissatisfaction with the present—what Robbins calls a "temporary discomfort . . . the kind of pain that you immediately transform into positive new actions"—requires its own remedy.[22] The promise of the literature of self-improvement—that one can imagine one's self anew and then invent the life one imagines, that one can act on "the before" to create "the after"—demands the sacrifice of the present moment. In such a construction, "the present" is displaced, at worst, and desolate at best. To mitigate the pain of forsaking the lived present for the imagined future, or of living in a present that is utterly lacking, many self-improvement authors, especially those who operate in the expressive tradition, offer prescriptions for cultivating gratitude. Thinking about what one appreciates provides a momentary relief from the relentless pursuit of a distant perfection.

Robbins, for example, suggests that people following his program use a series of "morning questions" to focus their power, including "What am I happy about in my life now? What am I grateful about in my life now? What am I enjoying most in my life right now?"[23] In her 1979 book *Creative Visualization*, Shakti Gawain advises readers to keep an appreciation list: "Make a list of everything that you can think of that you are especially thankful for, or that you especially appreciate having in your life. . . . It increases your realization of prosperity and abundance on every level, and thus your ability to manifest."[24] Mark Bryan and his coauthors of *The Artist's Way at Work*, are astute enough to focus the reader's sense of gratitude back on their book itself, turning the goodwill of this self-help practice back toward themselves: "List the many things you are grateful for about this work. What did you learn? What were the most important ah-hahs? . . . Please write this in your notebook and keep the answers to these exercises to excavate in about twenty-four months."[25] And perhaps most far-reaching in its effects is Sarah Ban Breathnach's development of the idea of keeping a "gratitude journal" as an integral part of her readers' paths to "simple abundance." In her daybook entry for January 14, she interpolates a quotation from the codependency popularizer Melody Beattie, and argues that this practice is the key to "simple abundance":

JANUARY 14: THE GRATITUDE JOURNAL

Gratitude unlocks the fullness of life. It turns what we have into enough, and more. It turns denial into acceptance, chaos to order, confusion to clarity. It can turn a meal into a feast, a house into a home, a stranger into a friend. Gratitude makes sense of our past, brings peace for today, and creates a vision for tomorrow.
—*Melody Beattie*

There are several tools that I'm going to suggest you use as you begin your inner exploration. While all of them will help you become happier and more content and will nurture your creativity, this first tool could change the quality of your life beyond belief: it's what I call a daily gratitude journal. I have a beautiful blank book and each night before I go to bed, I write down five things that I can be grateful [for] about that day. . . .

The gratitude journal has to be the first step on the Simple Abundance path or it just won't work for you. Simplicity, order, harmony, beauty, and joy—all the other principles that can transform your life will not blossom and flourish without gratitude. If you want to travel this journey with me, *the gratitude journal is not an option* [*sic*].[26]

Although Breathnach no doubt meant to write "the gratitude journal is not optional," her point is clear: victims, critics, ingrates, whiners, and complainers need not apply. Oprah Winfrey, among the most powerful promoters of contemporary self-culture, has taken on the cause of the gratitude journal, urging her viewers to engage in this practice and featuring some of them on her program, sharing from their gratitude journals. With the huge success of her magazine *O, The Oprah Magazine*, she devoted an issue to "The Gratitude Attitude." A pullout section in the November 2000 issue reads:

When you dwell on all the reasons you have to be grateful, you open yourself to receiving even more good—and more good comes to you. As you begin to feel abundant, you'll be willing and able to pass positive things on to others. Find a quiet spot to sit and consider the ideas below, then use the space to write down your thoughts.

1. Ask yourself: What are the good things in my life that I'm overlooking?
2. Each day for a month, write down one reason you're thankful for your mate or closest friend. At the end of the month, give him or her the list.[27]

Winfrey writes, in a related article in the same issue, "I keep a gratitude journal, as Sarah Ban Breathnach suggests in *Simple Abundance*, listing at least five things that I'm grateful for."[28] Gratitude sutures the gap between what one has and what one desires, a gap that would otherwise be ever widened by goal-oriented, instrumentalist self-improvement literatures.

Embracing Your Inner Corpse

Gratitude provides one way of escaping the constant striving and seeking in self-improvement culture. Death provides the other. The activist and satirist Andrew Boyd urges readers of his self-help sendup to embrace their "inner corpse" rather than their inner child.[29] And indeed, much of the literature of self-improvement does direct one to the contemplation of death. The imperative that one "be all one can be," an invocation of boundless opportunity driven by the specter of death, animates contemporary self-improvement literature. Death—and the threat of meaninglessness in the face of death—is the point of reference for nearly all self-improvement treatises. While the death threats take different forms, conjuring the possibility of imminent death is key for self-improvement authors. For example, Robert J. Ringer warns his readers:

In a matter of pages, the ball will be in your court. I wish I could be the bearer of good tidings and tell you that you have unlimited time to stare at the ball and decide what you're going to do with it. Alas, my friend, it isn't so. Like all games, this one, too, will end. And the clock is running as you read this sentence.

How much time? No one knows for sure, but I like to use age sixty-five as a nice round figure and look at anything beyond that as a bonus. That means if you're thirty-five years old and you theoretically could freeze time long enough to do some calculating, you have precisely 10,950 days left in your game; or 262,800 hours; or 15,768,000 minutes; or 946,080,000 seconds. Choose the time unit that makes you most comfortable, but do acknowledge the reality that the clock is running.[30]

Irene C. Kassorla's *Go For It!* (1984), which is aimed at a young female audience, suggests that readers should consider what they'd do if they had five hundred years to live—and then reminds her readers that they don't:

Do you have five hundred years to live? Are you one of those immortals who has almost unlimited time? If so, the first hundred years on this planet you could afford to spend your time according to your parents' needs and desires . . . you can "do it" for them. The second hundred, however, I think you ought to "do it" for your neighbors; they're nice people, find out what they would like you to be. . . . When you are mortal, you don't have unlimited time and you can't sacrifice your dreams and ideals for others, or you will hate yourself . . . and them.[31]

Or consider Wayne W. Dyer's comments in his 1976 book *Your Erroneous Zones*:

Look over your shoulder. You will notice a constant companion. For want of a better name, call him *Your-Own-Death*. You can fear this visitor or use him for your own personal gain. The choice is up to you.[32]

Dyer's "over the shoulder" figure of death, in keeping with the self-help tradition of direct appropriation, echoes an image from a bestselling book of the period, Carlos Castañeda's 1972 *Journey to Ixtlan: The Lessons of Don Juan*: "Death is our eternal companion. . . . The thing to do when you're impatient is to turn to your left and ask advice from your death. . . . Death is the only wise adviser we have."[33]

Generally the death threat—designed to instill a sense of urgency and immediacy, some would say to conjure the notion of a transcendent self—occurs fairly early in the self-improvement text, though occasionally it emerges midvolume. As was noted earlier, Stephen R. Covey deploys a funeral scene reminiscent of Cotton Mather's death-rattle sermon, and

Richard Nelson Bolles included a tombstone meditation until he shifted to a more upbeat tone. Julia Cameron counsels individuals to write their ideal "epithet"; presumably she means "epitaph."[34] Even Helen Gurley Brown, who insists she has no fear of death—only a fear of losing her desirability to male sexual partners—raises the issue of death when she touts the age-defying effects of exercise. After launching into a confession about how she'd rather die fucking—her word—than die undesirable, she abruptly stops and employs that rhetorical technique of drawing attention to a topic by denying its importance: "Heavens, I'd better get back to *you*, little friend. You *aren't* aging yet or thinking of dying. Let me try to tell you what else I know about exercise."[35] With the exception of New Age spiritual self-help literature, where death, like work, is denied because all binary categories (matter/energy, self/other, animate/inanimate) are negated, the invocations-of-mortality exercises are a staple of self-improvement culture. In the absence of a belief in an afterlife and a divine cosmic plan, the secular individual is subject to both the ravages of time and the vagaries of chance. The creation of a life, the notion of life as a work of art, offers some sense of meaning in the face of what might otherwise seem to be meaningless mortality. Wresting some control over one's life, including the forces of time and chance, is the background raison d'être of the self-improvement literature's admonitions to relentlessly work on the self, even if consolidating one's human capital is one of the material outcomes. Like the Protestant's tireless work that served to alleviate the meaninglessness of activity in the face of a doctrine of predestination, the contemporary imperative to invent one's life mitigates meaninglessness in the face of death.

The Maudlin Exemplar and the Doctrine of Self-Mastery

If the character of death—featured as a ticking clock, a shadowy figure behind you, or the members of the funerary party—figures prominently in much of the literature of self-improvement, another character, whom I call the Maudlin Exemplar, is never far from sight. Typically the Maudlin Exemplar appears in the form of a person with a catastrophic physical impairment: quadriplegics are ideal subjects. Like the specter of death, the specter of physical vulnerability encapsulated in the idea of a chance disability ("when bad things happen to good people") typically appears early in a text. Both Anthony Robbins and Robert H. Schuller introduce their accident-

victims-turned-heroic-survivors in their second chapters. Robbins introduces a quadriplegic character in the first paragraph of chapter 2 of *Unlimited Power*, with the story of a man massively injured and disfigured in a
motorcycle accident who goes on to become a millionaire and mounts a
campaign to run for Congress.[36] Schuller's chapter 2 quadriplegic character is an avid runner who works as a roofer and suffers a workplace fall that
leaves him paralyzed with a family to support.[37] When a story of paralysis
isn't invoked, blindness serves a similar function. At a promotional lecture
for her 1994 book *Take This Job and Love It: A Personal Guide to Career
Empowerment*, Diane Tracy recounted the story of an administrative assistant at the Pentagon who was, according to her supervisors, "the best administrative assistant" they'd ever had. When Tracy's client met the assistant
she was amazed to learn that the woman was blind but fulfilled her job functions "better than most assistants who have their sight." The story followed
of how the woman had lost her sight, sunk into a depression, thought of
killing herself, and finally transformed herself into the vision of productivity. The intended effects of stories of the Maudlin Exemplar are twofold.
First, the image of this kind of triumph over adversity can be read as an
injunction: "You think you've got problems? What have you got to complain
about?" Second, the role of the Maudlin Exemplar is to assure readers that
whatever the exigencies of fate and whatever their physical vulnerabilities,
they are each individually still in charge of their own lives, demonstrating
self-mastery in the face of unexpected events. The fact that there are forces
beyond one's own control is acknowledged and then dismissed with the
message that it's not what life hands you, it's how you handle it.[38]

The Maudlin Exemplar manages the notion of misfortune and suggests
that self-mastery is the fundamental prerequisite for success. For Anthony
Robbins, self-mastery consists of what he calls "managing one's state."[39] According to Robbins, the only thing that actually matters for one's quality of
life is the capacity to manage one's internal responses to events or circumstances. For Robbins, one's emotional state is to be brought completely under
one's conscious control so that external events have no impact. Paradoxically,
Robbins's own success has depended on his ability to alter others' states of
mind with his charismatic revival-style stadium performances.

While Robbins speaks about controlling one's "state," Covey's emphasis is on managing one's actions or responses. He remarks on the difference
between humans and other animals (though he omits the "other," since he
is squarely in the camp of those who place humans above animals, and above

human beings' own animal nature): "Between stimulus and response man has the freedom to choose."[40] Freedom, for Covey, is the capacity to respond independently to external circumstances. Rather than making a direct appeal in a Maudlin Exemplar story, Covey notes, with his characteristically cool, rational approach: "We have all known individuals with very difficult circumstances, perhaps with a terminal illness or a severe handicap, who maintain magnificent emotional strength. How inspired we are by their integrity."[41] Instead of invoking a Maudlin Exemplar in the story of injured individuals, Covey concentrates on the renowned heroics of imprisoned individuals and world leaders such as Victor Frankl, Anwar Sadat, and Mohandas K. Gandhi.[42] Leaving aside for a moment the politics of choosing these examples over, say, Nelson Mandela or Malcolm X, the imprisoned hero offers the finest example of oppressive external circumstances and "private victory." Mastery of the self in the face of profoundly asymmetrical power relations becomes the mark of the hero. But what is missing in the literature of self-improvement is the recognition that the achievements of a Gandhi or a Sadat occur within the context of larger social movements and forces. Individual praxis or action is meaningful in the context of larger social forces—in what Arendt would call the "space of appearance"—not in isolation from them.[43] But for Covey what matters most is the inviolability of a core self: "It's not what happens to us, but our response to what happens to us that hurts us. Of course, things can hurt us physically or economically and can cause sorrow. But our character, our basic identity, does not have to be hurt at all."[44]

Interestingly, when Foucault recounts the progression of concern with self-mastery among the Greeks, he notes a move from the kinds of non-reciprocal mastery that Robbins enacts in his charismatic performances to the rational self-mastery of Covey's characters:

> to be master of oneself meant, first, taking into account only oneself
> and not the other, because to be master of oneself meant that you
> were able to rule others. So the mastery of oneself was directly
> related to a dissymmetrical relation to others. You should be master
> of yourself in a sense of activity, dissymmetry, and nonreciprocity.
> Later on . . . mastery of oneself is something which is not primarily
> related to power over others . . . you have to be master of yourself
> not only in order to rule others, as in Alcibiades or Nicocles, but you
> have to be master of yourself because you are a rational being. And

in this mastery of yourself, you are related to other people, who are also masters of themselves. And this new kind of relation to the other is much less nonreciprocal than before.[45]

While self-mastery was necessary in the formation of oligarchic leaders, it was also necessary in the formation of rational democratic subjects.[46] In Covey's examples, self-mastery is offered as the only possible response to asymmetrical power and constitutes the rational democratic subject, while in the case of Robbins, self-mastery offers the capacity for mastery over others, as control of one's self allows one to control others who are less able to control themselves. As Robbins notes: "If you don't have a plan for your life, someone else does."[47] In this sense, Robbins brings an almost Nietzschean *übermensch* to the self-help discourse. Unless one "awakens the giant within," one is destined to join the herd.

Ordinary Self-Mastery: Watching the Clock, Watching the Scale

In the context of daily life, the heroic mastery of the self is reduced to the rational management of the self prescribed in the use of calendars and the adherence to diets and fitness regimens. One's body and time are one's limited "human capital." Covey's *Seven Habits* revolves around the time management system that he developed and markets through the FranklinCovey Company. For example, Covey provides detailed instructions on how to schedule one's time according to one's specific roles and values (see fig. 5.1).[48] Echoing Benjamin Franklin's daybook and book of virtues, in which he organized his days around cultivating various virtues, Covey's time management system updates the old-fashioned notion of "virtues" with the more modern idea of "priorities." Anthony Robbins suggests his morning and evening rituals of responding to various questions and prescribes a very specific diet regimen where "water-rich" foods are emphasized.[49] Helen Gurley Brown devotes three chapters of *Having It All* (more than a third of her total text) to her fitness and diet advice. "Effective" management of one's time and one's body enjoys the status of a moral imperative. Being thin is required for happiness as a "single girl":

> You don't have to do anything brassy or show-offy or against your nature. *Your most prodigious work will be on you—at home.* When I got married, I moved in with six-pound dumbbells, slant board, an

The WEEKLY WORKSHEET™		Week of:	Sunday	Monday		Tuesday	Wednesday	Thursday	Friday	Saturday
Roles	Goals	Weekly Priorities	Today's Priorities			Today's Priorities				
						② Send in seminar registration	⑫ Ken Peter		⑭ Visit Samuels	
			Appointments/Commitments			Appointments/Commitments				
			8	8		8	8	8	8	8 ⓐ Home mgmt. ④ Karla's class
			9	9		9	9 ⑦ Test market	9 ⑪ Bonding	9 ⑩ Test results	9
			10	10		10	10 parameters	10 problem	10 study	10
			11	11		11	11	11	11	11
			12	12		12	12	12	12 ⑱ Conklin	12
			1	1		1 ⑨ Study consumer	1	1	1	1
			2	2		2 survey	2	2	2	2
			3	3		3	3	3 ⑬ Performance	3 ⑮ EOM report	3
			4	4		4	4	4 review-Janie	4	4
			5	5		5	5	5	5	5
			6	6		6 ⑥ Tim's project	6	6 ⑰ United Way	6	6
			7	7		7	7	7 agenda	7	7
			8	8		8	8	8 ⑲ Next yrs. plans	8	8
SHARPEN THE SAW			Evening	Evening		Evening	Evening	Evening	Evening	Evening 7:00 Theater-Browns
Physical ___ Mental ___ Spiritual ___ Social/Emotional ___										

Figure 5.1. Scheduling by social role from *The Seven Habits of Highly Effective People* (Simon and Schuster, 1989) pp. 166–67. Excerpted from *The Seven Habits of Highly Effective People.* New York: Simon and Schuster. © 1989 Stephen R. Covey. Used with permission. All rights reserved.

electronic device for erasing wrinkles, several pounds of soy lecithin . . . and enough high powered vitamins to generate life in a statue. . . . Your figure can't harbor an ounce of baby fat. It never looked good on anyone but babies.[50]

Later Brown is no less adamant: "It is unthinkable that a woman bent on 'having it all' would want to be fat, or even plump."[51] Self-control, demonstrated in daily vigilance against fat, is a prerequisite for success. And daily labor in grooming is accorded a secondary role: after describing the endless and expensive day-in and day-out care needed by her pet Siamese cat, Brown says: "beauty routines are something like that . . . endless trouble, but they add pleasure to your life. . . . Maybe we can't be beautiful, but we can be better. Truly, if they *'freed'* us (no more makeup ever) I would go get 'back in my chains!'"[52] The relentlessness of labor of work on the self informs every aspect of daily life. Brown writes, referencing *How to Be Your Own Best Friend*, another bestseller of the period:

DON'T BE YOUR OWN BEST FRIEND

I think unconditional love is what a mother feels for her baby, and not what you should feel for yourself. Author Margaret Halsey said in a *Newsweek* editorial: "the [false] idea is that inside every human being, however unprepossessing, there is a glorious, talented, and overwhelmingly attractive personality. Nonsense. Inside each of us is a mess or unruly, primitive impulses, and these can sometimes, under the strenuous self-discipline and dedication of art, result in noble creativity."

I couldn't agree more. If we're too approving of ourselves too early, we may never be motivated to move onward. Yes, *of course*, you should feel pleased at the day's job well done, the face and body exercised and well-groomed, but heavy self-love must be *earned*.[53]

Baby fat and unconditional love are to be left in the nursery. Children, especially vulnerable infants, are the other, the antithesis, of the self-mastering autonomous self. Competent, capable, and rational adults shape their bodies and themselves—they whip themselves into shape—carefully warding off infantile incapacity and vulnerability in a vision of autonomous self-making. Mind is master, body is slave. Covey, Robbins, and Brown (and a host of others in bestselling diet and exercise manuals) offer an image of mind over matter, where the body is controlled by willpower or self-hypnosis.[54]

Authoring and Authorizing One's Self: Literacy as Legitimacy

Developing one's life as a work of art requires not only self-mastery but also authority. While the authority of the self-improvement expert is constructed both formally and informally—by drawing on either one's professional expertise as a psychologist, psychiatrist, or educated specialist of one kind or another or on oneself as an example of a "before"-to-"after" story—the authority of the individual reader is established through a series of activities of self-reflection, and most frequently through writing. Writing exercises, including lists, sentence completion exercises, inventories of skills or shortcomings, mission statements, "morning pages," deathbed reflections, fictional autobiographies, and fantasy ideal days, are the mainstays of self-improvement culture. Self-knowledge gleaned through these exercises is used to inform goal-setting and life-planning exercises. For example, Covey declares: "Writing is another powerful mental way to sharpen the mental saw. Keeping a journal of our thoughts, experiences, insights, and learnings [sic] promotes mental clarity, exactness, and context."[55] A written mission statement is a central component of Covey's approach, out of which one's life goals and weekly plans and schedules are to be drawn up. Drawing on the language of a popular psychology practice of the prior decade, transactional analysis, Covey suggests that one should develop new "scripts" for one's life choices.[56]

The daybooks that proliferated in the last two decades of the twentieth century, from Franklin Planners to Filofax, are reminiscent of the *hypomnemata* (literally, *hypo*, "under," and *mnemata*, "memory," therefore "under memory," or a support to memory)[57] that were employed by the literate ancient Greek population. As Foucault noted regarding the ancient Greeks:

> the *hypomnemata* could be account books, public registers,
> individual notebooks serving as memoranda. Their use as books of
> life, guides for conduct, seems to have become a current thing
> amongst a whole cultivated public. Into them one entered quota-
> tions, fragments of works, examples, and actions to which one had
> been witness or of which one had read the account, reflections or
> reasonings which one had heard or which had come to mind. They
> constitute a material memory of things read, heard, or thought,
> thus offering these to an accumulated treasure for rereading and
> later meditation. They also formed a raw material for the writing
> of more systematic treatises in which were given arguments and
> means by which to struggle against some defect (such as anger,
> envy, gossip, flattery) or to overcome some difficult circumstance
> (a mourning, an exile, downfall, disgrace).[58]

Writing became, for the ancient Greeks, a critical part of the work of creating one's life as work of art:

> No technique, no professional skill can be acquired without
> exercise; neither can one learn the art of living, the *techne tou biou*,

without an *askesis* which must be taken as a training of oneself by oneself. . . . Amongst all the forms this training took (and which included abstinences, memorizations, examinations of conscience, mediations, silence and listening to others), it seems that writing—the fact of writing for oneself and for others—came late to play a sizeable role.[59]

The self-authoring subject is assumed to be a literate subject, and literacy is assumed to be part of a successful life.[60] The significance of this point is not to be underestimated. Without literacy, the self-constructing itself loses the capacity to anchor its "truths." As the philosophy scholar Alexander Nehamas notes,

> it is difficult to imagine that one can formulate one's own art of living without writing about it because it is difficult to imagine that the complex views that such an art requires can be expressed in any other way. Further, unless one writes about it, one's art will not be able to constitute a model for others in the longer run.[61]

While one's identity might have formerly been anchored in (and limited by) a community where one's story was shared in spoken language and known informally, the self-creating self must create a written narrative of his or her life and secure it in written language. While literacy itself brings with it the possibility of the insularity or inwardness that some have labeled "narcissism," it also provides the possibility of leaving a written legacy—a work that outlasts one's own life. In this sense, the work of creating one's own life would not be a labor but rather, in Arendt's terms, a work—something that lasts.

But many written self-help exercises are by no means meant for others to read. These are not memoirs but rather aids in realizing one's internal states and desires. Julia Cameron calls this sort of writing "a tool for creative recovery."[62] Rather than existing as works of art, this writing is an ongoing daily labor. For example, Cameron's *Artist's Way* requires three pages of handwritten, uncensored, free-form language written first thing in the morning. The "morning pages" are a nonnegotiable part of the "recovery" process. But the contents of these stream-of-consciousness pages are informed by exercises and questions or exercises posed in the book. For example, in an exercise called "Goal Search," Cameron writes:

The simple act of imagining a dream in concrete detail helps us to bring it into reality. Think of your goal search as a preliminary architect's drawing for the life you would wish to have.

THE STEPS

1. Name your dream. That's right. Write it down. "In a perfect world, I would secretly love to be a _____."
2. Name one concrete goal that signals to you its accomplishment. On your emotional compass, this goal signifies true north.
   (Note: two people may want to be an actress. They share that dream. For one, an article in *People* magazine is the concrete goal. To her, glamour is the emotional center for her dream; glamour is true north. For the second actress, the concrete goal is a good review in a Broadway play. To her, respect as a creative artist is the emotional center of her dream; respect is true north. . . .
3. In a perfect world, where would you like to be in five years in relation to your dream and true north?
4. In the world we inhabit now, what action can you take, this year, to move you closer?
5. What action can you take this month? This week? This day? Right now?[63]

Another *Artist's Way* exercise involves imagining a perfect childhood and how your life might be different if you'd gotten "perfect nurturing."[64] And a decade earlier, Irene C. Kassorla instructed her female readers:

Start making a list: "WHAT I *DON'T* WANT TO BE." . . . Now start a second list. This list begins: "WHAT I *MIGHT* NOT MIND BEING." . . .
Now I ask them to write a third list, "I *THINK* I MIGHT LIKE."[65]

Individuals are asked to assess their current lives against imagined, presumably better, futures. But, far from writing their own scripts, individuals are guided through specific types of questions. The most extreme example of the self-improvement author directing individual writing is in the case of mission statements that are created by using an electronic form online at the FranklinCovey website (www.franklincovey.com). The person "writing" his or her mission statement uses pull-down menus and fills in blank spaces in forms to provide words describing his or her values, principles, assets, and liabilities, and then a "mission statement" is generated by a database template (see fig. 5.2). Similarly, Anthony Robbins and Oprah Winfrey each have had extensive journal writing sections on their websites, and Winfrey has launched an interactive online subscriber self-help program called "Live Your Best Life."[66] But, more typically, book-based self-improvement culture relies on a series of questions that invite the reader to revel in a pleasurable pornography of possibilities. "What would you do if money were no object?" "What would you do if you knew you could not fail?" "What would you want in your life if you'd had a perfect childhood?" Reality—the real world of financial constraints, failed plans, and typically insufficient childhoods—is jettisoned for a world of fantasy where any career or outcome is possible. Consider this exercise from *The Artist's Way*:

Figure 5.2. The FranklinCovey Company's online interactive "Mission Builder." On this page the form requires users to specify what admirable qualities in characters they want to use as role models. Viewed at www.franklincovey.com/cgi-bin/ mission_builder/mision-builder/mb8 on September 29, 2001. Excerpted from www.FranklinCovey.com. Used with permission. All rights reserved.

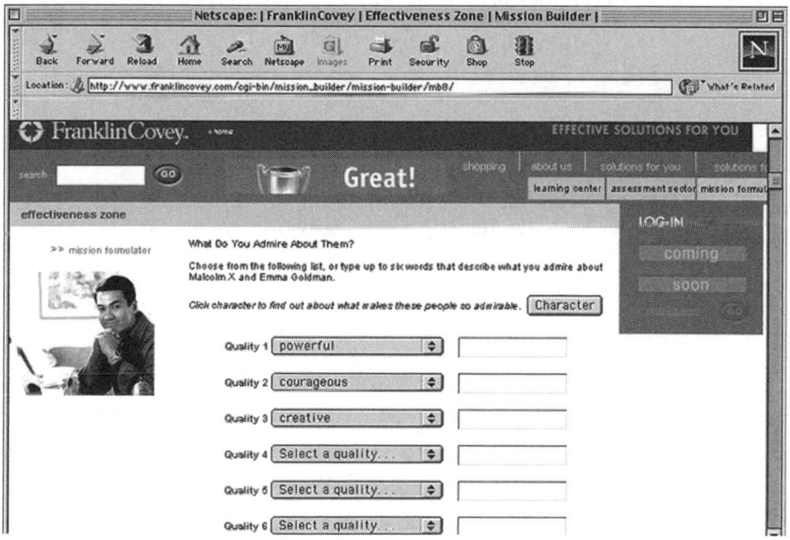

If you had five other lives to lead, what would you do in each of them? I would be a pilot, a cowhand, a physicist, a psychic, a monk. You might be a scuba diver, a cop, a writer of children's books, a football player, a belly dancer, a painter, a performance artist, a history teacher, a healer, a coach. . . . Whatever occurs to you, jot it down. Do not overthink this exercise. The point of these lives is to have fun in them—*more fun than you might be having in this one.*[67]

The trouble with these sorts of exercises is threefold. First, comparing one's current situation to some imagined perfect future is a recipe for dissatisfaction and constant striving. Second, it is striking that at precisely the moment when individuals are asked to imagine every possibility for their own individual lives in ever greater detail that one finds no exercises imagining a collective future. I have yet to find a bestselling self-improvement book that prompts one to consider, for example, the following: "If you could live in a world where profit were not the motivating force of production, what would your life look like?" or "How would your life be different if the nutritional, medical, and educational needs of children were the top priority of every individual, every group, and every institution?" or "How would your life be different if racism/sexism/anti-Semitism or other religious intolerance were no longer a structuring principle of social relations?" Were such questions part of the discourse of self-improvement culture, the writing exercises found in self-help books might be a remarkable tool for social transformation. One's realization of one's self might genuinely lead to societal change (though the steps between imagining the idealized future and realizing it would likely involve a good bit more effort than imagination.) However, in its current insularity, the literature of self-improvement directs the reader to familiar frameworks, namely, what one should seek for one's self narrowly conceived as a private individual rather than as a citizen or stakeholder in larger and more public arenas.

Finally, as a literature that is notable for its almost wholesale lack of imagination and its reliance on direct appropriation from others' works, self-help literature doesn't inspire the cultivation of new vocabularies, the broaching of new and more challenging questions, the development of what political theorists such as Richard Rorty call "strong poets"—individuals whose self-creation generates new vocabularies and new possibilities for others.[68] Even when self-help authors such as Anthony Robbins suggest that individuals analyze the metaphors that shape their thinking and enhance their vocabularies as a way of developing a range of responses, the questions are premised on the assumption of an autonomous, and often isolated individual whose self-mastery is central to his individual and isolated success.[69] Robbins writes:

In the back of this book you'll find some blank pages. You might find them ideal for this goal-setting session. Let's get down to business:

1. Pretend it's the holiday season—time for giving and receiving abundant gifts! Dream big! Write down *all* your dreams, all of the things you want to have, do, be, and share. Imagine the people, feelings, and places you want to be a part of your life. Sit down right now, grab your pencil, and start writing. Don't try to figure out how you're going to get there; *just write it down*. There are no limits.

2. Now go over the list you made and estimate when you expect to reach those outcomes: six months, one year, two years, five years, ten years, twenty years. It's helpful to see what sort of a time frame you're operating in.
Note how your list came out. Some people find that the list they made is dominated by things they want today. Others find their greatest dreams are far in the future, in some perfect world of total success and fulfillment. But a journey of a thousand miles begins with a single step, and it's important to be aware of the first steps as much as the final ones.

3. Once you've set some time frames, pick four goals that you can realize *this year*. Pick the things you're most committed to, most excited about, things that would give you the most satisfaction. On another sheet of paper, write them down again, and also write down *why* **you absolutely will achieve them.** *Why* to do something is much more powerful than *how*—if you get a big enough why, you can always figure out the how.[70]

Although authors such as Robbins understand the power of language and metaphor, they offer the prescribed language of self-improvement discourse, which corrals the reader back toward a predictable and limited set of concerns—back into what the French *fin de siècle* social theorist Gabriel Tarde called "the grooves of borrowed thought"[71]—patterns of thought that are unlikely to create any serious disruption of the status quo. In these labors that are purported to be labors of self-creation, the exercises provided are actually most effective not for the creation of newly invented selves but rather for the maintenance of existing notions of the self and its relation to the social and political worlds. Rather than authoring or inventing a new sort of self, these literatures tend to ensure that no one steps too far outside either the self-help genre or the generic lives it fosters.

"Imagineering": Visualizing One's Life and Managing One's Image

While authoring one's life—telling one's story in writing—is a central component of inventing the self, in an increasingly visual culture, more visual and figural forms of self-making have also come to play a central role. Much has been written on the impact and implications of the shift from an oral and aural culture to a literate text-based culture, a trend that is associated with the rise of modernity and the privileging of reason and rationality.[72] Similarly, much has been written regarding the shift from a literary culture to a visual and pictorial culture, or what some social theorists have called a shift from a discursive culture to a figural or iconic culture, a development that is tied to the emergence of postmodernity and is associated with an emphasis on sensation, feeling, and affect rather than reason.[73] There are important political implications in these developments. The literate subject engaged in dialogue, particularly written discourse, is said to have a greater capacity for reasoning and reflection, while the subject who is primarily visually oriented is imagined as more reactive and emotional. The former is an ideal for citizenship, while the latter is assumed to be easily swayed by the emotions and thus ideal for the development of supposedly "unruly" masses. Images are understood to speak more directly to unconscious desires, while language is assumed to foster rational decision-making. Thus this work of envisioning a self, rather than writing about one's self, is associated with pleasure and play, subject not to the rational processes of speech but rather to the perceptual world of image and sensation. Mind-power no longer takes the form of positive *thinking* alone but includes exercises in visualization and imagination. In her 1979 book *Creative Visualization*, Shakti Gawain writes:

Creative visualization is the technique of using your imagination to create what you want in your life. There is nothing at all new, strange, or unusual about creative visualization. You are already using it every day, every minute in fact. It is your natural power of imagination, the basic creative energy of the universe which you use constantly, whether or not you are aware of it. . . .

Imagination is the ability to create an idea or mental picture in your mind. In creative visualization you use your imagination to create a clear image of something you wish to manifest. Then you continue to focus on the idea or picture regularly, giving it positive energy until it becomes objective reality . . . in other words, until you actually achieve what you have been visualizing.[74]

Another typical example of a visualization exercise, making a "treasure map," is recommended by numerous self-help authors, Gawain among them:

Making a "treasure map" is a very powerful technique, and fun to do. . . . You can make a treasure map by drawing or painting it, or by making a collage using pictures or words cut from magazines, books, or cards, photographs, lettering, drawing, and so on. . . . Basically the treasure map should show you in your ideal scene, with your goal fully realized.[75]

In her 1998 *Take Time for Your Life*, Cheryl Richardson also advocates the use of a treasure map, but in a break with the self-help tradition of appropriating the ideas of others without attribution, Richardson, to her credit, attributes the exercise to an earlier inspirational author. "A treasure map," she writes, "is another way to keep your mind fueled with what really matters. In 1948, Robert Collier, in his book *The Secret of the Ages*, introduced the concept of creating a 'treasure map' as a way to visualize those things that you'd like to have in your life."[76]

The treasure map also figures prominently in Sarah Ban Breathnach's 1995 *Simple Abundance*:

JANUARY 29: YOUR PERSONAL TREASURE MAP

No self-respecting, swashbuckling buccaneer would set out in search of buried treasure without a map. Why should you? A personal treasure map is a collage of your ideal life that you create as a visual tool to focus your creative energy in the direction you wish to go.

First of all, you'll have to visualize your ideal life. Take a moment to get quiet and go within. Close your eyes. Now see how you live and who lives with you. What does your dream house look like? What part of the country is it in? Do you have children? How many? What type of garden do you have? Is there a gazebo in the backyard? A swimming pool? Do you have any pets? What kind of car is parked in the driveway? What kind of job do you have? Are you publishing your own newsletter, directing a feature film, or raising thoroughbred horses? Now see if you can't find pictures in magazines to match your ideal ones. Cut them out and create a collage on an eight- by ten-inch piece of posterboard.[77]

And Breathnach suggests that everyone create an "illustrated discovery journal":

One of the most pleasurable ways to start finding out your personal preferences is by creating an illustrated discovery journal. This is your explorer's log as you begin to make your way into the darkest terra incognita: your authentic inner world. . . . Here is an occasion where one picture speaks a thousand words. Meditating on one visual image a day can jump-start your creativity and lead to revealing insights.[78]

While on January 28—remember this is a daybook—one is exploring one's authentic, given, inner world, by January 29 one is creating "a wish list to the Universe" that bears a striking resemblance to a Christmas list, with a number of big-ticket items: house, car, swimming pool, Thoroughbred horses. One has gone from being an explorer to being a buccaneer, which is perhaps not at all a bad analogy for the directions suggested in *Simple Abundance*, which more often than not suggests shopping as a solution to problems.

In another, more high-tech exercise, Anthony Robbins suggests that one imagine oneself the director of one's own life, a film auteur rather than a text-based author:

Just as a movie director can change the effect his movie has on an audience, you can change the effect any experience in life has upon yourself. A director can change the camera angle, the volume and type of music, the speed and amount of movement, the color and quality of the image, and thus create any state he wants in his audience. You can direct your brain in the same way to generate any state or behavior that supports your highest goals or needs.

Let me show you how. [79]

Robbins's use of the idea of a film director's subjectivity recalls the work of the social theorist Walter Benjamin, who observed that the development of the printing press fostered the possibility of every person becoming an author. More recently, the advent of videotape recorders and computerized editing equipment renders everyone capable of imagining him or herself as an auteur: the director of his or her life. Mechanical reproduction, particularly the rise of photography and cinema, Benjamin argued, had diminished our access to singular experiences—to the presence of the living individual, to the unique "aura" of each thing and person:

> This situation might also be characterized as follows: for the first time—and this is the effect of the film—man has to operate with his whole living person, yet forgoing its aura. For aura is tied to his presence; there can be no replica of it. The aura which, on the stage, emanates from Macbeth, cannot be separated for the spectators from that of the actor. However, the singularity of the shot in the studio is that the camera is substituted for the public. Consequently, the aura that envelops the actor vanishes, and with it the aura of the figure he portrays.[80]

Mechanical reproduction, particularly filmmaking, sets the stage not only for a culture of celebrity, where the individual star's presence has been imbued with tremendous power,[81] but also for a world lived from the outside looking in that all the while harbors a nostalgia for the notion of an "authentic" world, lived from the inside out.[82] While modernity brought with it an inward turn—the rise of the psychological interiority associated with, for example, the novel—our increasingly visual culture brings with it the tendency to imagine oneself as one would appear.[83] Rather than living one's life in as unmediated a fashion as possible, the self-help reader engaged in Robbins's exercise imagines herself directing herself in a film, a ghostly puppeteer of a marionette that is her imagined self. One conceives of one's interiority by imagining how it might appear. This double gaze is not altogether new for women, who have long been charged with surveilling themselves as objects of masculine desire, or for other subordinated peoples, who must be mindful of the supervision of their masters.[84] It is not surprising, then, that Helen Gurley Brown suggests not a quest for authenticity but rather a pursuit of marketable appearances. She advocates cosmetic surgery among aging women for "anyone who cares how she looks."[85] And, under a heading entitled "Acceptable (Necessary!) Bullshit," she explains how overt lies are a necessary and acceptable part of courtship.[86] In Brown's business of life, feminine wiles and artifice are indispensable tools in the quest for a successful life. However, the extension of this image of self-surveillance to everyone is new, and is consistent with a culture that increasingly requires one to imagine one's self as a product. For example, embracing Tom Peters's idea of oneself as the CEO of Me, Inc., also requires a shift from plain packaging to a visually appealing one:

> Whatever you decide, you should look at your brand's power as an exercise in new-look résumé management—an exercise that you start by doing away once and for all with the word "résumé." You don't have an old-fashioned resume anymore! You've got a marketing brochure for brand You. . . .
>
> [Y]ou've got to be a broad-gauged visionary—a leader, a teacher, a farsighted "imagineer."[87]

Engineering one's image is part of self-mastery, but it is also, in the current context, critical to commodifying oneself—to keeping oneself marketable in a volatile labor market, or mastering the contingencies of the labor market. When Michel Foucault asked why not be a work of art, "like a lamp or a building," his metaphor offered the idea of the self as an object, as a commodity. This view, though it is likely that Foucault would protest, is completely consistent with Tom Peters's ideal of "brand You." Peters was among the first to observe that aestheticizing products would be increasingly important to their marketability.[88] This process is hardly limited to the inanimate: a 1996 *New York Times* headline kicker read: "Fearing the Ax, Men Choose the Scalpel."[89] Cosmetic surgery, the *Times* reported, was on the rise among men who feared that reaching middle age would make them candidates for downsizing. Maintaining an attractive, saleable image becomes critical in a culture saturated with media images.[90] When one imagines life as a sport or a battle, artifice, camouflage, ruse, and deception are legitimate means. Credibility, rather than authenticity, is the issue. Yet appearing authentic while conforming to external values produces for the self-creating self an endlessly contradictory task of reconciling incommensurable values. How does this self, caught between a newly expanded sense of interiority and faced with an increased demand that it shape itself for the marketplace, render itself "authentic"? What does the self-help literature advise, when there is not only a tension between appearing marketable and remaining authentic or true to oneself but also internal contradictions in the very notion of creating or inventing an authentic self? I want to look at each of these questions in turn.

Authenticating the Invented Self

Enthusiasm is the key to bolstering one's authenticity and promoting the appearance of self-mastery. Unlike authenticity, enthusiasm does not rely on any claim of origins, truthfulness, or integrity but instead depends upon energetic endorsement. Enthusiasm—the suggestion that one is infused with "theos," or supernatural inspiration—offers a serviceable substitute for authenticity. After all, what could be more authentic and masterful than to be infused with divine authority? Consider, for example, the characteristics of Tom Peters's prose in his most recent publications. Gone are the somber color schemes of the covers of *In Search of Excellence* or *Thriving on Chaos*. In their place are the orange, turquoise, and yellow colors of the covers of *The Pursuit of Wow!* and *The Tom Peters Seminar*. Peters's texts, which had already been notable for their use of exclamation marks, are riddled with them by the time of the publication of *The Pursuit of Wow!*[91] Peters is quoted in a recent interview on the importance of the exclamation mark: "Today, it's an exclamation-mark world. What is Silicon Valley but one big bright exclamation mark? If you had a Silicon Valley flag, isn't that what it would be?"[92]

Consider this passage from Peters's 1992 *Liberation Management*, which sits between *Chaos* and *Wow!* as a transitional work, where Peters proposes the notion of the company as carnival:

Dynamism. Say "carnival" and you think energy, surprise, buzz, fun. The mark of the carnival—and what makes it most different from a day at most offices—is its dynamism. Dynamism is a signature, the reason we go back. To create and maintain a carnival is never to get an inch away from dynamic imagery. As chief, you must feel the dynamics in your fingertips, be guided by them in *every* decision.[93]

Subtopics include "Toward Zany," "The Little Band of Jugglers," and "Bonkers Organizations." Peters's "wild and crazy" rhetoric substitutes an ethos of play for an ethos of "mission" or "life's purpose." Business is a pleasure and pleasure is a business for the CEO of Me, Inc. In *Wow*, Peters explains how to restructure a church for the 1990s:

> Typically dull white folks (of any denomination) could learn a lot from the best inner-city African-American churches, starting with Reverend Cecil Williams's inspiring, *energetic* Glide Memorial Church in San Francisco. (**Hint,** for starters: Glide doesn't have "services," it has "*celebrations*").[94]

African Americans are represented as the enthusiastic, passionate, feeling, and irrational other—aspects of the other that are to be incorporated into one's own business plan. Rational, thoughtful, careful economic planning is no longer sufficient: it must be infused and enhanced with enthusiasm. As in evangelical religions, where the emotional force of the conversion experience, along with impassioned public testimony about one's conversion, are the factors that authenticate and legitimize "salvation," the emotional enthusiasm of the entrepreneur legitimates his or her activity without the considerable inconvenience of an ethical stance. What Peters overlooks is that the enthusiasm of the African American church is made possible not simply by a dynamic, charismatic pastor but by the presence of an engaged community. His 1994 account of the entrepreneurial self is, by contrast, a lonely one, unmoored from community and the ethical values that are intrinsic to communities:

> Each of us is ultimately lonely. In the end, it's up to each of us alone to figure out who we are, who we are not, and to act more or less consistently with those conclusions.
>
> In my view, anyone who is not very confused all the time about ethical issues is out of touch with the frightful (and joyous) richness of the world. But at least being confused means that we are considering our ethical stance and that of the institutions we associate with.
>
> That's a good start.[95]

The CEOs of Me, Inc., ultimately alone and confused, are left to grapple with their problems, ethical and otherwise, entirely on their own. This is not only the ethical relativism of one culture in relation to another but also the ethical relativism of atomized individuals in relation to each other. Such a self, passionate though she or he may be, lives a life of alternating exhilaration and exhaustion:

> The life of an entrepreneur is occasionally exhilarating, and almost always exhausting. Only unbridled passion for the concept is likely to see you through the 17 hour days (month after month) and the painful mistakes that are part and parcel of the start-up process.[96]

Such isolated individuals—working seventeen-hour days—cannot, of course, engage in the labor of caring for others, or, it seems, even of caring for themselves. The work of producing oneself as the CEO of Me, Inc., requires that one belabor the self and leave care aside. Such atomized individuals, removed from any communities, may find themselves aggregated as a mass or a crowd. Robbins's seminars rely on this crowd experience, generating enthusiasm in the mass arena. Accounts of his preevent activities include reports of his "pumping up" for the event with a series of exercises.[97] Robbins explains:

> When I lead seminars, I always set off scenes of raucous, joyous, chaotic frenzy.
> If you walked in the door at the right moment, you would come upon perhaps three hundred people jumping up and down, screeching and hollering, roaring like lions, waving their arms, shaking their fists like Rocky, clapping their hands, puffing up their chests, strutting like peacocks, giving the thumbs-up sign, and otherwise acting as if they had so much personal power they could light up a city if they wanted to. . . .
> One way to get yourself into a state that supports your achieving any outcome is to act "as if" you were already there.[98]

The impossibility of finding one's "authentic" self is mitigated by the possibility of accessing, at least, one's most persuasive self. One does not need to be an authority if one can appear authoritative. "Awakening the Power Within"—accessing stores of energy—stands in for authenticity. "Congruity"—Robbins's version of authenticity—yields energy, and energy is, in turn, a sign of "congruity."

> Incongruity keeps me from being all I can be, from doing all I can do, and from creating my strongest state. Giving oneself contradictory messages is a subliminal way of pulling a punch. . . .

We've all experienced the price of incongruence when part of us really wants something but another part within seems to stop us. Congruence is power. People who consistently succeed are those who can commit all their resources, mental and physical, to work together toward achieving a task. Stop a moment now and think of the three most congruent people you know. Now think of the three most incongruent people you know. What is the difference between them? How do congruent people affect you personally versus people who are incongruent?[99]

The difficulty, of course, is that individuals who have multiple and often conflicting commitments—to families, to communities, and to their work—may find it all but impossible to reconcile these conflicting demands, to gain congruence, and thus may "fail" to "awaken the giant within." Paradoxically, Robbins's solution to finding what he calls "congruency" isn't to search one's soul for one's deepest values but rather to imitate other people:

> One way to develop congruency is to model the physiologies of people who are congruent. The essence of modeling is to discover which part of the brain an effective person uses in a given situation. If you want to be effective, you want to use your brain in the same way. If you mirror someone's physiology exactly, you will tap the same part of your brain.[100]

Producing this persuasive self was the topic of Arlie Russell Hochschild's 1983 study of the working conditions of flight attendants. Hochschild observed that presenting oneself as genuinely caring was a critical part of the flight attendant's work. This work, which Hochschild called emotional labor, was required by corporations wishing to represent "themselves"—their organizations—as friendly, and their service as superior. These corporations provided (and presumably continue to provide) service training to ensure that flight attendants learned the skills of emotional management necessary to present themselves as "caring professionals." Hochschild called this phenomenon "the managed heart" and observed: "The more the heart is managed, the more we value the unmanaged heart."[101] With the blurring of the boundaries between public and private life—evidenced in part by the rise of a construct like Peters's CEO of Me, Inc.—one is no longer compelled to manage the heart only in the context of the corporate workplace. Or rather, more accurately, the corporate workplace is interiorized:

one takes the workplace with one everywhere. Managing the heart while appearing completely natural (i.e., congruent) becomes even more important for success. In such a context, authenticating the invented self becomes a central, if futile, pursuit. Working on one's self while presenting an appearance of effortlessness, of seamless congruence and boundless energy, is critical to one's success. Moreover, engaging in the fantasy that one actually does "invent" oneself is an even more contradictory demand of the literatures of self-improvement.

Inventing the Authentic Self

To understand what the task of creating an authentic life might mean, it is useful to consider the varied meanings and the etymology of this term.[102] According to the *Oxford English Dictionary*, in its earliest forms, the word *authenticus* (Latin) referred to authority, as in "one who does a thing himself, a principal, a master, an autocrat." It was only later, in thirteenth-century France, that the term began to be conflated with the notion of something genuine or original. Thus "authenticity" can be understood in one of two ways. In the earlier case, authenticity is understood as the development of authority over oneself, or self-mastery. And in the second case, authenticity is understood as the quest for some kind of original ur-self unsullied by the impact of socialization. Such a self has to be "discovered," " uncovered," or "recovered" and figures prominently in the literatures of self-improvement, where one is urged to "excavate" and "unearth" one's true self or true desires. In the first case, the self is understood to be engaged in what Foucault would call a "practice of freedom"—the self creating itself as a work of art or inventing new forms of subjectivity (though Foucault himself eschews any notion of authenticity). This sort of authenticity requires not only freedom from the demands of the market—from the necessity of adapting oneself to the labor market—but also freedom from dependence on others. The ideal of creating a life of which one is the master, not the subject—of being self-creating rather than subject to the desires and discourses of others—would appear to be at the heart of any practice of freedom, and thus crucial for social change. But, as in any version of the self that assumes a highly autonomous individual agent, the belief in such an authoritative, authentic, self-authoring self requires the repression of any consideration of the contributions of others to one's self and one's world.

The quest for either of these sorts of authenticity, self-mastery or self-discovery, requires a disavowal of the value of the caring labor of others in shaping the self. One must be fully and completely independent or autonomous. In the first case, where one is to be master of oneself, the labor of others and the possibilities for freedom that it creates are denied or minimized. And in the second case, where one is to recover oneself from the damages of socialization, that labor is denigrated. Thus an important part of the work of the belabored self is to engage in a denial of the impact of, or the value of, others' contributions to oneself.[103] One must see one's self as either commanding, masterful, and in control and not subject to the exigencies of life or the labor market (thus authoritative, or self-authoring) or as given, unique, damaged by social forces, but recoverable (thus minimizing or denying the positive value of others). In the first case, one has no debt to these persons and institutions, because if the goal is to be singularly self-forming, one needs to deny the impact of others. In the second case, one has to deny the debt to, for example, one's parents and the social institutions that formed one, because this impact is seen as damage, as something to recover from.[104] In either case, these forms of authenticity are inconsistent with the reality that one is neither wholly a cause nor wholly an effect. Thus the literatures of self-improvement, and self-creations of other kinds, reliant as they are on the liberal notion of an autonomous self, require their adherents to engage in a denial of the importance of—even the existence of—the labors of others and the forces of history. In a repudiation of this notion of the self as its own author, Hannah Arendt wrote:

> Although everybody started his life by inserting himself into the human world through action and speech, nobody is the author or producer of his own life story. In other words, the stories, the results of action and speech, reveal an agent, but this agent is not an author or producer. Somebody began it and is its subject in the twofold sense of the word, namely its actor and sufferer, but nobody is its author.[105]

When Foucault imagined life as a work of art he imagined an art object. Arendt, in contrast, imagined life as a narrative, authored by the social collectivity rather than by the lone individual. While her metaphor brings along its own problematic (e.g., the potential aestheticizing of the political realm)[106] it offers a notion of agency that is both embedded and relational.

Fundamentally, it is our culture's fantasy of a disengaged, masterful, rational, and controlling self that creates the possibilities for endless and futile self-improvement. The work of belaboring the self consists not of the necessary activities of daily life—the labor that goes into sustaining and reproducing human life that Arendt describes as continuous until death. Rather, the work of this self-belaboring itself includes a labor of active forgetting, of denying the dependence, vulnerability, and contingency of this purportedly autonomous self. This liberal notion of the self, which took its cues from the philosophy of the ancient Greeks, relies, in its inception, on an ideal of self-mastery that necessarily required the mastery and exploitation of others. Whether this mastery is seen as creating one's life as a work of art or of realizing all of one's business opportunities or of winning at the game of life, this idea of self-mastery has its origins in a context of the alienation from and domination of others.

Up until the late twentieth century, the polite fiction of an autonomous individual who could direct his life course managed to sustain itself. When women, as well as others oppressed through racial and ethnic stereotyping, were required to operate as "the other" to this rational, self-authorizing self, the cultural landscape managed to sustain the myth of the self-making man, however wobbly and unsupportable the construct may have been. The extension of this particular notion of individual freedom to each and all has destabilized it. As the ideal of creating a life or leaving one's mark—arguably an appealing one—is made available to those people who have traditionally been excluded, the limitations of this ideal of a self-serving, autonomous individual are ever more apparent. Put simply, if everyone is busy making sure that they get to "be all they can be," then who will clean the house, cook the dinners, diaper the babies, and nurse the infirm, not to mention labor in the factories, sweep the streets, drive the taxis, and load the sanitation trucks? All the work of care—both the private and public labors of care—are rendered meaningless and debased when one is seeking some grander work of self-making, some vision of life as a permanent reified work of art. Ultimately, then, Arendt's categories of labor and work—as apt as they appear to be—may need to be understood as descriptive of ideological formations that we have inherited from the Greeks, and that we reproduce in our daily lives, rather than as prescriptive of an equitable way of organizing the world. The fiction of a masterful self that can make of its life a work of art ultimately fails us if the ideal is predicated on the privileging of work over labor and the dual refusal to recognize both the labor of others and the absolute, irrefutable vulnerabilities of corporeal, embodied selves. The ideal of life as a work of art is meant to insulate the self from the more economistic metaphor of life as a business, but in the end it fails to do so when it elevates work—understood as leaving a legacy— over labor, the reproduction of life itself.

Not only is it the labor of others, and the value of labor itself, that must be denied by the masterful self, but also it is the vulnerabilities of our bodies. In the model of the self-mastering self, the forms of selfhood that "fail" to be self-sufficient, self-reliant, and self-authoring are seen as somehow defective. As the ideal of an autonomous, self-serving, and masterful subject is applied to everyone, and as the values of the market overflow into every arena, "failed" and "defective" forms of selfhood—childhood, illness, disability, or aged infirmity—no longer find a safe haven. Whereas once the intimate sphere provided a refuge for these cast-off forms of selfhood, an increasingly market-oriented, gains-maximizing intimate arena offers no place of respite. Insulating the self from these affronts to its vulnerabilities through constant efforts at self-mastery and self-management is a central, if futile, undertaking of the belabored self. The belabored self grapples with the encroachment of market principles into every sphere of life, and finds that individual resources to fight such a battle are ultimately limited and ineffectual.

Maintaining the fiction of the autonomous self, a laborious fiction that is ultimately unsustainable, has become hard work. However, we are left with a tremendous problem if we are to abandon the notion of personal freedom at precisely the moment that this ideal has been extended to those who had formerly been excluded. Do we wish to reject the idea of a self with the freedom to create his or her own life at precisely the moment that this ideal has been extended to women and other oppressed groups?[107] Such a direction strikes me as suspect, even reactionary. In the final chapter, I will consider what might be recuperated from the notion of "being all one can be."

chapter 6

All You Can Be, or Some Conclusions

*[C]ontemporary seekers of authenticity often lack any but the
vaguest ethical or religious commitments. Their obsession with
"meaning" masks its absence from any frame of reference outside
the self. . . . The effort to re-create a coherent sense of selfhood
seems fated to frustration. Every failure inaugurates a new psychic
quest, until the seeker is embroiled in an interminable series of
self-explorations. . . . [T]he vision of a self in endless development
is perfectly attuned to an economy based on pointless growth and
ceaseless destruction.*
—T. J. Jackson Lears

The demand that one "be all one can be" is double-edged. On the one
hand, if one imagines oneself living in a democracy where every person's
self-development will benefit them individually as well as society as a whole,
then "being all one can be" is a social responsibility and privilege for each
and all. On the other hand, if one imagines oneself living in a market-driven
capitalism rapidly careening toward the annihilation of the planet, then
"being all one can be" is little more than another advertising slogan encouraging one to exploit the closest natural resource, in this case, one's self.[1] The
capitalist demand is that one "be all one can be": human capital, as with
any other natural resource, is to be developed and exploited. In such a context, the self is inevitably belabored. The democratic demand—and promise—is that one will get to "be all one can be": a human being reaching his
or her greatest potential in association with others. As it happens, we live in
a world that can be characterized by either of these representations—one
as an ideal that is only occasionally realized and the other as an unfortunate
reality all too readily available. Yet abandoning the notion of individual self-
determination that is at the center of self-help culture at exactly the moment

that this ideal is extended to those who have been historically excluded from the privileges of citizenship and the possibilities of self-invention seems a troubling proposal. On the other hand, embracing the prior models of self-making seems a faulty course if one is to allow for the possibility of self-making that embraces autonomy and connection, individual freedom and an abiding sense of community.

Tired Models of the Self

Prior, tired models of the self have fostered the belabored self. These ideas of self-making—ideals inherited from our Enlightenment philosophical traditions—populate the literatures of self-improvement culture. Whether driven by stark economic motives, as is the Number One of *Looking Out for Number One*, or operating according to a set of abstract moral principles, as do Stephen Covey's "highly effective people," this self-mastering self is an ideal that was revived by Enlightenment gentlemen philosophers who'd taken up where Greek philosophers had left off.[2] These rational-economic and rational-ethical versions of the self included the desire for self-mastery, the suppression of the bodily, the denial of the importance of the caring labor of others, and, at least in the case of the *Homo economicus*, the privileging of the individual over the collective. As an alternative to these two rational versions of the self, the late nineteenth century also offered two aesthetic alternatives: a version of the self that is best exemplified by the mystical, transcendental vision of the poet Walt Whitman and the more bracing aestheticism of the philosopher Friedrich Nietzsche. The transcendental version of the self neither mastered itself nor sought control over anything but instead operated in tune with a higher Source or Power, Nature standing in for God. Operating outside boundaries, rejecting categories, and denouncing distinctions, this Romantic version of the self (and post-Romantic in the case of Nietzsche) privileged the creative potential in each individual and provided an alternative to the rational approach.

While these versions of the self are not new, what is new, as I noted at the outset, is that the ideal of self-fulfillment and self-mastery has been extended more broadly. In that process, two things have occurred. First, within the cultures of self-improvement, values from the competitive world of the marketplace have been transplanted to the personal world of intimate life, and vice versa. Second, and perhaps more important, the serious flaws in the notions of a self-mastering and self-creating self have grown more apparent. The first development—the hybridization of personal and commercial values—was eminently evident in the texts of self-improvement culture. A calculating rationality was imported into the private sphere under the aegis of recovery from "codependency." And, reciprocally, the full-scale entry of women into the labor force (coupled with the historical coding of the aesthetic as "feminine") fostered a newly invigorated aesthetic orientation in both intimate and workplace domains. In the intimate domain of personal life, the ideal of life as work of art was increasingly offered as a source of solace for individuals whose life courses were unpredictable, while in the workplace the artist has come to serve as a new workforce ideal.

The second development—that the idea of a self-mastering self cannot be sustained when it is extended to everyone—is less apparent in the context of the literatures of self-improvement. In scholarly circles, this has appeared as what one hears called "the crisis of the liberal subject" or "the death of the subject." For example, Michel Foucault's famous and often-quoted assertion that the self will fade like a face drawn in the sand offers an image of selfhood as an ephemeral phantom borne of our particular historical epoch.[3] But in the literatures of self-improvement, one does not read of a crisis of the subject. In this literature, proclamations of the death of the subject, as with the death of God, seem to be either premature or, as the joke goes, greatly exaggerated. Instead, in this milieu, that crisis of subjecthood is not articulated but enacted—demonstrated in ever expanding self-help book sales and, presumably, enacted in the lives of subjects who find that it is difficult or impossible to manage mastery of themselves and their life courses in the face of volatile social and economic forces.[4] For these individuals, the self is belabored: caught in a cycle of seeking individual solutions to problems that are social, economic, and political in origin.

In the mid 1980s "women who loved too much" were urged to be "codependent no more." Two decades and thousands of self-help books later, a rather different directive is needed. Rather than renouncing or denying our interdependence, perhaps it has come to the point where anxious readers of self-help literature need to refuse to participate in futile efforts at individual self-improvement and instead focus collectively on eliminating the vast social and economic inequities that have rendered us such a ready market for this literature. In short, we need to become belabored no more. But as this is not a standard lifestyle makeover project, it cannot be undertaken by individuals acting in isolation. Rather, it calls for newer models of the self and new social movements.

The first of these requirements is a model of the self that is fully embodied, relational, and emotional, that imagines the self as part of a constellation of relationships in which contributing to the advancement of others is seen as necessary and inseparable from contributing to one's own advancement. The second and related necessity would be the development of social movements committed to making the possibility of this kind of interdependent self-development available to each and all. Although these requisites are interconnected, I want to consider them each in turn.

Newer Models of the Self: Maternal and Internal Multitudes

In developing newer models of the self to replace the inadequate prior representations, a good place to start would be to consider the lives of those who have been traditionally un- or underrepresented in the previous representations: the various Maria Coveys whose lives are rendered unmanageable by our culture's blindness to the amount of caring labor required to reproduce ourselves as individuals, communities, and a species. Some feminist theorists and philosophers have suggested that motherhood offers an improved metaphor or model for a new vision of self-making.[5] One engages in the "making" of others and the making of one's self, neither to the exclusion of the other, and both irrevocably intertwined. In the act of fostering another, one creates not one life but two. Metaphorically it is perhaps not overreaching to observe that the word "mother" has "other" contained within it. While such a metaphor risks the possibility of falling into a kind of biological essentialism with all its clichés (e.g., the pure and selfless mother),[6] this pitfall can be avoided if one recalls that *mother* is both noun and verb, and that the verb form is available to anyone, regardless of his or her gender or reproductive history.[7] Mothering, not mother or motherhood, is the model.

The point is not to idealize mothers—sentimental literatures and popular culture of the last two centuries have done a thorough job of that. Rather, the point is to find a central role for the nurturance of others in the models of the self and then generate a multiplicity of caring selves. Although the literatures of self-improvement occasionally rely on metaphors of mothering (as in caring for one's "inner child"), this inward turn of mothering, focused back on the individual self, saps the mothering metaphor of its ethical and political potential. Curiously, Nietzsche, a philosopher not known for his high regard for women, proposed the image of mothering as the model for a new ethics: "Let yourself be in your deeds as a mother is in her child, let that be your *word* concerning virtue."[8] The somewhat cryptic imperative is consistent with his vision of selves within selves: "not one immortal soul, but many mortal souls."[9] Like Walt Whitman, who proclaimed: "I am large . . . I contain multitudes," [10] Nietzsche's assemblage of mortal souls makes multiple identifications and allegiances the model. His version of the self, supported by the artificial intelligence work of theorists such as Marvin Minsky, suggests that the individual be understood as a constellation of agendas or "agents" that compete for one's resources.[11] Internal conflict, rather than the "congruence" urged by Anthony Robbins, is recognized as necessary and inevitable in developing a multifaceted self. Governing the self is seen as a process of both contestation and coalition building, much as contemporary political efforts call for a politics of coalitions—the possibility of community without the requirement of a false or forced unity or oneness.

Related and interdependent models of the self have started to enter the self-help literature: Stephen Covey's "highly effective person" is one such model. However, the interdependence Covey advocates is limited to particular social roles and, as such, is "scripted" or formulated out of normative expectations: what one ought to do in one's role as spouse or parent, employee or manager, student or teacher. Beyond that, the self that Covey proposes is one that privileges reason and self-control. Covey's model is that of a rational ethical subject guided by fixed universal principles rather than the particulars of specific contexts or the needs of his internal coalition of agents. His emphasis on a rational self that "manages" a variety of roles significantly overestimates the role of reason and willpower while underestimating the irrational or "bio-*logical*."[12] This planning, managing, and calculating version of the self is, by Covey's own admission, unable to accommodate the messy realities of mothering. Perhaps most important, what is missing in Covey's model is any acknowledgement of the actually existing inequitable distribution of resources and power, any concern about how the gendered division of labor in family life might lead to limited opportunities for women, as well as any acknowledgement that where there is an inequitable distribution of power, resources, and opportunities, that conflict is not only likely, but perhaps inevitable, if not desirable.

Covey's conflict-averse cosmology requires a focus on the internalized versions of the external world. Social relations are reduced to roles, and conflicts are internal—between the roles one fulfills rather than with actually existing others in the world. This reduction of conflict is tracked by the sociologist Irene Taviss Thomson, who undertook a content analysis of self-improvement literature from the 1920s through the 1990s.[13] Taviss Thomson argues that the literature of self-improvement demonstrates that Americans have already moved away from a model of the lone individual in conflict with society to a newer model of a relational self that forms and reconfirms itself within small voluntary groups.[14] Taviss Thomson understands this development as the end of the conflict paradigm—the end of the notion of the individual pitted against an overarching "society." And if individuals had only to live within small self-constituted communities, her argument would appear incontrovertible. The hitch is that while individuals are clearly constituting themselves in small self-created communities of interest—Twelve-Step groups, reading groups, and groups along the lines of what Gloria Steinem proposed and the sociologist Robert Wuthnow documents[15]—they continue to have involuntary relationships with a whole group of institutions that are neither voluntary nor self-constructed. For example, legislative and juridical institutions limit the use of controlled substances, and increasingly regulate even traditionally accepted drugs such as tobacco; the taxes that support wars one opposes are not optional; and so on. Conflict will inevitably continue, not only between individuals and larger institutional structures but also between the self-constituted groups and established institutional forces. In such a setting, "becoming oneself" or "being all one can be" could potentially challenge existing power structures.[16]

Newer Versions of Selves, Newer Social Movements

Cultivating groups in which individuals might become themselves—multiple, complex, and interrelated selves—as well as insisting on a world in which they can be themselves would seem to be the work of progressive social movements. If one imagines self-help culture not only as means of social control but also as a symptom of social unrest that has not found a political context, then, given the exponential growth of self-help reading, there is no shortage of unrest or dissatisfaction. Understood in these terms, self-help culture could potentially offer an enormous opportunity for cultivating social change. Indeed, some would argue that the rise of the Twelve-Step groups constitutes one of the most significant American social movements of the late twentieth century.[17] Tapping into this vast reserve of discontent has been, some suggest, one of the secrets of the conservative rise to power in the late twentieth century.[18] For those who might wish for a more progressive, even radical, political agenda, mobilizing this dissatisfaction would surely be an important undertaking. Toward such an end, a number of factors would be of vital importance.

Perhaps the most important shift that would be required would be a change in the ways in which we understand the self, which has already been considered at some length. Individuals who have been urged to imagine themselves as self-directing would need to come to understand the fundamental flaws in this ideal. Not only does this notion of the self overstate the individual capacity for willed actions[19] but, as I've shown, this characterization relies on the unacknowledged, and typically un- or undercompensated, labor of others. Those who have been exhorted to become the CEOs of Me, Inc., would come to acknowledge the underside of their ideal—a belabored self demanding boundless effort from one's self and from those around one. Individuals would understand themselves and each other not as the failed CEOs of Me, Inc., but rather as disenfranchised members of a group of people who have been "liberated" from the possibility of stable jobs and careers (that is, from stable sources of a livelihood) and deprived of a social safety net, much as serfs and peasants were once freed from their indenture to lords *and* deprived of the lands on which their livelihoods depended.

While this shift of consciousness would be necessary, it is also insufficient, as there are notable limits to developing a politics out of a sense of victimization. The difficulty of operating from a politics of "victimhood" is at least threefold. First, there is the tendency of this formation to reinscribe and perpetuate precisely the categories it is meant to eliminate.[20] For example, if disability activists achieved genuine success at full access and opportunities, the category of "disability" would fade into something akin to differences of ability to which everyone is subject. "Reasonable accommodations" for differences in learning styles, or mobility, or sensory capacities would no longer be exceptional demands, they would be commonplace. If antiracist politics were to succeed, then these completely ideological categories built on skin tones and facial features would likewise fade, and racial categorization would vanish. And so on with any category of difference. Second, a politics of victimization requires good guys and bad guys, and historically it has been all too easy for one exploited group to imagine another exploited group as its oppressor. Anti-immigrant sentiments are one popular version of this tendency, as are claims that women and other formerly excluded groups in the labor force have "taken" the good jobs once reserved for able-bodied white men. While there may indeed be good guys and bad guys, correctly identifying those who are genuinely operating against one's interests can be a risky undertaking. Finally, unless one can imagine the possibilities of redressing one's grievances, feeling that one is a victim simply feels bad. Individuals who feel they have some control over their lives—what psychologists call "self-efficacy"—are more likely to exercise whatever control they may have, as well as to join with others to change the conditions of their lives.[21]

Self-improvement culture, as it actually exists, derails the opportunities for individuals to understanding injuries or grievances as part of systematic social problems. In this sense, it offers a worldview that is precisely the inverse of the "sociological imagination" that C. Wright Mills proposed.[22] The literatures and practices of self-improvement culture do this in two ways: first, in self-improvement literature, victims are anathema, and second, when victimization occurs, it is almost exclusively located in the past, in the lost world of childhood, where the family, imagined as isolated from society as a whole, is named as the cause of the violence or injustice. Apart from the juridical arena of civil court, where victims can be channeled into the manageable and profitable category of plaintiffs, and the nationalist arena of combat casualties and their bereaved families, where the loss of loved ones can be transmuted into patriotism, victims are notoriously loathed. Viewers of talk show television are told—by, for example, Dr. Philip McGraw on the *Oprah Winfrey Show*—that "there are no victims, only volunteers."[23] If one "volunteered" to be abused, then there is really no one to blame but oneself. Thus the usual political strategy of organizing individuals around their grievances is short-circuited, and culpability is turned back on the self. Problems and grievances are cast as personal "challenges" that the individual must strive to overcome. Second, in the culture of recovery, victimization exists, but only in the past, where it cannot be remedied. The sources of one's problems, in this milieu, occurred only in childhood; thus no political action in the present is possible. The injured party is not an adult who may have equal measures of agency and vulnerability but rather is located in the arena of lost childhood, where vulnerability and dependence are still accepted conditions.[24] What the literatures of self-improvement do offer is the promise of power, however limited in scope and mistakenly located it may be in isolated individual action. Traditional political organizing, for example, the recruitment strategies of labor organizers, builds on a sense of aggrievement and then moves the aggrieved individual to locate his or her power in the group, forging a sense of collective identity that is not wholly a function of victimization but that takes victimization as its starting point.[25]

Beyond the challenges associated with forming individual and collective identities within the framework of political grievances—beyond this politics of recognition—what is also necessary is a commitment to the equitable distribution of wealth and resources.[26] Demands for recognition without a parallel demand for economic justice is at the heart of why the self is belabored. The demand for individual self-development and realization without the possibility of economic security can never be more than an ideological carrot or a bludgeon. For those who have some measure of middle-class access to resources, however tenuous this access may be during the ebbs and flows of the economy, the ideal of self-fulfillment serves as an enticement. And for those who do not, particularly for those recently "liberated" from public assistance, the ideal gives way to a punishing rhetoric of individual self-reliance. Either way, in the absence of a social safety net and in the face of profound economic injustice, any discussion of self-actualization is rendered absurd. Even the psychologist Abraham Maslow, who popularized this term, would consider the pursuit of self-actualization without some measure of economic security to be a tenuous, if not impossible, undertaking. The demand for an equitable distribution of resources would be central to any politics emerging from the fatigue of the belabored self. A social safety net with a guaranteed minimum living allowance would be a necessary component of a politics of self-realization. Without forced labor—without the requirement that one scurry about to pursue a livelihood like the desperate rodents of *Who Moved My Cheese?*—work might be genuinely recast as an expression of identity and self-fulfillment, and the self would lose its belabored quality.

For the most part, self-improvement culture continues to operate on a belief that wealth is a sign of industry, intelligence, competence, or attunement with the universe. Poverty, bred of economic injustice, remains a marker of laziness, stupidity, immorality, or some sort of cosmic dissonance. As with much of American culture that finds its roots in Christian traditions, self-help culture suggests that inequitable distributions of wealth ought to be remedied through charity rather than through any process of distributive justice. Charitable foundations, rather than a progressive tax code or the elimination of untaxed wealth transfers through inheritance, are offered as the solution to the social problem of economic inequity.[27] Even the most visible social justice movements of the late twentieth century have tended to eschew struggles over the distribution of goods and resources, focusing instead on issues that involve symbolic or representational issues (sexist or racist representations, for example).[28] More recently, with the antiglobalization movement that burst onto the public landscape in Seattle in 1999, this may be changing. Fostering a politics of economic justice will require that we remember a crucial axiom: any politics of equitable distribution necessarily includes a politics of identity, insofar as particular identities are denied equitable access to material and symbolic resources. However, the obverse does not hold true: a politics of identity does not necessarily encompass a commitment to economic justice.[29] One can, for example, be concerned about equal rights for women without being concerned about economic justice for women of all backgrounds. However, if one is committed to economic equality for all people, one is necessarily concerned with the impact that an array of categorical distinctions—for example, "woman" and racial and ethnic categories such as "African American" or "Latino"—have had on women's earning power and access to other economic resources. Or, to use a more contemporary example, the desire of same-sex couples to gain access to the institution of marriage is at once a question of identity or recognition, specifically the public recognition of one's choice of a life partner, and of material concerns or redistribution of resources, in that an unmarried partner is routinely denied access to the healthcare and pension plans of his or her employed partner. When one conceives of the problem solely in terms of recognition—in terms of sexual identity—one misses the covalent and coalition-building concern for equitable access to healthcare and to secure retirement.

Common Vulnerabilities, Mutual Recognitions

A politics that encompassed a commitment to redistribution would require mutual, reciprocal recognition.[30] While one demands recognition for one's self and the members of groups with which one is aligned, one must necessarily be willing to offer recognition to others. One way to foster this mutual recognition would be to focus not on one's differences but rather on the common vulnerabilities that we experience as embodied, corporeal creatures. These vulnerabilities are elided and eliminated in the rhetoric of self-help culture with its can-do, bootstrapping proposals. Mind is supposed to trump body at every juncture. Recognition of our own and each other's repressed corporeal vulnerabilities suggests an immediate basis for locating common ground. Rather than rising above the challenges of physical limitation through some sort of mind-power, as does the Maudlin Exemplar identified earlier in inspirational self-help literature, we might attend to the fragility of embodied existence. Such attention ought to foster a culture of care and mutual interdependence. Although you may not be mobility-impaired today, you or someone you love may be tomorrow; thus the "disabled self" is one that you carry within you as a real, even likely, possibility. Disability rights, though perhaps not an immediate concern to you as a discrete, able-bodied person, would necessarily be a concern.

Another way to cultivate mutual recognition is to foster public spaces for discussion and dialogue. The much-lamented vanishing of a public sphere may need to be understood somewhat differently as the distinctions between public and private, and commercial and intimate life, are eroded. Indeed, it may need to be reimagined not as a disappearing act but rather as a redistribution of public spaces to multiple constituencies. Rather than one public sphere, political organizing may be most fruitful in multiple and overlapping spheres. The unstable and often confusing dichotomy of public and private, which was traditionally understood as paired spaces of citizenship (public) and commerce (private), respectively, would need to be refigured to encompass the radical ways in which commerce has entered into intimate life (as in the emergence of concepts such as codependency and the financialization of daily life) and the ways in which intimate life has become part of the public discourse (talk show confessionals being only one of many examples). An effective politics in the current context would necessarily embrace the demise of the public-private split for all of its possibilities, rather than mourning its passing. For example, rather than attempting to maintain the family or intimate sphere as a retreat from the demands of the market, one might instead "take parenting public" and argue that the nonmarket values formerly confined to the intimate sphere (or otherwise articulated only in religious contexts) must be upheld in every arena of life. One might argue that the caring work provided by stay-at-home parents be adequately compensated through a modified tax structure or by other adjustments.

Self-improvement culture, particularly the culture of recovery based in the Alcoholics Anonymous tradition, has contributed much in the formation of small groups where dialogue is possible.[31] The difficulty with these groups is that the political possibilities are radically short-circuited by several factors: (1) the anonymous groups have a strong commitment to remaining apolitical and focused solely on individual recovery; (2) the very requirement of anonymity cuts off the individual from any of his or her other identities; and (3) modes of dialogue are necessarily short-circuited by the speech guidelines set down by the Twelve-Step "Traditions."[32] The sociologist Anthony Giddens suggested that these groups served as a sign of the "transformation of intimacy" and a "democratisation of the private sphere."[33] And in broad strokes, that may indeed be correct. But in the details, in the fine-tuning, the structures of these groups have largely mitigated against progressive social change. Alcoholics Anonymous has an inviolable tradition of remaining apolitical, while the requirement of anonymity ensures that the individual separates his or her "addict" identity from his or her other social roles. Inside the groups themselves, speech rules that require individuals to refrain from responding to other members' comments short-circuit dialogue and maintain a series of related monologues strung together by the medical metaphor of addiction and the Protestant tradition of testimony.[34]

On the other hand, one of the virtues of these groups is that they have fostered a notion of individual self-mastery or self-control as limited.[35] The premise of these groups is that one is powerless over the particular "addiction" being battled. In other words, the self that operates in the Twelve-Step framework is not a fully rational agentic self but rather a self that is subject to irrational behaviors, subject to "temptations," subsumed under the general medicalized category of "addictions." The self proposed in these groups is not all-powerful but rather admits that there is a power (or powers) greater than the self that shape(s) the individual's life. Individuals are encouraged to develop their own notion of a higher power, typically understood as unitary and benevolent, encouraging a traditional monotheistic understanding. However, if the individual were asked to consider that there are multiple, and not necessarily beneficent, powers greater than the self shaping his or her life—for example, an out-of-control economic market or the erratic weather patterns borne of global warming—then there could be a space for political discourse. This admission of powerlessness offers the paradoxical point from which to gather new sources of power—

from the group and from a particular set of ideals or values. In the case of AA, the value is sobriety, but for groups adopting this model, other values might prevail.

Citizen-Artists as Agents of Social Change?

Along with new spaces of dialogue, what will also be needed are new ways of envisioning the world: ways of making over culture rather than remaining subject to makeover culture. For new visions of the world, our culture has often turned to various avant-garde artists and poets. The political philosopher Richard Rorty borrows the literary critic Harold Bloom's ideal of the "strong poet" as the most effective agent of social transformation.[36] In this model, the artist is no longer the ideal model for the new knowledge-labor economy, nor is she simply composing a life—rather, the "strong poet" has the power to transform culture and society through his own self-creation or self-transformation via new metaphorical constructs. The concept of the "strong poet" suggests that cultural vanguards are the last best hope for political transformation. The strong poet's goal is to overcome the given world, the inherited world, and, in Bloom's words, "give birth to one's self."[37] Leaving aside for the moment this metaphorical usurpation of maternal powers—this powerful image of mothering turned back on the self—there are obvious limits to the virtue of the new, particularly when it is cast as the work of lone individuals. In an effort to avoid these problems, Rorty proposes a partition of private and public, a continuing separation of spheres. In the former, the pursuit of private self-creation and self-fulfillment is made possible, limited only by a liberal public sphere where only cruelty and intolerance are not allowed. The trouble with Rorty's private-public partition is that it imagines self-creation as an individual's private project rather than a social endeavor.[38] Rorty imagines a private self construction, an individual "becoming what one is," rather than a community-based dialogue that moves our understandings of social possibilities forward. But self-realization is seldom a private endeavor, particularly when the individual who is attempting to realize herself bumps up against limiting normative expectations. It was not individual self-creation in isolation but self-invention in the context of consciousness-raising groups that made the feminism of the 1970s and 1980s a social movement to be reckoned with. Feminist groups were among the first to recognize that personal change was catalyzed by group participation, while group participation could also forge larger social and political agendas. That these groups were able to wed a culture of collective self-help with political actions offered a model for other social movements.[39]

The ideal of political change through imaginative transformation—the vision of the artist as an agent of social change—must be joined to a culture of collective dialogue to forge effective political transformation. "Cultural citizenship," to use the term offered by the cultural theorist Toby Miller, recuperates citizenship from the traditional sphere of electoral politics and transports it to the arena of the representational, suggesting that citizenship operating in multiple arenas offers the best possibilities for fostering social and political change. The effective cultural citizen, in this model, joins together with others to articulate not their similarities and unity but rather their differences from normative social categories. By locating and articulating these spaces of disjunction—of the differences between one's own experience and the predictable, stereotypical categories of borrowed thought, by operating against the cultural grain—the cultural citizen engages in a kind of autoinvention that challenges existing norms and modalities, generating new and emancipatory possibilities for self-construction.[40] Such challenges to normative categories, when they occur in spaces of public dialogue, constitute an engaged cultural citizenship.[41]

Ironically, self-help culture, particularly Twelve-Step culture, has provided some of our most robust new language: recovery, dysfunctional families, and, of course, codependency are all concepts that emerge from this vital, if depoliticized, context. The difficulty with these formulations is that they do not operate out of a disjunction with cultural norms but rather are hybridizations of religious traditions of testimony and medical discourse. These formulations necessarily produce some measure of social transformation, but in the process of hybridization rather than disjunction, the tendency is for their formulations to maintain, rather than disrupt, the status quo. The literatures of self-improvement are, as I've demonstrated throughout this consideration, in the main, uninventive, liberally appropriating from prior inspirational literature. The developments we've seen have been not so much new inventions but expansions and adaptations.[42] The actually existing culture of self-improvement, while its prevalence fairly shouts the need for progressive social movements, does not yet offer much possibility for progressive social change. What would be required to tap into the unrest in self-improvement culture would be a politics committed to economic justice (redistribution) as well as to mutual recognition.[43] Such a politics would be forged in public dialogue, where both imagination and dialogue would formulate new ways of thinking, acting, and behaving.[44]

What Activists Might Learn from Self-Help Culture

Finally, a radical or progressive agenda committed to relief for belabored Americans would ask why the growth of self-improvement groups and culture have far outpaced the growth of either progressive or radical political movements throughout the last part of the twentieth century. Why have people embraced self-help groups—what do they get there that they don't get in political organizations? Anyone who has ever worked in an alternative political context can answer this question. There are long hours and low pay—pay that is often lower than one would find in the most menial of jobs. Often there is no pay at all. Individuals without access to independent financial resources are asked to choose between economic security for themselves and their families and their commitment to the group's cause. Frequently one finds precisely the hierarchical and authoritarian power structures one rejects in the dominant culture, complete with a recapitulation of privileges dispensed along race, gender, class, and heterosexist categories glossed over in a rhetoric of equality. Often there is a sense that any concern with individual personal well-being is simply self-indulgence. Any skilled political organizer knows that when people are asked to choose between their own well-being and a political cause, they will necessarily choose themselves.[45] When political organizations fail to meet personal needs—economic, social, and emotional—individuals will drop out. Self-help groups, on the contrary, suggest that they will do nothing but meet the individual's needs for safety and well-being, for community and connection, and for hope about the future.

There is reason to be optimistic that political organizers have already begun to learn these lessons. Analysts of recent social movements observe that traditional, or older, social movements were focused primarily on the economic interests of particular groups of working people. In contrast, what are called "new social movements" have focused primarily on issues of identity. But newer, more effective social movements will necessarily focus on both. Operating in a realm where public and private domains are no longer even remotely distinct, individuals in these movements require that their political organizations not simply function as a means to an end but rather operate as a manifestation of the principles they espouse—as a model form of collective action.[46] Absent a public/private divide, living differently and changing society are seen as complementary. Working for an abstract and distant goal or principle at the expense of the present is no longer a viable option. Some social movement theorists, for example Barbara Epstein and Verta A. Taylor, observe that feminist modes of organizing, despite their middle-class and white origins (and possible obliviousness to issues of economic and racial injustice), offered a model for taking the personal into the political arena.[47] Gloria Steinem's image of revolution from within, though perhaps overstated and somewhat mired in the language of recovery, offered a model where individual needs would be consistent with, rather than contradictory to, a progressive or radical social agenda. The personal-political politics of direct action groups such as the AIDS Coalition to Unleash Power (ACT UP) demonstrate the power of these personal-political formations when both a politics of recognition and redistribution are in play. Committed not only to fostering a powerful image of people with HIV-infection but also to the equitable distribution of resources (medical research funds, pharmaceutical products), ACT UP served (and continues to serve) as a model for direct-action anti-globalization efforts, as well as a host of other issues.[48] Similarly, the geographically and hierarchically dispersed political organizing that marked the breakout campaign mounted by Howard Dean for the 2004 Democratic presidential nomination or the flourishing recent online political action groups such as Moveon.org suggests that the decentralizing effects of the internet may help foster a new politics across what was once a public/private divide.[49] The most successful newer political movements will increasingly capitalize on the erosion of the partition between public and private needs, ensuring that their organizations serve the needs of their constituents in the present as well as in the long term.[50]

An effective mobilization of the millions of Americans who find they must constantly upgrade themselves simply to hold their ground in an increasingly competitive economy would have as its agenda a politics of recognition wedded to a politics of economic justice. The American myth of equal opportunity for self-development would need to be rendered plausible with a politics of economic justice. Accomplishing this will be no mean feat, and will call on multiple resources and dimensions, including: (1) sustaining a model of the self that is relational and multiple; (2) cultivating the capacity to move from aggrievement to a collective identity and power; (3) fostering of new spaces for public dialogue and mutual recognition; (4) promoting imagination—not only political imagination but social and sociological imagination as well; and (5) assessing and embracing what the cultures of political organizing can learn from the cultures of self-improvement. Tapping into the discontent that the literatures of self-improvement evidence may be the work of the radical and progressive movements of the coming decades.

The questions asked at the outset—whether one could observe changes in the American ethos around self and work roughly corresponding to the emergence of new postindustrial or knowledge-based economic structures—seem at least provisionally answered. Faced with a new economic climate of increased competition between individuals for fewer and less stable employment opportunities, a literature of self-improvement has emerged that counsels self-fulfillment and self-improvement as an antidote to economic uncertainty. On the whole, this literature recycles images from prior self-improvement and inspirational literatures. However, the large-scale entry of women into the paid labor force encouraged a new emphasis on the metaphor of life as a work of art, while changing work conditions suggest that the artist may be the emerging model for the postindustrial, contingent labor force. Although these emerging tropes—the metaphor of life as work of art, and the model of artists as ideal workers—suggest a Romantic, antimodernist refusal of the domination of market forces, paradoxically they contribute to the expansion of a culture of work without end. Cast in the upbeat literature of self-improvement as "creators of their own work of art" or as the "chief executive officers" of their own enterprises, the reality for most readers of self-improvement literature is less one of creative adventure and entrepreneurial enthusiasm than of constant vigilance against individual obsolescence and expendability. One might hope that inside every person imagining himself or herself the creator of his or her own life-artworks—inside every CEO of Me, Inc.—is a belabored self finally weary and fed up enough to throw off the fantasy of self-sufficiency and to demand instead, sufficiency for each and all. In such a world, we might find that, in the place of endless struggles for private self-improvement couched in a language of entrepreneurial uplift, a nearly forgotten imperative emerges: the demand for a world in which the free development of each is understood as the condition for the free development of all.

Some Notes on Method

As with so many books that have spent part of their development ful-filling the requirements of dissertations, this book had a rather more detailed outline concerning method in an earlier iteration. While space pro-hibits the inclusion of detailed records of sampling methods and bestseller lists, I want to briefly explain the considerations that went into selecting the titles discussed in this study.

Given the vast quantity of self-improvement literature that has been published, as well as the shifting meanings of the term "self-help" during the period of this study, defining the boundaries for this study constituted both a theoretical and a practical question. Sociologists who have studied self-help literature and its readers, such as Wendy Simonds, Stuart Lichter man and Steven Starker, have reported that subjects in their studies named the Bible as their most important self-help book, raising the important question of whether "self-help" ought to be a category defined by the reader's use of a text or the particular characteristics of the text itself.[1] If one defines self-help literature as a mode of reading, rather than as a genre, then nearly any publication—fiction, poetry, autobiography, philosophy, history, or social science—could fall within the category. For example, a young woman coming to terms with her sexual identity might read Rita Mae Brown's

Rubyfruit Jungle. Or someone coming to terms with the suicide of a loved one might happen upon the sociologist Emile Durkheim's treatise on the topic and search therein for answers. And, of course, people of many cultures have turned to their religious texts for inspiration, guidance, and consolation.[2] The advantage of defining a text in terms of its use, rather than its characteristics, is that a text is understood within a social and historical context—reading is understood as a situated activity—and meanings are not fixed or reified. The disadvantages, in terms of research methodology, are twofold: not only can categories become vast and untenable but the reader's imaginative use of a text isn't subject to direct observation. It relies instead on the empathic imagination of the researcher or the reader's own subjective reporting.

The classification of particular books in terms of their social uses, rather than in terms of their genre and overt content, also results in categorical distinctions that reflect gendered divisions in the public and private spheres. Consider the following seeming anomaly: *The Authoritative Guide to Self-Help Books*—a survey of more than a thousand self-help titles designed to assist librarians, mental health professionals, and self-help readers evaluate the quality of popular titles—included Arlie Russell Hochschild's *The Second Shift*, Carol Tavris's *The Mismeasure of Woman*, and Susan Faludi's *Backlash* as self-help titles.[3] Works that might be classified elsewhere as sociology or, in the case of Faludi's book, investigative journalism, were reframed as advice to women. Strikingly, no other works of sociology or journalism are included in this list of self-help titles. Sociologists looking at self-help literature, among them both Starker and Simonds, have included Betty Friedan's book *The Feminine Mystique* in their examples of self-help books, despite the fact that it was not written using the "how-to" conventions of the genre and included the kind of extensive historical and sociological analysis that is rarely found in self-help books.[4] In *Women and Self-Help Culture*, Simonds even selects Friedan's bestseller as the chronological starting point for her research on self-help books. She argues that Friedan's book was the first in the recent wave of self-help books, in part because the book was marketed as a self-help book.[5] These categorical choices seem to suggest that feminist political issues are quite readily reduced to the realm of personal, private problems to be answered with advice, rather than understood as political issues worthy of (wo)manifestos and collective action. Thus setting definitive boundaries for self-help literature becomes not only a methodological concern but a political question as well. In a more idiosyncratic example, on a recent visit to New York's Strand Bookstore, I discovered a copy of Stanley Aronowitz's *False Promises* in the section labeled "Career: Self-Help." While arguably Aronowitz's discussion of the shortcomings of American trade unions offers some of the most effective advice available, such a title would hardly appear to be a self-improvement book to any but the most mischievous or subversive shop clerk or customer. Indeed, among academics whose books find their way to the *New York Times* bestseller list, it has become customary to deny that the book in question is a self-help book. For examples, see Juliet B. Schor's disclaimer in the paperback edition of *The Overworked American* or Deborah Cameron's discussion of Deborah Tannen's denial of the self-help role of her books.[6]

To develop a list of self-help books from which to choose, I reviewed the *New York Times* bestseller lists during the period of 1973 and 1997 and identified books that were designed to help readers improve themselves and their prospects in the world through particular, practical prescriptions. Books that were specifically about fitness, dieting, weight loss, and beauty regimes were excluded, as were books about enhancing one's sexual prowess or improving one's intimate relationships. Although our cultural emphasis on personal appearance is pronounced, I was confident that there would be ample evidence of this phenomenon in the general literatures of self-improvement, as turned out to be the case. Advice on intimate relationships was excluded from the sample, as it had been well addressed by others.[7] However, a discussion of the concept of codependency, a phenomenon too important to overlook, was needed, and was developed primarily from the considerable scholarly literature on this topic. Similarly, a discussion of spiritual or inspirational self-help, which has been thoroughly covered by Simonds and Starker, was not included, with the exception of a consideration of the longest running bestseller on the *New York Times* bestseller list, M. Scott Peck's *The Road Less Traveled*, which provides a counterpoint to the literatures of worldly success.

Although others who have reviewed the literature of self-improvement have narrowed their focus by limiting titles to those that have made the bestseller lists,[8] I chose to include several titles in my review that, while not *Times* bestsellers, have remained in print continuously since their date of publication and sold more than one million copies. My hunch was that the consideration of titles that have had a long shelf-life, but have perhaps received limited promotional efforts, may help reflect something more than the impact of successful marketing efforts. Of particular interest are titles that started out self-published and gradually found an extensive audience. For example, Julia Cameron's *The Artist's Way* was originally self-published and has now sold in excess of 1.5 million copies. Similarly, Marsha Sinetar's book *Do What You Love, The Money Will Follow*, while not originally self-published, became an unexpected bestseller at the religious publishing house that first issued the book. In the case of the career advice books considered, stepping away from the requirement that a book hit the bestseller list has generated a more interesting and representative sample. Finally, after the initial version of this study was completed in 2002, I returned to the bestseller lists to assess whether the bestselling self-help literature from 1997 to the present differed in any significant ways from the prior sample. Not surprisingly, the turn-of-the-century literatures of self-improvement were quite similar to those of prior years, with the important exception of an increasingly financial approach to daily life[9] and the emergence of the phenomenon of life coaching (these are considered in chapter 3.) A number of titles from this period (1998–2003) were included to bring the sample up to date for this publication.

Prologue: Covey's Daughter and Her Dilemma

1. *First Things First*, written with A. Roger Merrill and Rebecca R. Merrill, is actually the eighth book in Covey's oeuvre, including his doctoral dissertation, completed at Brigham Young University in 1976, on the topic of American success literature since 1776. See Timothy K. Smith, "What's So Effective About Stephen Covey?" *Fortune*, December 12, 1994, 122. In addition to the bestselling *The Seven Habits of Highly Effective People* (New York: Simon and Schuster, 1989), Covey's publications include *How to Succeed with People* (Salt Lake City: Deseret Books, 1971); *Spiritual Roots of Human Relations* (Salt Lake City: Deseret Books, 1976); *The Divine Center* (Salt Lake City: Bookcraft, 1982), *Principle-Centered Leadership* (New York: Summit, 1990), and, with Truman G. Madsen, *Marriage and Family: Gospel Insights* (Salt Lake City: Deseret Books, 1983).

2. Stephen R. Covey, A. Roger Merrill, and Rebecca R. Merrill, *First Things First* (New York: Simon and Schuster, 1994), 15.

3. While it is customary to think of gender as a variety of features and characteristics related to sex and sexuality, it will be helpful for the purposes of my argument to think of gender in terms of its relationship to labor: gender roles operate as a caste system in which particular types and forms of labor are devalued and under- or uncompensated. Typically these

forms of labor are performed by women, and, because of the power of this caste system, any work or labor performed by women may be similarly discounted. The power of these gendered roles emerges because they are inscribed everywhere and in every way—they are so potent because they appear to be natural arrangements.

4. Eccles, Chapter 3, verse 1. All biblical references are to the King James version.

5. That Covey's moral counsel has not only biblical but Mormon roots has not gone unnoticed in the popular and business press. See, for example, Elizabeth A. Schick, ed., *1998 Current Biography Yearbook* (New York: Wilson, 1998), 129; Leslie Kaufman-Rosen, "Getting in Touch with Your Inner President," *Newsweek*, January 16, 1995; Mark Lasswell, "Habit Former," *People*, June 12, 1995; Timothy Smith, "What's So Effective About Stephen Covey?"; and Alan Wolfe, "White Magic in America," *New Republic*, February 23, 1998, 26–34.

6. Elizabeth L. Eisenstein, *The Printing Press as an Agent of Change*, vol. 1 (Cambridge: Cambridge University Press, 1979), 87–88; Norbert Elias, *The Civilizing Process*, trans. Edmund Jephcott (New York: Urizen Press, 1978), 54.

7. Paul Lichterman, "Self-Help Reading as Thin Culture," *Media, Culture and Society* 14, no. 3 (1992): 435; Wendy Simonds, *Women and Self-Help Culture: Reading Between the Lines* (New Brunswick, N.J.: Rutgers University Press, 1992), 49; Steven Starker, *Oracle at the Supermarket: The American Preoccupation with Self-Help Books* (New Brunswick, N.J.: Transaction, 1989), 158.

8. Louis Schneider and Sanford M. Dornbusch, *Popular Religion: Inspirational Books in America* (Chicago: University of Chicago Press, 1958); Starker, *Oracle*.

9. Covey, Merrill and Merrill, *First Things First*, 16.

10. The social theorist Teresa Brennan writes: "capital seeks to avoid paying for the costs of reproduction. This is . . . why capital tends to substitute space for time." If workers demand compensation and services to meet their reproductive needs—healthcare, time off and subsidies for dependent care, adequate vacation time and retirement—capital readily relocates to sites where the supply of human capital has not yet grown so demanding as it has not yet been so depleted. Teresa Brennan, *Globalization and Its Terrors: Daily Life in the West* (London: Routledge, 2003), 125–26. See also David Harvey's extensive discussion of time-space compression in late modernity, in *The Condition of Postmodernity: An Enquiry into the Origins of Cultural Change* (Cambridge, Mass.: Blackwell, 1989), and Fredric Jameson's discussion of the what he calls "the spatialization of temporal-

ity," in *Postmodernism, or, the Cultural Logic of Late Capitalism* (Durham, N.C.: Duke University Press, 1991), 156.

11. The FranklinCovey Company acquired its name in 1997 when the Franklin Quest Company, founded by Hyrum Smith to produce and promote the Franklin Planner, a time management system inspired by Benjamin Franklin's day planner, merged with Stephen Covey's Covey Leadership Center.

12. Benjamin Franklin, "The Autobiography of Benjamin Franklin," in *The Autobiography and Other Works* (New York: Viking Penguin, 1986 [1791]), 98.

13. Franklin, *Autobiography*, 217.

14. Ibid., 88.

15. Roz Chast, "The Last Word: Mom's World," *Ladies' Home Journal*, May 1997, 192.

16. Actually, there is a second important difference. While Dr. Covey is publicly concerned with his daughter's well-being and self-fulfillment, Dr. Franklin quite famously provided a minimal, if practical, education for his daughter, Sarah "Sally" Franklin Bache, who, like her mother, Deborah Read Franklin worked primarily to maintain her father's Philadelphia household. Walter Isaacson, *Benjamin Franklin: An American Life* (New York: Simon and Schuster, 2003), 119, Mary Kelley, "Petitioning with the Left Hand: Educating Women in Benjamin Franklin's America," in *Benjamin Franklin and Women*, ed. Larry E. Tise (University Park: Pennsylvania State University Press, 2000), Claude-Anne Lopez and Eugenia W. Herbert, *The Private Franklin: The Man and His Family* (New York: Norton, 1975), 70–71.

Introduction

Epigraph from George Carlin, "People Who Oughta Be Killed: Self-Help Books," *Complaints and Grievances* (Atlantic, 2001), audio compact disc.

1. Tammy Tierney Allison, "'Self-Help' Satisfies Need for Quick Fix," *Business First-Buffalo*, September 14, 1998, v. 14, no. 49, B-2. Available online at: http://buffalo.bcentral.com/buffalo/stories/1998/09/14/editorial2.html. Last viewed: January 5, 2005.

2. Marjorie Coeyman, "Everybody Can Use a Little Help," *Christian Science Monitor*, August 8, 2000, 13; James B. Stewart, "Bestseller: The Agent from Texas That New York Can't Ignore," *New Yorker*, September 8, 1997, 45.

3. Daniel McGinn, "Self Help U.S.A.," *Newsweek*, January 10, 2000, 42.

4. Leonard Wood, "The Gallup Survey: Self-Help Buying Trends," *Publishers Weekly* 234, no. 16 (1988), 33.

5. Measurements of the shelf space devoted to self-improvement titles were taken at the Barnes and Noble bookstore at Union Square in New York City in February 1997 and included the following subject categories: addiction and recovery; diets and fitness; career planning; parenting; personal motivation; self-improvement; psychology; and human sexuality and relationships.

6. In "Self-Help Books and the Quest for Self-Control in the United States 1950–2000," (Ph.D. diss., Oxford University, 2004) Christine Whelan observed that between 1972 and 2000, the number of self-help books listed in R. R. Bowker's *Books in Print* increased from 1.1 percent to 2.4 percent of the total number of books in print. Her data in this respect support my assertion that self-help publishing has boomed during the same period when economic circumstances for the average American worker have declined. Whelan's categories included a wide array of self-improvement books, from diet and fitness guides to popular psychology books to children's etiquette books. Specifically, the categories she included in her sample included: conduct of life; Christian life; psychology, applied; success; self-culture; youth; women—conduct of life; men—conduct of life; youth—conduct of life; self-help techniques; self-actualization; self-realization; change (psychology); behavior modification; affirmations; self-talk; meditation; stress management; Twelve-Step programs; character; spiritual life; business ethics; etiquette; interpersonal relations; self-control, self-respect; young men; young women; adult children; Alcoholics Anonymous; child rearing; codependence; compulsive behavior; courtship; dating; depression; diet; etiquette—kids; fathers; happiness; hygiene—sexual; intimacy; mind and body; mothers; parent and child; personality; reducing; relationship; addiction; self-acceptance; self-confidence; self-esteem; self-reliance; self-perception; sex instruction; sex instruction—kids; youth—religious; young men—religion; young women—religion. Personal correspondence, May 9, 2003.

7. See, for example, Gershen Kaufman, Lev Raphael, and Pamela Espeland, *Stick Up for Yourself: Every Kid's Guide to Personal Power and Positive Self-Esteem* (Minneapolis, Minn.: Free Spirit, 1999) aimed at preteens, or the newly burgeoning category of self-help books for teenagers, including Sean Covey, *The Seven Habits of Highly Effective Teens* (New York: Simon and Schuster, 1998); Richard Carlson, *Don't Sweat the Small Stuff for Teens* (New York: Hyperion, 2000); and Jay McGraw, *Life Strategies for Teens* (New York: Fireside, 2000).

8. Jerald Wallulis, *The New Insecurity: The End of the Standard Job and Family* (Albany: State University of New York Press, 1998).

9. Ibid., xv.

10. Americans now outpace even the famously industrious Japanese by two work weeks each year. Lonnie Golden and Deborah M. Figart, eds., *Working Time: International Trends, Theory, and Policy Perspectives* (London: Routledge, 2000), 5. Juliet Schor was among the first to demonstrate that Americans are working longer shifts and more hours overall with a book that struck a chord and spent numerous weeks on the *New York Times* bestseller list: Juliet B. Schor, *The Overworked American: The Unexpected Decline of Leisure* (New York: Basic Books, 1991). While some sociologists have challenged her work, arguing that that television viewing and perceived time deficits, rather than work time, account for the idea that work time has increased—notably John P. Robinson and Geoffrey Godbey, *Time for Life: The Surprising Ways Americans Use Their Time* (University Park: University of Pennsylvania Press, 1997)—Schor demonstrates that their research methods conflate involuntary time off (unemployment and underemployment) with actual leisure time. Juliet B. Schor, "Working Hours and Time Pressure: The Controversy About Trends in Time Use," in *Working Time: International Trends, Theory, and Political Perspectives*, 73–86. While work time has clearly increased, the perception of increased working time may also be linked to the blurring of the distinction between work and leisure time. See Charles Sabel, "Mobius-Strip Organizations and Open Labor Markets: Some Consequences of the Reintegration of Conception and Execution in a Volatile Economy," in *Social Theory for a Changing Society*, ed. Pierre Bourdieu and James S. Coleman (Boulder, Colo.: Westview, 1991), 43.

11. For discussions of the ideal of the self-made man, see John G. Cawelti, *Apostles of the Self-Made Man* (Chicago: University of Chicago Press, 1988 [1965]); Judy Hilkey, *Character Is Capital: Success Manuals and Manhood in Gilded Age America* (Chapel Hill: University of North Carolina Press, 1997); Donald B. Meyer, *The Positive Thinkers* (Middlebury, Conn.: Wesleyan University Press, 1988 [1965]); Richard Weiss, *The American Myth of Success* (Urbana: University of Illinois Press, 1988 [1969]), Irvin G Wyllie, *The Self-Made Man in America: The Myth of Rags to Riches* (New York: Free Press, 1966 [1954]).

12. See Robert K. Merton, *Social Theory and Social Structure* (New York: Free Press, 1968), 122, for a pointed version of this observation.

13. Hilkey, *Character Is Capital*, 5, 159; Meyer, *Positive Thinkers*; Wyllie, *Self-Made Man in America*, 29–30; and Mary P. Ryan, *Cradle of the Middle Class: The Family in Oneida County, New York, 1790–1865* (Cambridge: Cambridge University Press, 1981), 145–185.

14. Hilkey, *Character Is Capital,* 142–65.

15. See, for example, Daniel Bell, *The Cultural Contradictions of Capitalism* (New York: Basic Books, 1976); Harry Braverman, *Labor and Monopoly Capital: The Degradation of Work in the Twentieth Century* (New York: Monthly Review Press, 1974); Peter F. Drucker, *Post-Capitalist Society* (New York: HarperCollins, 1993; reprint, New York: Harper Business, 1994); David Harvey, *The Condition of Postmodernity: An Enquiry into the Origins of Cultural Change* (Cambridge, Mass.: Blackwell, 1989); and Ernest Mandel, *Late Capitalism,* trans. Joris De Bres (Atlantic Highlands, N.J.: Humanities Press, 1975).

16. Stanley Aronowitz and William DiFazio, *The Jobless Future: Sci-Tech and the Dogma of Work* (Minneapolis: University of Minnesota Press, 1994); Jeremy Rifkin, *The End of Work: The Decline of the Global Labor Force and the Dawn of the Post-Market Era* (New York: Putnam, 1995).

17. The self American has been described variously as: mutable, in Louis A. Zurcher, Jr., *The Mutable Self: A Self-Concept for Social Change,* vol. 59, Sage Library of Social Research (Beverly Hills, Calif.: Sage, 1977); protean, in Robert J. Lifton, *The Protean Self* (Chicago: University of Chicago Press, 1993); autotelic and evolving, in Mihaly Csikszentmihalyi, *The Evolving Self: A Psychology for the Third Millennium* (New York: HarperCollins, 1993), and *Flow: The Psychology of Optimal Experience: Steps Toward Enhancing the Quality of Life* (New York: HarperPerennial, 1990); multiple, in Jon Elster, ed., *The Multiple Self: Studies in Rationality and Social Change* (Cambridge: Cambridge University Press, 1985); marginal, in René J. Muller, *The Marginal Self: An Existential Inquiry into Narcissism* (Atlantic Highlands, N.J.: Humanities Press International, 1987); postmodern, in Michael R. Wood and Louis A. Zurcher, Jr., *The Development of a Postmodern Self,* vol. 70, Contributions in Sociology (New York: Greenwood Press, 1988), and elsewhere; narcissistic and minimal, in Christopher Lasch, *The Culture of Narcissism: American Life in an Age of Diminishing Expectations* (New York: Warner Books, 1979), and *The Minimal Self: Psychic Survival in Troubled Times* (New York: Norton, 1984); hungry, in Kim Chernin, *The Hungry Self: Women, Eating and Identity* (New York: Perennial Library, 1985); empty, in Philip Cushman, *Constructing the Self, Constructing America: A Cultural History of Psychotherapy* (Reading, Mass.: Addison-Wesley, 1995), and "Why the Self Is Empty: Toward a Historically Situated Psychology," *American Psychologist* 45, no. 5 (1990): 599–611; saturated, in Kenneth J. Gergen, *The Saturated Self: Dilemmas of Identity in Contemporary Life* (New York: Basic Books, 1991); seeking, in Richard E. Lind, *The Seeking Self: The Quest for Self Improvement and the Creation of Personal Suffering* (Grand Rapids, Mich.:

Phanes Press, 2000); invented and enterprising, in Nikolas Rose, *Governing the Soul: The Shaping of the Private Self*, 2nd ed. (London: Free Association Books, 1989), and *Inventing Our Selves: Psychology, Power, and Personhood* (Cambridge: Cambridge University Press, 1998 [1996]); well-tempered, in Toby Miller, *The Well-Tempered Self: Citizenship, Culture, and the Postmodern Subject* (Baltimore: Johns Hopkins University Press, 1993); playing, in Alberto Melucci, *The Playing Self: Person and Meaning in the Planetary Society* (Cambridge: Cambridge University Press, 1996); and "decentered." This last self-description, in which the experience of a unified self is imagined as fiction, as a function of language, is widely embraced in contemporary critical theory but nowhere evident in the vast literature of self-improvement. See Jacques Lacan, *Écrits: A Selection*, trans. Alan Sheridan (New York: Norton, 1977 [1966]); Carolyn J. Dean, *The Self and Its Pleasures: Bataille, Lacan, and the History of the Decentered Subject* (Ithaca, N.Y.: Cornell University Press, 1992); and, in particular, Jacques Derrida, "Structure, Sign and Play in the Discourse of the Human Sciences," in *Writing and Difference* (Chicago: University of Chicago Press, 1978 [1967]), 278–93.

18. Lasch's argument was that diminishing material expectations in the context of a culture that was increasingly secularized resulted in a "narcissistic" self preoccupied with individual happiness. By framing the problem in terms of the problem of the rise of psychological culture, Lasch finds himself nostalgic for a moral order that hailed from theistic traditions. Instead of an analysis of the material conditions that required an inward turn, Lasch finds himself the author of a jeremiad that rails against the selfishness of "narcissistic" individuals, rather than recognizing that what he sees as narcissism is increasingly required for survival. To address the problems created by the idea of the narcissistic personality, Lasch came up with the idea of a minimal self that is preoccupied with survival. Lasch, *Culture of Narcissism;* Lasch, *Minimal Self.*

19. A good example of this buttressing comes in the figures of prominent "self-made" women. While figures such as Oprah Winfrey, Madonna Ciccone, and Martha Stewart suggest to women that the ideal of the self-made man was actually gender neutral—available to them as well as to men—these exceptions operated according to existing categories of appropriate feminine roles. Each of these figures "succeeds" by taking the central elements of intimate life—emotional support, sexuality, and homemaking activities, respectively—that had traditionally been the uncompensated area of domestic life and rendering them larger than life and highly profitable. While these figures capitalize on women's roles—best girlfriend, femme fatale turned mother, and homemaker par

excellence—in their own private lives the actual labors of daily life are likely to be delegated to others. But for the preponderance of women, the activities of care, sexuality, and homemaking remained in the realm of intimate, unwaged life, where the ideal of an autonomous, self-making woman was largely incompatible with the actual laborious work of caring for others. Stephen Covey's daughter Maria was conflicted not because she was female but as a consequence of the expectation that she, as a woman and as a mother, would be available to engage both in the laborious care of newborns and in the care and creation of an autonomous, rational, well-organized self. In short, the myth of the self-made man was transferable to women only as long as the women engaged in and valorized traditional "feminine" activities while outsourcing them in their private lives. Thus female executives may find themselves vilified when they require strong performances from their employees, while their male counterparts are rewarded for similar behavior. The myth of the autonomous self-made man that served to motivate and cajole male workers has been deployed to motivate women, but with mixed, partial, and contradictory effects.

20. Describing the impact of early advertising strategies on American consciousness, the cultural historian Stuart Ewen observed that advertising evoked social anxiety, only to offer solutions in the forms of commodities. In place of the "social self," Ewen noted, advertising sold "the next best thing—a commodity self—to people who were unhappy or could be convinced that they were unhappy about their lives. Each portion of the body was to be viewed critically, as a potential *bauble* in a successful assemblage." *Captains of Consciousness: Advertising and the Social Roots of the Consumer Culture* (New York: McGraw-Hill, 1976), 47.

21. Philip Seldon, *The Complete Idiot's Guide to Wine* (Indianapolis: Alpha Group, 1997); Eric Tyson, *Personal Finance for Dummies* (San Mateo, Calif.: IDG Books Worldwide, 1994).

22. Alan Gartner and Frank Riessman, eds., *The Self-Help Revolution*, Community Psychology Series, vol. 10 (New York: Human Sciences Press, 1984); Alfred H. Katz and Eugene I. Bender, *The Strength in Us: Self-Help Groups in the Modern World* (New York: Franklin Watts, 1976).

23. Leslie Berger, "*Our Bodies* Is Recast for Latina Culture," *New York Times*, February 13, 2000, F-8.

24. Another sign of this shift can be detected in the subject headings in *The Reader's Guide to Periodical Literature*, a source of evidence whose topic headings and subtopics offer a way of tracking the changes in the popular consciousness. In 1974, the subject heading for "Self-Help Programs" was crosslisted only with the heading "Economic Assistance, Domestic" (34,

83). "Self-Help Action" referred to an article on a food marketing club and was crosslisted with "Cooperative Associations." By 1978 (and on and off through 1987) the subject heading "Self-Help Groups" is crosslisted with a variety of specific self-improvement and human potential organizations, including "Erhard Seminar Training (EST)," "Esalen," and the motivational "coach" Anthony Robbins's company, the "Robbins Research Group." The shift in the meaning of the term "self-help" seems to emerge from the social context, rather than to lead it. By 1985 the topic heading "Self-Help Literature" appears in the *Reader's Guide,* and by 1987 the term "self-improvement" emerges triumphant as its own subject heading, displacing the arguably less achievement-oriented topic "self-culture." Around the same time, specifically in 1988, the category "self-help groups" becomes refocused on the family, with numerous listings for family support groups over the following decade, until 1997, when Erhard Seminar Training (EST) returns, reinvented as the Landmark Forum.

25. Philip Rieff, *The Triumph of the Therapeutic: Uses of Faith After Freud* (New York: Harper and Row, 1966).

26. Rose, *Governing the Soul.* See also earlier arguments about the use of psychiatry and psychotherapy for social control: R. D. Laing, *The Divided Self: An Existential Study in Sanity and Madness* (Middlesex, England: Penguin Books, 1965); Thomas S. Szasz, *The Manufacture of Madness: A Comparative Study of the Inquisition and the Mental Health Movement* (New York: Harper and Row, 1977 [1970]); *The Myth of Mental Illness: Foundations of a Theory of Personal Conduct* (New York: Hoeber-Harper, 1961); and Michel Foucault, *Madness and Civilization: A History of Insanity in the Age of Reason*, trans. Richard Howard (New York: Vintage, 1973 [1965]).

27. Lichterman, "Self-Help Reading as Thin Culture"; Simonds, *Women and Self-Help Culture,* 49; Starker, *Oracle.*

28. Charles Taylor, *The Ethics of Authenticity* (Cambridge, Mass.: Harvard University Press, 1991); Charles Taylor, *Sources of the Self* (Cambridge, Mass.: Harvard University Press, 1989). In *Portrait of a Lady,* Henry James makes a similar point when his character Gilbert Osmond suggests that Isabel Archer think of her life as a work of art. *The Portrait of a Lady* (New York: Oxford University Press, 1999 [1880]), 362.

29. Arlie Russell Hochschild, "The Commercial Spirit of Intimate Life and the Abduction of Feminism: Signs from Women's Advice Books," *Theory, Culture and Society* 11, no. 2 (1994): 1–24. Republished in Arlie Russell Hochschild, *The Commercialization of Intimate Life: Notes from Home and Work* (Berkeley: University of California Press, 2003).

30. Richard Florida, *The Rise of the Creative Class* (New York: Basic Books, 2002); Arlie Russell Hochschild, *The Time Bind: When Work Becomes Home and Home Becomes Work* (New York: Metropolitan, 1997); and Andrew Ross, *No Collar: The Humane Workplace and Its Hidden Costs* (New York: Basic Books, 2003).

31. Connie Glaser and Barbara Steinberg Smalley, *Swim with the Dolphins: How Women Can Succeed in Corporate America on Their Own Terms* (New York: Warner Books, 1995).

32. Michael Lewis, "The Artist in the Grey Flannel Pajamas," *New York Times Magazine*, March 5, 2000; Andrew Ross, "The Mental Labor Problem," *Social Text*, no. 63 (2000): 1–33.

33. Andy Warhol, *The Philosophy of Andy Warhol (from A to B and Back Again)* (New York: Harcourt Brace Jovanovich, 1975), 92.

34. David Brooks, *Bobos in Paradise: The New Upper Class and How They Got There* (New York: Simon and Schuster, 2000).

35. Florida, *Rise of the Creative Class*; Lewis, "Artist in the Grey Flannel Pajamas"; Ross, "Mental Labor Problem."

36. Henri Lefebvre, *Everyday Life in the Modern World*, trans. Sacha Rabinovitch (New York: Harper and Row, 1971), 204; Herbert Marcuse, *An Essay on Liberation* (Boston: Beacon Press, 1969).

37. Wendy Kaminer, *I'm Dysfunctional, You're Dysfunctional* (Reading, Mass.: Addison-Wesley, 1992); Lasch, *Culture of Narcissism*; Rose, *Governing the Soul*; Rose, *Inventing Our Selves*. While these authors differ in the substance of their critiques, they all observe the impact of a culture of self-improvement in stifling social change. For Lasch and many other critics of "psychological man," the concern was with the loss of moral grounding, as well as the loss of the sense of communal expectations that was fostered in the intimate sphere of the family and reinforced by religious and civic institutions. The rise of "psychological man" heralded a new concern with what came to be known as "the vanishing public sphere." The public spaces where middle-class and bourgeois men had been able to participate as supposedly rational citizens in civic affairs—their private emotional and intimate lives essentially curtained off and sustained by the unacknowledged contributions of women—were threatened not only by an emphasis on intimate psychological life but also by the blurring of the boundaries between intimate and public life—by an idea that emerged from feminist political discourse: that personal life was itself political.

Thus, while on the face of things it appears that Lasch was concerned that individuals had turned inward and away from their collective social responsibilities, a good case can be made that it was not so much the inward turn of men that alarmed Lasch as the demands by women for recognition and equity. He lamented a late-twentieth-century America that, in his mind, moved from a moral culture that celebrated the characters of Horatio Alger to a hedonistic and pecuniary culture that applauded the exploits of the Happy Hooker. "If Robinson Crusoe embodied the ideal type of economic man, the hero of bourgeois society in its ascendancy," Lasch wrote, "then the spirit of Moll Flanders presides over its dotage," *Culture of Narcissism*, 109. Though Lasch had concerns about *Homo economicus*, he was clearly disturbed at the emergence of economic woman. The application of market values to the intimate sphere of the family threatened what Lasch saw as a "haven in a heartless world"; the last holdout from the principles of market economics but also the site of the unwaged and usually unacknowledged labor of women. The traditional morality that Lasch was missing was premised on the idea of an intimate domain—maintained through the unwaged labor of women— that could be sequestered from the imperatives of the marketplace.

More recent critics of psychological man, such as British social theorist Nikolas Rose, argue that individuals are repressed and oppressed by what Rose calls "psy-culture." This position downplays the extent to which socialization, although constraining, is also enabling: that social norms and values enable individuals only to the extent that they are also constrained. Consider a most mundane example: learning to read and write is a laborious social process—a disciplinary process—that requires the individual to shape his or her body to the task. Yet the capacity to read and write provides new kinds of freedoms and possibilities for the individual. In Rose's formulation, which builds on the work of the French theorist Michel Foucault, these "disciplinary processes" have advanced into a form of "governmentality," where the interests of the state or government are seamlessly internalized by individuals, making it less necessary for the state to resort to totalitarian restraints. The collective constitution of individuals in sites such as the family and schools is characterized as largely a repressive function of the state rather than as a means of enhancing individuals' capacities and capabilities in all sorts of ways. In short, socialization—traditionally the work of women—is seen as the enemy.

38. Marshall Berman, *The Politics of Authenticity: Radical Individualism and the Emergence of Modern Society* (New York: Atheneum, 1970); Anthony Giddens, *The Transformation of Intimacy: Sexuality, Love and Eroticism in Modern Societies* (Stanford, Calif.: Stanford University Press, 1992); Arlie Russell Hochschild, *The Managed Heart: Commercialization of Human Feeling* (Berkeley: University of California Press, 1983); Fredric Jameson, *The Political Unconscious: Narratives as a Socially Symbolic Act* (Ithaca,

N.Y.: Cornell University Press, 1981); Miller, *Well-Tempered Self*, Gloria
Steinem, *Revolution from Within: A Book of Self-Esteem* (New York: Little,
Brown, 1992).

39. See, for example, Miller, *Well-Tempered Self*, 180.

40. Berman, *Politics of Authenticity*; Hochschild, "Commercial Spirit of
Intimate Life"; Alberto Melucci, *Nomads of the Present* (Philadelphia:
Temple University Press, 1989); Melucci, *Playing Self*; Taylor, *The Ethics of
Authenticity*; Verta A. Taylor, *Rock-a-by Baby: Feminism, Self-Help and
Postpartum Depression* (New York: Routledge, 1996). The historian
Marshall Berman and the communitarian philosopher Charles Taylor each
see the pursuit of individual authenticity as central to the development of
democratic polities. And while the social theorist and cultural critic Toby
Miller sees the cultivation of a "well-tempered" self as means of state
governance, he also sees culture—cultural citizenship—as an arena for
democratic participation. While these social observers differ in their
conceptions of the self and the social world, they share the conviction that
the impulse toward self-determination ought not be underestimated, even
in the face of capitalism's enormous capacity to incorporate its opposition.

41. The feminist scholars among them, notably Arlie Russell Hochschild,
Wendy Simonds, Elayne Rapping, and Verta A. Taylor, see self-improvement practices as a prepolitical form of protest that might be rechanneled
toward political ends. The activist Gloria Steinem contends that self-help
not only offers prepolitical protests but also can potentially foster a
"revolution from within": political change grounded in individual self-
discovery. Similarly, the social theorist Anthony Giddens sees a "democratisation of personal life" in the rise of Twelve-Step groups organized
around the themes of codependence and sexual "addiction." Giddens,
Transformation of Intimacy; Hochschild, "Commercial Spirit of Intimate
Life"; Elayne Rapping, *The Culture of Recovery: Making Sense of the Self-
Help Movement in Women's Lives* (Boston: Beacon, 1996); Simonds,
Women and Self-Help Culture; Taylor, *Rock-a-by Baby*. Hochschild
suggests that the ways in which self-help culture emphasizes emotional life
operates to contradict the fact that these aspects of life are typically
devalued in masculinist cultures that privilege reason over the expressive
dimensions of life; *Managed Heart*, 192–193.

42. The idea of "prepolitical protest" comes from the work of the historian
Eric Hobsbawm, who describes prepolitical protest among peasant
populations "who have not yet found, or only begun to find, a specific
language in which to express their aspirations about the world"; *Primitive
Rebels* (New York: Norton, 1959), 2. Hochschild adopts this term in her
study of flight attendants when she describes the loss of sexual interest

among female flight attendants as a revolt against the use of their sexuality as a selling point. *Managed Heart*, 183.

43. Maurizio Lazzarato, "Immaterial Labor," in *Radical Thought in Italy: A Potential Politics*, eds. Paolo Virno and Michael Hardt (Minneapolis: University of Minnesota Press, 1996).

Chapter 1

Epigraph from Max Weber, *The Protestant Ethic and the Spirit of Capitalism*, trans. Talcott Parsons (New York: Scribner's, 1958 [1904]), 182.

1. The social theorist Jacques Donzelot writes of a similar phenomenon in the French context; "Pleasure in Work," in *The Foucault Effect: Studies in Governmentality*, ed. Graham Burchell, Colin Gordon, and Peter Miller (Chicago: University of Chicago Press, 1991 [1980]), 251–280.

2. Weber, *Protestant Ethic*, 79.

3. Cotton Mather, "A Christian at His Calling," in *The American Gospel of Success*, ed. Moses Rischin (Chicago: Quadrangle Books, 1965 [1701]), 23–24 (emphasis in original).

4. In addition to the dubious distinction of presiding over the Salem witch trials, Mather also served as an inspiration to Benjamin Franklin, who notes the impact of the clergyman's 1710 *Bonifacius, or An Essay To Do Good*, had on his thinking. "Autobiography," 13.

5. Mather asserts:

   We are not under the Law as a *Covenant of Works*. Our own Exactness in doing of *Good Works*, is not now the *Condition* of our *Entring into Life. Wo unto us if it were!* But still, the *Covenant of Grace* holds us to it, as our *Duty*; and if we are in the *Covenant of Grace*, we shall make it our *Study*, to *Do* those *Good Works* which once were the Terms of our *Entring into Life*."
   Bonifacius: An Essay . . . To Do Good (Gainesville, Fl.: Scholar's Facsimiles and Reprints, 1967 [1710]), 36.

6. "Indeed," wrote Mather in the first chapter of his *Bonifacius*, "no *Good Works* can be done by any man until he be *Justified*. Until a Man be United into Glorious Christ, who is *our Life*, he is a *Dead Man*. And, I pray, what Good Works to be expected from Such a Man? They will be *Dead Works*." Ibid., 25.

7. Weiss, *American Myth*, 28–29; Wyllie, *Self-Made Man in America*, 55.

8. Hilkey, *Character Is Capital*, 3.

9. For a classic and still relevant discussion of Jonathan Edwards, see Perry Miller, *Jonathan Edwards* (New York: Sloane, 1949).

10. The image of Franklin as an "avant-garde of one" comes from Meyer, *Positive Thinkers*, 130.

11. Colin Campbell, *The Romantic Ethic and the Spirit of Modern Consumerism* (Cambridge, Mass.: Blackwell, 1987), 219.

12. Ibid., 101.

13. The doctrine of separate spheres, as it has come to be called, has come under thoughtful scrutiny from feminist scholars: Susan Gal, "A Semiotics of the Public/Private Distinction," *Differences* 13, no. 1 (2002): 77–95; Linda K. Kerber, "Separate Spheres, Female Worlds, Woman's Place: The Rhetoric of Women's History," *Journal of American History* 75, no. 1 (1988): 9–39; V. Spike Peterson, "Rereading Public and Private: The Dichotomy That Is Not One," *SAIS Review* 20, no. 2 (2000):11–29; Michelle Zimbalist Rosaldo, "The Use and Abuse of Anthropology: Reflections on Feminsim and Cross-Cultural Understanding," *Signs* 5 (Spring 1980): 389–417; Rosalind Rosenberg, *Beyond Separate Spheres* (New Haven, Conn.: Yale University Press, 1982); Joan W. Scott, "Comment: Conceptualizing Gender in American Business History," *Business History Review* 72, no. 2 (1998): 242–49. A central concern is that in using categories that were prescriptive ideological categories one risks reinscribing history with the oppressive dualism that constrained women in the past; ideology may be represented as historical fact. Drawing on Kerber, "Separate Spheres," Scott notes: "the separate spheres notion conflates ideological precept with analytical category," ("Comment," 243). Thus, one must remain cognizant that the idea of separate spheres reflects both an ideological category imposed upon women during a period of social upheaval and a category that allowed middle-class women, who enjoyed the luxury of not joining the ranks of factory workers, to also enjoy a sense of superiority, both moral and otherwise. See, for example, Nancy Fraser, "Rethinking the Public Sphere: A Contribution to the Critique of Actually Existing Democracy," in *Habermas and the Public Sphere*, ed. Craig Calhoun (Cambridge, Mass.: MIT Press, 1992), 109–42; and Mary P. Ryan, "Gender and Public Access: Women's Politics in Nineteenth Century America," in Calhoun, ed., *Habermas and the Public Sphere*, 259–88. Still, Scott observes, even if a doctrine of separate spheres is not quite appropriate, some kind of segregation between the sexes did exist. For the purposes of this analysis, the broad categories of the dual spheres—male/female, public/private, mind/body, rational/emotional—will be understood as ideological constructs that, while not representative of any "true reality," have also served to a great extent to shape our realities and experiences of social worlds.

14. Catherine Hall, "The Early Formation of Victorian Domestic Ideology," in *Fit Work for Women*, ed. Sandra Burman (London: Croom Helm, 1981),

15–32; Mary P. Ryan, *Cradle of the Middle Class: The Family in Oneida County, New York, 1790–1865* (Cambridge: Cambridge University Press, 1981). The feminist philosopher Teresa Brennan observes that when production moves out of the domestic space, out of the place where childrearing tasks have traditionally taken place, women tend to experience economic setbacks. *Exhausting Modernity: Grounds for a New Economy* (London: Routledge, 2000), 145.

15. Ryan, *Cradle of the Middle Class*, 65.

16. Robert N. Bellah, Richard Madsen, William M. Sullivan, Ann Swidler, and Stephen M. Tipton, *Habits of the Heart: Individualism and Commitment in American Life* (New York: Harper and Row, 1985).

17. For example, Campbell, *Romantic Ethic*.

18. Johan Huizinga, *Homo Ludens* (London: Routledge and Kegan Paul, 1949).

19. See, for example, Bellah, Madsen, Sullivan, Swidler, and Tipton, *Habits of the Heart*, Campbell, *The Romantic Ethic*, Taylor, *Sources of the Self*.

20. In addition to Campbell, *Romantic Ethic*, see, for example, T. J. Jackson Lears, *No Place of Grace: Antimodernism and the Transformation of American Culture 1880–1920* (New York: Pantheon, 1981).

21. See, for example, some requiems for the public sphere: Richard Sennett, *The Fall of Public Man: On the Social Psychology of Capitalism* (New York: Vintage, 1974); Lasch, *Culture of Narcissism*; and the ongoing discussions surrounding Jürgen Habermas, *The Structural Transformation of the Public Sphere*, trans. Thomas Burger and Frederick Lawrence (Cambridge, Mass.: MIT Press, 1992), for example, Calhoun, *Habermas and the Public Sphere*; Bruce Robbins, ed., *The Phantom Public Sphere*, vol. 5, *Cultural Politics* (Minneapolis: University of Minnesota Press, 1993). For a bracing feminist corrective to the long faces around the demise of the public sphere, see Nancy Fraser's (1989) "What's Critical About Critical Theory? The Case of Habermas and Gender," in Fraser, *Unruly Practices* (Minneapolis, Minn.: University of Minnesota Press), 93–119.

22. See, for example, Harvey, *Condition of Postmodernity*; Scott Lash and John Urry, *The End of Organized Capitalism* (Madison: University of Wisconsin Press, 1987); David Neumark, ed., *On the Job: Is Long-Term Employment a Thing of the Past?* (New York: Russell Sage Foundation, 2000); Paul Osterman, *Securing Prosperity, the American Labor Market: How It Has Changed and What to Do About It* (Princeton, N.J.: Princeton University Press, 1999).

23. Literacy was vital to Franklin's rise, and he makes numerous references in his autobiography to the importance of his library as a means of social mobility and affiliation. Franklin, *Autobiography*, 9, 18, 36.

24. Cawelti, *Apostles of the Self-Made Man*, 12.

25. Ibid., 101.

26. Ibid., 123; and Weiss, *American Myth*, 58.

27. Ralph Waldo Emerson, *Self Reliance* (Boston: Thomas Nelson, 1841; reprint, New York: Dover, 1993), 35.

28. Ibid., 32 (emphasis in original).

29. Ralph Waldo Emerson, *Success, Greatness, Immortality* (Boston: Houghton, Osgood and Company, 1880 [1870]), 14–15.

30. Ryan, *Cradle of the Middle Class*, 65.

31. Meyer, *Positive Thinkers*, 336–67.

32. Hilkey, *Character Is Capital*, 101.

33. Weiss, *American Myth*, 98.

34. Russell H. Conwell, *Acres of Diamonds* (New York: Harper, 1915), 18.

35. Weber, *Protestant Ethic*, 178–79.

36. Cawelti, *Apostles of the Self-Made Man*, 87; Emerson, *Success, Greatness, Immortality*, 13.

37. The historian Donald B. Meyer suggests that New Thought, positive thinking, and the popularity of various spiritualist practices emerged out of the confinement of middle-class women to the domestic sphere. *Positive Thinkers*, 46.

38. This undifferentiated oneness is associated with what psychoanalytic theorists call "primary narcissism"—the state in which the infant perceives no separation between herself and her mother. In this infantile state, which psychoanalysts describe as pre-Oedipal, bounds, limits, and moral strictures are unnecessary because all is one.

39. Ibid., 197.

40. C. Wright Mills, *White Collar* (London: Oxford University Press, 1951), 272.

41. William H. Whyte, Jr., *The Organization Man* (Garden City, N.Y.: Doubleday, 1957 [1956]).

42. Starker, *Oracle*, 62–66.

43. Betty Friedan, *The Feminine Mystique* (New York: Norton, 1974 [1963]).

44. Wyllie, *Self-Made Man in America*, 30.

45. See, for example, Stuart Ewen, *All Consuming Images: The Politics of Style in Contemporary Culture* (New York: Basic Books, 1988), 185–232; Hillel Schwartz, *Never Satisfied: A Cultural History of Diets, Fantasies and Fat* (New York: Anchor Books, 1986).

46. Hilkey, *Character Is Capital*, 163. See also Ryan, *Cradle of the Middle Class*, 145–85.

47. Ryan, *Cradle of the Middle Class*, 166, 168, 173, 184–85.

48. Wyllie, *Self-Made Man in America*, 29–30.

49. William James, *The Letters of William James* (Boston: Little, Brown, 1926),

260. Even Progressive critiques of the pecuniary nature of the Gilded Age success mythology relied on the conventional dichotomies of madonna and whore. One such example is an often-quoted letter from William James to H. G. Wells in which James denounced the "moral flabbiness born of the exclusive worship of the bitch-goddess SUCCESS. That—with squalid cash interpretation put on the word success—is our national disease." Muscular rigor is akin to moral rectitude, and the self-making man is seen as prey to a pecuniary siren, the bitch goddess, the inverse of the virtuous wife sequestered in the purity of the domestic realm. The repressed material role of women in the social mobility of their husbands and sons returns, cast in the role of the bitch goddess.

50. See, for example, Jeffrey Louis Decker, who considers the stories of Jane Addams, Harriet Hubbard Ayer, and others *Made in America: Self-Styled Success from Horatio Alger to Oprah Winfrey* (Minneapolis: University of Minnesota Press, 1997); while Dorothy Pennino explores "self-reliant women" in nineteenth-century success literature. "Engendering the Text: Self-Reliant Women in American Self-Help Literature (1848–1896)" (Ph.D. diss., George Washington University, 1991).

51. There is yet another reason for understanding this isolated, agentic self as "masculine." A number of feminist theorists, among them Teresa Brennan, *Exhausting Modernity,* 6, 21–40; Nancy Chodorow, *The Reproduction of Mothering: Psychoanalysis and the Sociology of Gender* (Berkeley: University of California Press, 1978); Dorothy Dinnerstein, *The Mermaid and the Minotaur: Sexual Arrangements and Human Malaise* (New York: Harper and Row, 1976); and Jessica Benjamin, *The Bonds of Love: Psychoanalysis, Feminism, and the Problem of Domination* (New York: Pantheon Books, 1988) expand on the work of the psychoanalyst Melanie Klein to argue that the desire to imagine the self as separate from others has its roots in the infant's ambivalent dependence on the mother. Brennan also draws on the work of the French psychoanalyst Jacques Lacan and calls the fantasy of a separate, agentic self the "foundational fantasy," since, she asserts, all other ideological constructs depend upon it.

52. Smith's caveat "for others in the society similarly excluded" opens the door for us to understand this accidental or contingent model of agency in terms of not only gender but race and class as well. Beyond the ideology of the self-made man—in the realities of working-class men and women's lives—contingency, rather than self-mastery, is perhaps the rule rather than exception. The gendered distinction we might make is that even when middle- and ruling-class women were not contingent to the general forces of the economy, their life courses were still contingent on the particular choices of their husbands. And for working-class women, their

lives were contingent on not only the overarching forces of the economy but also the choices made by their husbands. In general, the "realm of freedom" for women was considerably more bounded than that of their male counterparts: to a great extent, biology *was* destiny, Dorothy E. Smith, "A Sociology for Women," in *The Prism of Sex*, eds. Julia A. Sherman and Evelyn Torton Beck (Madison: University of Wisconsin Press, 1977), 151.

53. Helen Gurley Brown, *Sex and the Single Girl* (New York: Avon Books, 1962), 77 (emphasis in original).

54. An observation made elsewhere by Barbara Ehrenreich, Elizabeth Hess, and Gloria Jacobs, *Re-Making Love: The Feminization of Sex* (Garden City, N.Y.: Anchor Press, 1986) 56–57.

55. Friedan, *Feminine Mystique*, 344.

56. See also Simonds, *Women and Self-Help Culture*, 56; and Starker, *Oracle*, 109.

57. Barbara Sher, with Barbara Smith, *I Could Do Anything, If I Only Knew What It Was* (New York: Delacorte, 1994), 7–8.

58. Friedan, *Feminine Mystique*, 348.

59. As the social theorist Nikolas Rose observes:

> A new vocabulary of the employment relation has been articulated by organizational psychologists and management consultants, in which work has been reconstrued, not as a constraint upon freedom and autonomy, but as a realm in which working subjects can express their autonomy. Workers are no longer imagined merely to endure the degradations and deprivations of labor in order to gain a wage. Nor are workers construed as social creatures seeking satisfaction of needs for solidarity and security in the group relations of the workplace. Rather, the prevailing image of the worker is of an individual in search of meaning and fulfillment, and work itself is interpreted as a site within which individuals represent, construct, and confirm their identity, an intrinsic part of a style of life.

> *Inventing Our Selves*, 160.

60. Abraham H. Maslow, *The Farther Reaches of Human Nature* (New York: Viking Press, 1971), 45.

61. Abraham H. Maslow, *Eupsychian Management: A Journal* (Homewood, Ill.: Dorsey Press, 1965), 1.

62. Maslow, *Farther Reaches*, 43 (emphasis added).

63. Ibid., 7. Maslow's 1964 *Religions, Values and Peak Experiences* (New York: Viking) suggested that mystical experiences were signs of advanced human development rather than evidence of psychosis.

64. Mather, "Christian at His Calling," 23.

65. Indeed, when the sociologist Robert Bellah and his collaborators developed their typologies of "habits of the heart," they proposed four figures to characterize the American psyche and ethos: the independent citizen, the entrepreneur, the manager, and the therapist. While these figures cover many of the trends in American thought, I suspect that if Bellah and his team were working together today, they would have to consider adding at least a fourth character: the artist. Indeed, in light of recent activities in corporate America, they might add another: the con artist.

66. For example, Laurie Beth Jones, *The Path: Creating Your Mission Statement for Work and Life* (New York: Hyperion, 1996); and Beverly Potter, *Finding a Path with a Heart: How to Go from Burnout to Bliss* (Berkeley: Ronin, 1995) are only two of the numerous self-help life and career planning books available. A search of the Amazon.com "self-help" inventory uncovers 154 titles that include the word "path." M. Scott Peck's bestseller *The Road Less Traveled: Spiritual Growth in an Age of Anxiety* (New York: Simon and Schuster, 1978) and Julia Cameron's book *The Artist's Way: A Spiritual Path to Higher Creativity* (New York: Tarcher, 1992) will be considered in greater detail in chapters 2 and 4, respectively.

67. See, for example, the feminist theorist Teresa de Lauretis, who writes:
    the hero must be male regardless of the gender of the text-image, because the obstacle, whatever its personification, is morphologically female. . . . The implication here is not inconsequential. For if the work of the mythical structuration is to establish distinctions, the primary distinction on which all others depend is not, say, life and death, but rather sexual difference. In other words, the picture of the world produced in mythical thought since the very beginning of culture would rest, first and foremost, on what we call biology. Opposite pairs such as inside/ outside, the raw/the cooked, or life/death appear to be merely derivatives of the fundamental opposition between boundary and passage. . . . [A]ll these terms are predicated on the *single* figure of the hero who crosses the boundary and penetrates the other space. In so doing the hero, the mythical subject, is constructed as a human being and as male; he is the active principle of culture, the establisher of distinction, the creator of differences. Female is what is not susceptible to transformation, to life or death; she (it) is an element of plot-space, a topos, a resistance, matrix and matter. (emphasis in original)
    While one might quibble with de Lauretis over her assertion that the primary distinction from which all others follow is sexual difference (as this seems

developmentally secondary to the distinction between self and other), her central point, that the narrative structure assumes a male hero, remains apt. Individual agency, a masculine sense of agency, is central to the metaphor of the journey or the path. Teresa de Lauretis, *Alice Doesn't: Feminism, Semiotics, Cinema* (Bloomington: Indiana University Press, 1984), 118–19.

68. *The Compact Oxford English Dictionary* (Oxford: Oxford University Press, 1971), 1818.

69. Current data on the gender of self-help book readers are difficult to obtain, as they are closely guarded by the book industry. The most recent survey released publicly was the 1988 Gallup survey that demonstrated that self-help book–buying was not an overwhelmingly female activity, with a relatively insignificant 6 percent difference between the number of women and men reading self-help literature. Leonard Wood, "The Gallup Survey, 33. See also Simonds, *Women and Self-Help Culture*, 23. Despite these data, the misconception that these books are primarily purchased by women is widely repeated. In a 2001 review of Tom Tiede, *Self-Help Nation* (New York: Atlantic Monthly Press, 2001), Julia M. Klein writes that "most self-help books are geared toward—and purchased by—women, who are eager (sometimes overly so) to modify themselves as society demands." "A Noodler's Chicken Soup," *Nation* 272, no. 10 (2001): 31.

70. For the classic discussions of this split consciousness, see Simone de Beauvoir, *The Second Sex*, trans. H. M. Parshley (New York: Vintage Books, 1974 [1952]), xv–xxxiv; W.E.B. Du Bois, *The Souls of Black Folks* (New York: Bantam, 1989 [1903]), 1–9.

71. Mike Featherstone, "Postmodernism and the Aestheticization of Everyday Life," in *Modernity and Identity*, eds. Scott Lash and Jonathan Friedman (Oxford: Blackwell, 1992), 269.

72. The bourgeoisie return dressed up as bohemians—the "bobos" described by the journalist David Brooks, *Bobos*.

73. Mary Catherine Bateson, *Composing a Life* (New York: Penguin, 1990 [1989]), 9.

74. Discussions of the shift from a text-based to a visual culture abound. Several useful sources are Martin Jay, "Scopic Regimes of Modernity," in Scott Lash and Jonathan Friedman, *Modernity and Identity*; Scott Lash, "Discourse or Figure? Postmodernism as a 'Regime of Signification,'" *Theory, Culture and Society* 5 (1988): 311–36; and Ewen, *All Consuming Images*. For a few seminal works from diverse traditions, see Marshall McLuhan, *Understanding Media: The Extensions of Man* (Cambridge, Mass.: MIT Press, 1994 [1964]); and Jean François Lyotard, *Discours, Figure* (Paris: Klincksieck, 1971). Decker, *Made in America*, also applies the rise of a visual culture in his consideration of American self-making.

75. Weber, "Religious Rejections of the world and Their Directions." *From Max Weber*, eds. Hans H. Gerth and C. Wright Mills (New York: Oxford University Press, 1946 [1915]), 342.

76. See, for example, Taylor, *Sources of the Self,* (Cambridge, Mass.: Harvard University Press, 1989), part 2.

Chapter 2

Epigraph from John G. Cawelti, *Apostles of the Self-Made Man* (Chicago: University of Chicago Press, 1988 [1965]), 47.

1. *Economic Report of the President* (Washington, D.C.: U.S. Government Printing Office, 2003), 352.

2. See, for example, Michael B. Arthur and Denise M. Rousseau, eds., *The Boundaryless Career: A New Employment Principle for a New Organizational Era* (New York: Oxford University Press, 1996); Harvey, *Condition of Postmodernity*; Lash and Urry, *End of Organized Capitalism*; Neumark, *On the Job*; Osterman, *Securing Prosperity*.

3. Hochschild, *Time Bind*; and Arlie Russell Hochschild, with Anne Machung, *The Second Shift* (New York: Avon, 1990 [1989]).

4. In fact, one of the features of the general self-help literature is its almost complete lack of innovation, along with the tendency of authors to borrow liberally from others' work without attribution. Historians have made the same observation about earlier self-improvement literatures. See Hilkey, *Character Is Capital*, 48; Wyllie, *Self-Made Man in America*, 126–28. There are abundant contemporary examples of this seemingly sanctioned appropriation. For example, Stephen Covey parses the word *responsibility*: "Look at the word responsibility—'response-ability'—the ability to choose your response." *Seven Habits*, 71. Five years later, Deepak Chopra writes: "responsibility then means the *ability* to have a creative *response* to the situation as it is now." *The Seven Spiritual Laws of Success* (San Rafael, Calif.: New World Library, 1994), 59 (emphasis in original). On a grander scale, the self-help author Laurie Beth Jones wrote a 1996 book called *Jesus CEO: Using Ancient Wisdom for Visionary Leadership* (New York: Hyperion, 1996) that revisits the premise of Bruce Barton's 1924 bestseller *The Man Nobody Knows* (Indianapolis: Bobbs-Merrill, 1924), in which Jesus is portrayed as the world's greatest business executive. While one might applaud these authors for their "open source" approach—for preserving a tradition of the intellectual and cultural commons that is increasingly enclosed with the expansion of copyright laws—the overall lack of innovation in these literatures may also suggest a lack of ingenuity or resourcefulness.

5. Rose, *Inventing Our Selves*.

6. Bellah, Madsen, Sullivan, Swidler, and Tipton, *Habits of the Heart*; Diane

Rothbard Margolis, *The Fabric of Self: A Theory of Ethics and Emotions* (New Haven, Conn.: Yale University Press, 1998); Taylor, *Sources of the Self*; Steven M. Tipton, *Getting Saved from the Sixties: Moral Meaning in Conversion and Cultural Change* (Berkeley: University of California Press, 1982).

7. For a discussion of feminist critiques of the masculinist bourgeois versions of the self, see Diana Meyers, "Feminist Perspectives on the Self," in *The Stanford Encyclopedia of Philosophy*, ed. Edward N. Zalta (2000), Available online at: http://plato.stanford.edu/archives/sum2000/entries/feminism-self/. Last viewed: January 15, 2005.

8. See, for example, Lasch, *Minimal Self*.

9. Robert J. Ringer, *Winning Through Intimidation*, 2nd ed. (New York: Funk and Wagnalls, 1974), 3–4.

10. Michael Korda, *Power! How to Get It, How to Use It* (New York: Ballantine, 1975), 40.

11. Ringer, *Winning Through Intimidation*, 21.

12. Ibid., 34–35.

13. Wayne Dyer, *Pulling Your Own Strings* (New York: Crowell, 1978), 4.

14. Korda, *Power! How to Get It, How to Use It*, 37.

15. Ringer, *Winning Through Intimidation*, 26–27.

16. Robert J. Ringer, *Looking Out for Number One* (Beverly Hills, Calif.: Los Angeles Book Corp., distributed by Funk and Wagnalls, 1977), 109–110.

17. Ibid., 132, emphasis in original.

18. Smith's invocation of an "invisible hand" guiding self-interest in the free market appears in *The Wealth of Nations* (1776), 4.2.9, and in his earlier *Theory of Moral Sentiments* (1759), 4.1.10.

19. Ringer, *Looking Out for Number One*, 197.

20. Herb Cohen, *You Can Negotiate Anything* (New York: Bantam, 1980); Roger Fisher and William Ury, *Getting to Yes: Negotiating Agreement Without Giving In* (New York: Penguin, 1981).

21. Fisher and Ury, *Getting to Yes*, 13.

22. Covey, *Seven Habits*, 204–05.

23. It is perhaps not altogether fair to characterize spiritual books in the terms of the metaphor of the game—as consolation prizes. Such a rhetorical position privileges the metaphor of the game and material rewards as the criteria for evaluating success, when the preponderance of the literature of self-improvement suggests that spiritual and material values vie equally for readers' attention and allegiance. One of the problems of the metaphor of the journey, as well as the linear text, is that the sequence of encounters privileges one position over another. As it happens, this landscape of the

last three decades necessarily begins with the books that come first: those that privilege the material metaphor of the game.

24. John W. Donohue, "The Book Much Read," *America*, April 19, 1997, 26.

25. See, for example, Susan Bolotin, "God and Freud: What Makes a Bestseller?" *Vogue*, December 1985, 317; John Colapinto, "M. Scott Peck at the End of the Road," *Rolling Stone*, October 19, 1995, 80–82, 86, 164; William Grimes, "Mega-Seller, Great Gift," *New York Times*, November 8, 1992, sec. 9, 11; Charles Leerhsen, "Peck's Path to Inner Peace," *Newsweek*, November 18, 1985, 79; John Skow, "The Fairway Less Traveled," *Time*, September 19, 1994, 96.

26. Carolyn Anthony, "Story Behind the Bestseller: The Long, Winding and Happy Fate of *The Road Less Traveled*," *Publishers Weekly* 228, no. 13 (1985), 75.

27. Phyllis Theroux, "A Psychotherapist's Guide for Living." Review of *The Road Less Traveled*, by M. Scott Peck. *Washington Post*, September 29, 1978, A-1.

28. This hybridization of religious and spiritual doctrines is also observed in the development of Twelve-Step groups; John Steadman Rice, *A Disease of One's Own: Psychotherapy, Addiction, and the Emergence of Co-Dependency* (New Brunswick, N.J.: Transaction, 1996).

29. M. Scott Peck, *The Road Less Traveled* (New York: Simon and Schuster, 1978), 15.

30. Ibid., 273.

31. Ibid., 306–7.

32. Harold S. Kushner, *When All You've Ever Wanted Isn't Enough* (New York: Simon and Schuster, 1986).

33. Cawelti, *Apostles of the Self-Made Man*; Weiss, *American Myth*; Wyllie, *Self-Made Man in America*.

34. Starker, *Oracle*, 51–54.

35. Simonds, *Women and Self-Help Culture*, 49.

36. Lichterman, "Self-Help Reading as Thin Culture," 427.

37. Stewart, "Bestseller, 44."

38. While the similarity of Covey's thinking to that of Franklin might lead one to think that Ben had been reincarnated to serve as the company's co-CEO, the actual co-CEO was Hyrum Smith, a great-great-grandnephew of Joseph Smith, founder of the Church of Jesus Christ of Latter-Day Saints. Hyrum Smith founded the Franklin Quest Company in 1984 to foster the principles expounded by Franklin by marketing time management seminars and a day planner system called the Franklin Planner, which became one of the most successful day planning systems, displacing

the less ideologically embellished Daytimer system. In 1992 the Franklin Quest Company went public with an initial public offering that raised $78 million. Five years later, in May 1997, Franklin Quest merged with Covey's privately held, $100 million Covey Leadership Center to form the FranklinCovey Company.

39. Doug Stanton, "Aren't You Glad You're Anthony Robbins?" *Esquire*, April 1994, 106.

40. N. Griffin, "The Charismatic Kid," *Life*, March 1985, 42.

41. Stanton, "Aren't You Glad You're Anthony Robbins," 100.

42. See, for example, Anthony Robbins, *Unlimited Power* (New York: Fawcett Columbine, 1986), 11.

43. See, for example, Anita Clair Fellman and Michael Fellman, *Making Sense of Self: Medical Advice Literature in Late Nineteenth-Century America* (Philadelphia: University of Pennsylvania Press, 1981); Meyer, *Positive Thinkers*.

44. Starker, *Oracle*, 114.

45. The Psycho-Cybernetics Foundation, Inc., dedicated to continuing Maltz's work, makes these estimates. Available online at: www.psycho-cybernetics.com/about.html Last viewed: August 16, 2003.

46. Robbins, *Unlimited Power*, 26.

47. Carolyn Merchant, *The Death of Nature: Women, Ecology, and the Scientific Revolution* (San Francisco: Harper and Row, 1980), cited in Margolis, *Fabric of Self*, 27.

48. Robbins, *Unlimited Power*, 254.

49. Taylor, *Ethics of Authenticity*, 103.

50. Robbins, *Unlimited Power*, 84–85.

51. Stephen R. Covey, "Three Resolutions" (1991). Available online at: www.franklincovey.com/ez/library/three.html Last viewed: August 16, 2003.

52. Friedrich Nietzsche, *The Gay Science*, trans. Walter Kaufmann (New York: Vintage, 1974), 232, passage 290.

53. Stanton, "Aren't You Glad You're Anthony Robbins," 106.

54. Art Levine, "Peak Performance Is Tiring," *U.S. News and World Report*, February 24, 1997, 53.

55. Alex Berenson, "Motivating Investors: Anthony Robbins Makes an Internet Play," *New York Times*, January 8, 2000, C-1. As with many online ventures, his internet startup, dreamlife.com, collapsed in 2001 and was restructured through the purchase of a toy company; Don Bauder, "Dreamlife Has Trouble Making Its Dreams Come True," *San Diego Union-Tribune*, January 21, 2001, H-2; Don Bauder, "Robbins Donates Millions of Shares Back to Ailing Dot-Com," *San Diego Union-Tribune*, February 3, 2001, C-3; and Tony Robbins, "Tony Robbins: Practicing

What He Preaches," Interview by Beverly Schuch, *Pinnacle*, CNN-FN, March 10, 2001. Transcript available online at http://www.cnn.com/TRANSCRIPTS/0103/10/pin.00.html. Last viewed: August 14, 2003.

56. Simonds, *Women and Self-Help Culture*, 98–99; Starker, *Oracle*, 63–64.

57. Stanton, "Aren't You Glad You're Anthony Robbins," 105–6.

58. Robbins, *Unlimited Power*, 200.

59. Ralph Waldo Trine, *In Tune with the Infinite, or Fullness of Peace, Power, and Plenty* (New York: Crowell, 1897), 176.

60. T. J. Jackson Lears, *Fables of Abundance: A Cultural History of Advertising in America* (New York: Basic Books, 1994); Meyer, *Positive Thinkers*; David M. Potter, *People of Plenty: Economic Abundance and the American Character* (Chicago: University of Chicago Press, 1954).

61. Hilkey, *Character Is Capital*, 4; Richard Sennett, *The Corrosion of Character: The Personal Consequences of Work in the New Capitalism* (New York: Norton, 1998); Warren Susman, *Culture as History: The Transformation of American Society in the Twentieth Century* (New York: Pantheon, 1984 [1979]), 271–85.

62. Covey, *Seven Habits*, 19.

63. Ibid., 32.

64. See, for example, Hilkey, *Character Is Capital*; Sennett, *Corrosion of Character*.

65. Examples of the fiscal metaphor of the emotional bank account can be found on p. 188; the agrarian metaphor of harvesting what one sows is evident on p. 22, while the computer programming metaphor is used frequently, for example on pp. 70, 129, and 169. Covey, *Seven Habits*.

66. Covey, Merrill, and Merrill, *First Things First*, 51.

67. Covey, *Seven Habits*, 103.

68. Ibid., 128.

69. Ibid., 169.

70. Mather, *Bonifacius*, 45–46.

71. Covey, *Seven Habits*, 96–97.

72. Mather writes:

> Perhaps almost every *Proposal* to be now mentioned, may be like a *Stone* falling on a *Pool*; *Reader*, Keep thy Mind *Calm*, and see, whether the Effect prove not so! That one *Circle* (and *Service*) will produce another, until they Extend, who can tell, how far? and they cannot be reckoned up. The men who give themselves up to Good Devices, and who take a due Notice of their *Opportunities to Do Good*, usually find a strange Growth of their *Opportunities*. *Bonifacius*, 42.

73. Covey, *Seven Habits*, 81–87.

74. Ibid., 118.

75. Ibid., 128.

76. Covey, Merrill and Merrill, *First Things First*, 260.

77. Wolfe, "White Magic in America," 32.

78. Covey, Merrill and Merrill, *First Things First*, 201.

79. Ibid., 202.

80. Charles Sabel, "Mobius-Strip Organizations and Open Labor Markets: Some Consequences of the Reintegration of Conception and Execution in a Volatile Economy," in *Social Theory for a Changing Society*, ed. Pierre Bourdieu and James S. Coleman (Boulder, Colo.: Westview Press, 1991), 25.

81. Ibid., 43.

82. Deepak Chopra, *The A-to-Z Steps to a Richer Life* (New York: Barnes and Noble, 1993), 27–28.

83. Chopra, *Seven Spiritual Laws of Success*, 10 (emphasis in original).

84. Ibid., 97–99.

85. Ibid., 57.

86. Ibid., 58–59.

87. Shakti Gawain, *Living in the Light* (Mill Valley, Calif.: Whatever Publishing, 1986), 142.

88. Ibid., 145.

89. Indeed, Mihaly Csikszentmihalyi's bestselling *Flow: The Psychology of Optimal Experience: Steps Toward Enhancing the Quality of Life*, while not a New Age book, comes to mind as another example of the language of liquidity.

90. Ralph Waldo Trine, *The Best of Ralph Waldo Trine* (Indianapolis: Bobbs-Merrill, 1957), 17.

91. Karl Marx and Friedrich Engels, "Manifesto of the Communist Party," in *The Marx-Engels Reader*, ed. Robert C. Tucker (New York: Norton, 1978 [1848]), 469–91.

92. Zygmunt Bauman, *Liquid Modernity* (Cambridge: Polity Press, 2000), 6.

93. Harvey B. Mackay, *Swim with the Sharks Without Being Eaten Alive* (New York: Ballantine, 1988), xxxiii.

94. Ibid., 25.

95. Ibid., 51.

96. Ibid., 117.

97. Ibid., 53–54.

98. Spencer Johnson, *Who Moved My Cheese? An Amazing Way to Deal with Change in Your Work and in Your Life* (New York: Putnam, 1998), 46.

99. For two hilarious parodies that make this point, see Mason Brown, *Who Cut the Cheese? A Cutting-Edge Way of Surviving Change by Shifting the Blame* (New York: Simon and Schuster, 2000); Ilene Hochberg, *Who Stole*

My Cheese? An A-Mazing Way to Make More Money from the Poor Suckers That You Cheated in Your Work and in Your Life (New York: Union Square Press, 2002).

100. Johnson, *Who Moved My Cheese*, 88.

101. Many thanks to Nina Eliasoph for pointing out this sharp contradiction in the self-help literatures of childrearing compared with those of professional advancement.

102. Johnson, *Who Moved My Cheese*, 34.

103. See Karl Polanyi, *The Great Transformation: The Political and Economic Origins of Our Time* (Boston: Beacon Press, 1957 [1944]), or the more recent anthology on this question, Paul Heelas, Scott Lash, and Paul Morris, eds., *Detraditionalization: Critical Reflections on Authority and Identity* (Oxford: Blackwell, 1996).

104. See, for example, Eisenstein, *Printing Press as an Agent of Change*; Walter J. Ong; *Orality and Literacy: The Technologizing of the Word* (New York: Routledge, 1991 [1982]); Taylor, *Sources of the Self.*

105. Bell, *Cultural Contradictions of Capitalism*; Lasch, *Culture of Narcissism*; Sennett, *Fall of Public Man*, 323–36.

Chapter 3

Epigraph from Letty Cottin Pogrebin, "Can Women Really Have It All? Should We?," *Ms.*, March 1978, 48.

1. Ringer, *Looking Out for Number One*, x.

2. Ibid., 155.

3. Ibid., 41.

4. Peck, *Road Less Traveled*, 102.

5. Covey, Merrill, and Merrill, *First Things First*, 15.

6. Ibid., 183–184, 297.

7. Ruth Sidel, *Women and Children Last* (New York: Penguin, 1986), 15.

8. Hilda Scott, *Working Your Way to the Bottom: The Feminization of Poverty* (London: Pandora Press, 1984).

9. The economist Sylvia Anne Hewlett described these changes in *A Lesser Life: The Myth of Women's Liberation in America* (New York: Morrow, 1986).

10. Hochschild, *Second Shift*, 11.

11. Helen Gurley Brown, *Having It All* (New York: Pocket Books, 1982), 355 (ellipsis and emphasis in original).

12. Kassorla has inadvertently secured her place in history's footnotes as Monica Lewinsky's psychotherapist.

13. Irene C. Kassorla, *Go for It! How to Win at Love, Work and Play* (New York: Delacorte, 1984), ix–x.

14. Brown, *Having It All*, 25 (emphasis in original).

15. Ringer, *Looking Out for Number One*, 41.

16. Covey, *Seven Habits*, 296.

17. Brown, *Having It All*, 7.

18. Ibid., 2.

19. Ibid., 7, 21, 61, 63.

20. Ibid., 361.

21. Ibid., 307.

22. Ibid., 29 (emphasis in original).

23. Ibid., 33.

24. Ibid., 35.

25. Ibid., 34 (emphasis in original).

26. Helen Gurley Brown, *I'm Wild Again: Snippets from My Life and a Few Brazen Thoughts* (New York: St. Martin's Press, 2000), 12.

27. Ibid., 5.

28. Jeffrey Louis Decker, *Made in America*, 127–30, 132.

29. James, *Letters of William James*, 260.

30. Interestingly, Brown's emphasis on physical fitness and ability may be overdetermined by her own personal situation, in which she was responsible for supporting her mother and a physically disabled sister.

31. Brown, *Having It All*, 34 (emphasis in original).

32. Ibid., 99.

33. Brown, *Having It All*, 46 (emphasis in original).

34. Brown, *Having It All*, 50 (emphasis in original).

35. Ibid., 67.

36. Elias, *Civilizing Process*, 54.

37. See, for example, Susan Faludi, *Backlash: The Undeclared War Against American Women* (New York: Crown, 1991).

38. Marguerite Babcock and Christine McKay, eds., *Challenging Codependency: Feminist Critiques* (Toronto: University of Toronto Press, 1995); Constance Fabunmi, Loretta Frederick and Mary Jarvis Bicknese, "The Codependency Trap," in Babcock and McKay, eds. *Challenging Codependency*, 88–92; Kay Hagen, "Codependency and the Myth of Recovery: A Feminist Scrutiny," in Babcock and McKay, *Challenging Codependency*, 198–206; Hochschild, "Commercial Spirit of Intimate Life"; Jo-Ann Krestan and Claudia Bepko, "Codependency: The Social Reconstruction of Female Experience," in Babcock and McKay, *Challenging Codependency*, 93–110; Bette S. Tallen, "Codependency: A Feminist Critique," in Babcock and McKay, *Challenging Codependency*, 169–76.

39. See also Connell Cowan and Melvyn Kinder, *Smart Women, Foolish*

Choices: Finding the Right Men, Avoiding the Wrong Ones (New York: Signet, 1985); and *Women Men Love, Women Men Leave* (New York: Signet, 1987).

40. See, for example, Melody Beattie, *Codependent No More: How to Stop Controlling Others and Start Caring for Yourself* (New York: Harper: 1987), and her followup *Beyond Codependency: And Getting Better All the Time* (San Francisco: Harper: 1989); Susan Forward and Craig Buck, *Toxic Parents: Overcoming Their Hurtful Legacy and Reclaiming Your Life* (New York: Bantam, 1989); and John Bradshaw, *Homecoming: Reclaiming and Championing Your Inner Child* (New York: Bantam, 1990).

41. Since many social critics and scholars have considered the development of the idea of codependency, this is not the focus of this investigation. For further considerations of the concept of codependence, see Babcock and McKay, eds., *Challenging Codependency*; Leslie Irvine, *Codependent Forevermore: The Invention of Self in a Twelve Step Group* (Chicago: University of Chicago Press, 1999); Kaminer, *I'm Dysfunctional, You're Dysfunctional*, Rapping; *Culture of Recovery*; Craig Reinarman, "The Twelve-Step Movement and Advanced Capitalist Culture: The Politics of Self-Control in Postmodernity," in *Cultural Politics and Social Movements*, eds. Marcy Darnovsky, Barbara Epstein, and Richard Flacks (Philadelphia: Temple University Press, 1995); Rice, *Disease of One's Own*.

42. Rice, *Disease of One's Own*.

43. Micki McGee, "Hooked on Higher Education and Other Tales from Adjunct Faculty Organizing," *Social Text 70*, vol. 20, no. 1 (2002): 73.

44. Hochschild, " Commercial Spirit of Intimate Life," 12.

45. Ibid., 2.

46. Ibid., 13.

47. Ibid., 16–17.

48. See, for example, Nietzsche's insistence that "we want to be the poets of our life—first of all in the smallest, more everyday matters" (*Gay Science*, sec. 299) and that "One thing is needful.—To 'give style' to one's character—a great and rare art!" (*Gay Science*, sec. 290).

49. Richard Rorty, *Contingency, Irony and Solidarity* (Cambridge: Cambridge University Press, 1989), 35. Rorty goes on to quote the literary critic Leo Bersani's observation that "psychoanalytic theory has made the notion of fantasy so richly problematic that we should no longer be able to take for granted the distinction between art and life." 36.

50. Daniel Yankelovich, *New Rules: Searching for Self-Fulfillment in a World Turned Upside Down* (New York: Random House, 1981), 59.

51. Ibid., 81.

52. Shakti Gawain, *Creative Visualization* (New York: Bantam, 1985 [1979]), 123.

53. Ibid.

54. Bateson, *Composing a Life*, 3.

55. Ibid., 5–7.

56. Weber writes:

> The development of intellectualism and the rationalization of life change this situation. For under these conditions, art becomes a cosmos of more and more consciously grasped independent values which exist in their own right. Art takes over the function of a this-worldly salvation, no matter how this may be interpreted. It provides a *salvation* from the routines of everyday life, and especially from the increasing pressures of theoretical and practical rationalism.
>
> With this claim to a redemptory function, art begins to compete directly with salvation religion. Every rational religious ethic must turn against this inner-worldly, irrational salvation. For in religion's eyes, such salvation is a realm of irresponsible indulgence and secret lovelessness. As a matter of fact, the refusal of modern men to assume responsibility for moral judgments tends to transform judgments of moral intent into judgments of taste ("in poor taste" instead of "reprehensible"). The inaccessibility of appeal from esthetic judgments excludes discussion. This shift from the moral to the esthetic evaluation of conduct is a common characteristic of intellectualist epochs; it results partly from subjectivist needs and partly from the fear of appearing narrow-minded in a traditionalist and Philistine way.

"Religious Rejections," 343 (emphasis in original).

57. This interview appears in multiple locations: Michel Foucault, "How We Behave: Sex, Food and Other Ethical Matters," interview by Hubert L. Dreyfus and Paul Rabinow, *Vanity Fair* 46, no. 9 (1983), 60–69; also available as "On the Geneaology of Ethics: An Overview of a Work in Progress," in Hubert L. Dreyfus and Paul Rabinow, *Michel Foucault: Beyond Structuralism and Hermeneutics*, 2nd ed. (Chicago: University of Chicago Press, 1983), 229–52; in Paul Rabinow, ed., *The Foucault Reader* (New York: Pantheon, 1984), 340–72; and in Michel Foucault, *The Essential Works of Michel Foucault*, vol. 1, *Ethics: Subjectivity and Truth*. ed. by Paul Rabinow, trans. Robert Hurley and others, (New York: New Press, 1994), 253–80. For this question, see Dreyfus and Rabinow, *Beyond Structuralism and Hermeneutics*, 237. All citations are to the version published in Dreyfus and Rabinow, which will be noted hereafter as Foucault, "Genealogy of Ethics."

58. Foucault, "Genealogy of Ethics," 245.

59. Friedrich Nietzsche, *Human, All Too Human*, trans. R. J. Hollingdale (Cambridge: Cambridge University Press, 1996 [1878]), 218 (emphasis in original).

60. Friedrich Nietzsche, "Ecce Homo," in *Basic Writings of Nietzsche* (New York: Modern Library, 1992 [1908]), 710.

61. Foucault, "Genealogy of Ethics," 246.

62. Sarah Ban Breathnach, *Simple Abundance: A Daybook of Comfort and Joy* (New York: Warner Books, 1995), unpaginated; citations hereafter by entry date. At the end of 1997, the closing date for the first set of materials sampled for this study, Breathnach's book had enjoyed ninety weeks on the *New York Times* bestseller list.

63. Carolyn G. Heilbrun, *The Education of a Woman: The Life of Gloria Steinem* (New York: Dial Press, 1995), 390–393.

64. Steinem, *Revolution from Within*, 8.

65. Rice, *Disease of One's Own*, 213.

66. Ibid., 213. See also Robert Wuthnow, *Sharing the Journey: Support Groups and America's New Quest for Community* (New York: Free Press, 1994); Rapping, *Culture of Recovery*.

67. Steinem, *Revolution from Within*, 347. Steinem, like communitarian philosopher Charles Taylor, was calling for synthesis of the positions of the self-improvement "knockers" and "boosters." Taylor, *Ethics of Authenticity*, 11.

68. Steinem, *Revolution from Within*, 25.

69. Ibid., 348.

70. Rosalind Franklin is the molecular biologist whose imaging of DNA was vital to the discoveries attributed to Watson and Crick. Watson and Crick are reported to have borrowed her work without attribution. Brenda Maddox, *Rosalind Franklin: Dark Lady of DNA* (New York: HarperCollins, 2002).

71. Indeed, Steinem's diffused cellular notions of power are not unlike those articulated by Michael Hardt and Antonio Negri, *Empire* (Cambridge, Mass.: Harvard University Press, 2000).

72. Berman, *The Politics of Authenticity*.

73. Paul H. Ray and Sherry Ruth Anderson, *The Cultural Creatives: How Fifty Million People Are Changing the World* (New York: Harmony Books, 2000).

74. See, for example, Elias Canetti, *Crowds and Power*, trans. Carol Stewart (New York: Seabury Press, 1978); Gustave Le Bon, *The Crowd: A Study of the Popular Mind* (London: Unwin, 1896).

75. Stuart Ewen, *PR! A Social History of Spin* (New York: Basic Books, 1996).

76. Irene Taviss Thompson, *In Conflict No Longer: Self and Society in Contemporary America* (Lanham, Md.: Rowman and Littlefield, 2000), argues that the self-help literature and groups of the late twentieth century demonstrate a new sense of community that marks a change in the idea of the individual against society. Instead, she suggests, this new relational and embedded self would necessarily contribute to conflict-free social change.

77. Steinem, *Revolution from Within*, 348 (emphasis in original).

78. Ibid., 348.

79. Breathnach, *Simple Abundance*, January 11.

80. Ibid., January 12.

81. Lawrence Chenoweth, *The American Dream of Success: The Search for Self in the Twentieth Century* (North Scituate, Mass.: Duxbury Press, 1974), 72.

82. Meyer, *Positive Thinkers*, 369.

83. Catherine Ponder, *The Dynamic Laws of Prosperity: Forces That Bring Riches to You* (Englewood Cliffs, N.J.: Prentice-Hall, 1962), xiii.

84. Breathnach, *Simple Abundance,* April 9.

85. Ibid., section entitled "Joyful Simplicities for February," immediately following the February 29 entry.

86. Ibid., section entitled "Joyful Simplicities for June," immediately following the June 30 entry.

87. Ibid., section entitled "Joyful Simplicities for July," immediately following the July 31 entry.

88. Ibid., section entitled "Joyful Simplicities for November," immediately following the November 30 entry.

89. Examples include: Andrea Van Steenhouse, with Doris A. Fuller, *A Woman's Guide to a Simpler Life* (New York: Harmony Books, 1996); Dave Babbitt, *Downscaling: Simplify and Enrich Your Lifestyle* (Chicago: Moody Press, 1993); Georgene Lockwood, *The Complete Idiot's Guide to Simple Living* (Indianapolis: Alpha, 2000); and Elaine St. James's numerous guides to simplicity: *Simplify Your Life: One Hundred Ways to Slow Down and Enjoy the Things that Really Matter* (New York: Hyperion, 1994); *Inner Simplicity: One Hundred Ways to Regain Peace and Nourish Your Soul* (New York: Hyperion, 1995); *Living the Simple Life: A Guide to Scaling Down and Enjoying More* (New York: Hyperion, 1996).

90. For example, Duane Elgin, *Voluntary Simplicity: Toward a Way of Life That Is Outwardly Simple, Inwardly Rich* (New York: Quill, 1993).

91. See, for example, Campbell, *Romantic Ethic*; Potter, *People of Plenty*; David E. Shi, *The Simple Life: Plain Living and High Thinking in American Culture* (New York: Oxford University Press, 1985).

92. Hochschild, *Time Bind*, 227.

93. Ibid., 229.

94. John de Graaf, ed., *Take Back Your Time: Fighting Overwork and Time Poverty in American* (San Francisco: Berrett-Koehler, 2003).

95. See the websites of Thomas Leonard and Coach University: www.thomasleonard.com/cli/assess/12.html or www.coachinc.com/local/files/Resources/ CoachU/Forms/FB281QAZ.pdf Last viewed: August 16, 2003.

96. Suze Orman, *The Nine Steps to Financial Freedom* (New York: Crown, Three Rivers Press, 2000 [1997]), 2.

97. The advent of the life-coaching phenomenon is interesting as it: (1) repopularizes the metaphor of life as a game, and (2) seems to be partially driven by reductions in mental healthcare funding under the HMO model. Therapists, seeking to reposition themselves outside this newly parsimonious healthcare economy, repackage themselves as coaches—part of the personal service industry—rather than as mental health professionals. And others, often without training in psychology, psychiatry, or pastoral counseling, develop careers as "life coaches" from backgrounds as financial planners, career counselors, or fitness experts. In these examples, one sees members of the new flexible or contingent professional labor markets refashioning themselves as advisors to other members of the contingent labor market.

98. Orman, *Nine Steps*, xi.

99. "Lifestyle Makeovers: Energy Drains," *Oprah Winfrey Show*, first aired June 12, 2000, Burrell's transcripts.

100. Ibid.

101. Ibid.

102. For example, Gergen, *The Saturated Self*; James Gleick, *Faster: The Acceleration of Just About Everything* (New York: Random House, 1999); Jeremy Rifkin, *Time Wars: The Primary Conflict in Human History* (New York: Holt, 1987).

103. "Lifestyle Makeovers: Energy Drains."

104. Ibid. (emphasis added).

105. See Nina Eliasoph's thoughtful discussion of this process in *Avoiding Politics: How Americans Produce Apathy in Everyday Life* (Cambridge: Cambridge University Press, 1998).

106. Working Today—the organization founded by the labor lawyer and activist Sara Horowitz to advocate on behalf of contingent and freelance workers—recently launched an advertising campaign focused on middle-class poverty: the poverty endured by middle-class working people as wages have retrenched and costs for healthcare, housing, and education have far outpaced the overall rate of inflation.

107. "Lifestyle Makeovers: Energy Drains."

108. Orman, *Nine Steps*, 4.

109. Orman offers a striking description of what Marx calls commodity fetishism, where relations between one individual and another appear not as direct social relations but rather as a relationship between things: "material relations between persons and social relations between things." *Capital*, vol. 1, trans. Ben Fowkes (New York: Vintage, 1997 [1867]), 166.

110. Orman, *Nine Steps*, 133.

111. Or what Arlie Russell Hochschild has called "the commercialization of intimacy" and Randy Martin has called the "financialization of everyday life." Hochschild, "Commercial Spirit of Intimate Life"; Randy Martin, *Financialization of Daily Life* (Philadelphia: Temple University Press, 2002).

Chapter 4

Epigraph from Warren Buffett, quoted in Mark Bryan, with Julia Cameron and Catherine Allen, *The Artist's Way at Work: Riding the Dragon* (New York: William Morrow, 1998), v.

1. Brooks, *Bobos*.

2. For an account of increased working hours, see Schor, *The Overworked American*. While working hours have increased, real wages remain well below their 1973 high point, despite recent gains from the technology boom. *The Economic Report of the President* (2003), 332, table B-47.

3. With the 1997 edition of *Parachute*, the publisher dropped the subtitle ("A Practical Manual for Job Hunters and Career Changers") that had described the book in the first quarter-century of its publication.

4. Kevin McManus, "Making a Career of Careers," *Forbes*, March 15, 1982, 144, Ray Walters, "Paperback Talk," *New York Times Book Review*, February 18, 1979, 41.

5. As a result, Richard Nelson Bolles, *What Color Is Your Parachute?* (Berkeley, Calif.: Ten Speed Press) suggests itself as a unique data set, providing an opportunity to track continuity and divergence across three decades. My initial sample included editions from 1972, 1977, 1979, 1981, 1982, 1987, 1988, 1989, 1990, 1992, 1996, and 1997. I have subsequently reviewed the 1998–2004 editions.

6. *Economic Report of the President* (2003), 326, table B-42.

7. Edwin L. Herr, "The Emerging History of Career Education: A Summary View Prepared for the National Advisory Council on Career Education" (Washington, D.C.: 1976), 70.

8. By 2004 the book was pruned back to a more manageable 411 pages and a website, www.jobhuntersbible.com, provided additional information.

9. See "job-hunting while on the job" in the 1981 edition, p. 54, and as a full appendix in the 1987 edition, pp. 281–282.

10. Raymond Williams, *Keywords: A Vocabulary of Culture and Society* (New York: Oxford University Press, 1976), 44.

11. Bolles, *Parachute*, 1990 ed., xvii.

12. McManus, "Making a Career of Careers," 144.

13. Bolles, *Parachute*, 1988 ed., 295–296 (emphasis in original).

14. Mather, *Bonifacius*, 34 (emphasis in original).

15. Bolles, *Parachute*, 1972 ed., 64; 1977 ed., 65; 1982 ed., 34.

16. Bolles, *Parachute*, 1987 ed., 64 (emphasis in original).

17. Bolles, *Parachute*, 1982 ed., 336.

18. Bolles, *Parachute*, 1988 ed., xviii.

19. Ibid., 395.

20. Bolles, *Parachute*, 1992 ed., 14–15.

21. My thanks to the staff at Ten Speed Press, for checking previous editions of *Parachute* for 1991, 1993, and 1994 that were not available to me.

22. Polanyi, *The Great Transformation*, 177.

23. Bolles, *Parachute*, 1996 ed., 248

24. Ibid., 248

25. Bolles, *Parachute*, 1992 ed., 163 (emphasis in original).

26. Bolles, *Parachute*, 1996 ed., 255 (emphasis in original).

27. Margaret Langstaff, "Beating Those Workplace Blues," *Publishers Weekly* 241, no. 15 (1994), 36. Langstaff mistakenly dates the original publication of *Do What You Love, The Money Will Follow,* at 1980. Paulist Press first published the book in 1987.

28. Ibid., 36.

29. Marsha Sinetar, *Do What You Love, the Money Will Follow: Discovering Your Right Livelihood* (Mahwah, N.J.: Paulist Press, 1987), 1–2.

30. Acts 9: 3–5: "And as he journeyed, he came near Damascus: and suddenly there shined round about him a light from heaven: / And he fell to the earth, and heard a voice saying unto him, Saul, Saul, why persecutest thou me? / And he said, Who art thou, Lord? And the Lord said, I am Jesus."

31. Sinetar, *Do What You Love,* 144.

32. Ibid., 8–9.

33. Ibid., 9 (emphasis added).

34. Claude Whitmyer, ed., *Mindfulness and Meaningful Work* (Berkeley, Calif.: Parallax, 1994), 17.

35. Ibid., 15.

36. Sinetar, *Do What You Love*, 71.

37. Hilkey, *Character Is Capital*, 101. The dignity-of-all-labor doctrine is a double-edged belief. On the one hand, the idea has been misused to undercut Aid to Families with Dependent Children, where the care of one's own children is not regarded as labor and taking a minimum-wage job or participating in so-called workfare is considered dignified. On the other hand, the idea is used to honor the contributions of the workers engaged in the less glamorous labors that our daily lives require.

38. Sinetar, *Do What You Love*, 144–145.

39. See, for example, Bolles, *Parachute*, 1997 ed., 208 and 13.

40. Sinetar, *Do What You Love*, 91.

41. *Creative America: A Report to the President* (Washington, D.C.: President's Committee on the Arts and the Humanities, 1997), 13. Available online at the website of the President's Committee on the Arts and the Humanities: www.pcah.gov/publications.htm. Last viewed: January 5, 2005.

42. Lewis Hyde, *The Gift: Imagination and the Erotic Life of Property* (New York: Vintage Books, 1979).

43. Donohue, "The Book Much Read," 26.

44. Julia Cameron, *The Artist's Way: A Spiritual Path to Higher Creativity* (New York: Tarcher, 1992), 10.

45. Ibid., 189.

46. Ibid., 18.

47. Ibid., 189.

48. For a valuable analysis of the logical inconsistencies in using a Twelve-Step recovery model for so-called process addictions (codependency, shopaholism, workaholism), see Rice, *Disease of One's Own*, 199–200. Rice notes that in the logic of Twelve-Step programs, society and culture are viewed as immutable sources of oppression, yet participating as a member of a Twelve-Step group—participating in a new social formation—is required for recovery.

49. Greta Beigel, "The Path to the Person Inside," *Los Angeles Times*, July 23, 1995, E1.

50. Donna Zerner, "The Artist's Way," *Yoga Journal*, March-April 1995, 96.

51. In 1997, a number of creativity support groups based on *The Artist's Way* were operating in online bulletin board communities or, as they called themselves, "clusters." Among them were www.everydayartist.com and www.artistway.com. As this book goes to press, these sites are no longer operating as online bulletin board communities for artists, but others have emerged, on the Yahoo and eGroups bulletin board sites.

52. Bryan, *Artist's Way at Work*, xv.

53. Laurence G. Boldt, *Zen and the Art of Making a Living: A Practical Guide to Creative Career Design* (New York: Penguin, 1993 [1992]); see especially pages xivii–lxiii.

54. James Servin, "Is Nice Back?" Harper's *Bazaar*, January 1997, 101.

55. Of course I am neither groundbreaking nor alone in these observations. By March 5, 2000, the *New York Times Magazine* published an article entitled "The Artist in the Grey Flannel Pajamas," by the journalist Michael Lewis, that clearly articulated the "artist exemplar" model. And in the summer of 2000, the cultural theorist Andrew Ross presented a similar thesis in an article entitled "The Mental Labor Problem." Although Ross's article was published shortly after the Lewis article appeared, he had presented these ideas earlier, in a paper presented at "The Privatization of Culture," working group sponsored by the Rockefeller Foundation and hosted by New York University and the New School University in November 1999.

56. Ross, "Mental Labor Problem," 22.

57. "His" because this was a profoundly gendered mythology: the male artist was supposed to locate his legacy in his artmaking—sublimating his drives into artmaking—while ignoring the demands of paternity whenever possible. George Bernard Shaw puts it aptly in his *Man and Superman*:

> The true artist will let his wife starve, his children go barefoot, his mother drudge for his living at seventy, sooner than work at anything but his art. . . . Since marriage began, the great artist has been known as a bad husband. But he is worse: he is a child-robber, a bloodsucker, a hypocrite and a cheat. Perish the race and wither a thousand women if only the sacrifice of them enable him to act Hamlet better, to paint a finer picture, to write a deeper poem, a greater play, a profounder philosophy! . . . Of all human struggles there is none so treacherous and remorseless as the struggle between the artist man and the mother woman.

Man and Superman: A Comedy and a Philosophy (Edinburgh: Penguin Books, 1946 [1903]), 65.

58. Abraham H. Maslow, *Toward a Psychology of Being*, 3rd ed. (New York: Wiley, 1999 [1968]), 190.

59. *Economic Report of the President* (2003), 327, table B-43.

60. James Heintz, Nancy Folbre, and the Center for Popular Economics, *The Ultimate Field Guide to the U.S. Economy* (New York: New Press, 2000), 35.

61. Tom Peters, *Thriving on Chaos* (New York: Knopf, 1987), 341.

62. Ibid., 342.

63. Ibid., 416 (underlining and italics in original).

64. Ibid., 423.

65. Ibid., 416.

66. Ibid., 423.

67. Ibid., 426 (emphasis in original).

68. Ibid., 435. While I have not yet decided what to make of it, it seems striking that the elimination of large numbers of middle management positions just as women and minorities gained access to these positions seems to parallel the loss of "self" and authority discussed by Nancy Hartsock, "Foucault on Power: A Theory for Women?" in *Feminism/ Postmoderisn*, ed. Linda J. Nicholson (New York: Routledge, 1990 [1987]).

69. Tom Peters, "The Brand Called You," *Fast Company*, August 1997, 83 (emphasis in original).

70. Ibid.

71. Brown, *Having It All*, 36 (emphasis in original).

72. Ibid., 36.

73. Ibid., 37.

74. Ibid., 39 (emphasis added).

75. Donald Meyer, *Positive Thinkers*, 130.

76. Warhol, *Philosophy of Andy Warhol*, 92.

Chapter 5

Epigraph from Michel Foucault, "Genealogy of Ethics," in *Michel Foucault: Beyond Structuralism and Hermeneutics*, eds. Hubert L. Dreyfus and Paul Rabinow (Chicago: University of Chicago Press, 1983), 236.

1. Hannah Arendt, *The Human Condition* (Chicago: University of Chicago Press, 1958), 80n5.

2. Ibid., 81fn.

3. Ibid., 83.

4. Ibid.,128.

5. Ibid., 99.

6. Ibid., 104.

7. For example, Michael Hardt and Antonio Negri, *Labor of Dionysus: A Critique of the State-Form* (Minneapolis: University of Minnesota Press, 1994).

8. As Arendt points out, Marx uses this biological metaphor throughout his work. Arendt, *The Human Condition*, 99n34. For example, see *Capital*, vol. 1, 33.

9. Anthony Robbins, *Awaken the Giant Within*, 293 (bold and italics in original).

10. Covey, Merrill and Merrill, *First Things First*, 240 (emphasis added).

11. Peck, *The Road Less Traveled*, 55.

12. Covey, *Seven Habits*, 291.

13. Ibid., 289.

14. Brown, *Having It All*, 6.

15. Chopra, *The Seven Spiritual Laws of Success*, 54–55.

16. Ibid., 62–64.

17. Ibid., 79.

18. Richard Carlson, *Don't Sweat the Small Stuff . . . And It's All Small Stuff* (New York: Hyperion, 1997), 19.

19. Ibid., 29.

20. Eckhart Tolle, *The Power of Now* (Novato, Calif.: New World Library, 1999), 41.

21. Ibid., 40.

22. Robbins, *Awaken the Giant Within*, 293.

23. Ibid., 204.

24. Gawain, *Creative Visualization*, 87.

25. Bryan, *Artist's Way at Work*, 264.

26. Breathnach, *Simple Abundance*, January 14 (emphasis in original).

27. *O, The Oprah Magazine*, November 2000, pullout.

28. Oprah Winfrey, "What I Know for Sure," *O*, November 2000, 298.

29. Andrew Boyd, *Daily Afflictions: The Agony of Being Connected to Everything in the Universe* (New York: Norton, 2002), 83.

30. Ringer, *Looking Out for Number One*, 16–17.

31. Kassorla, *Go for It*, 3–4.

32. Wayne W. Dyer, *Your Erroneous Zones* (New York: Funk and Wagnalls, 1976), 7 (emphasis in original).

33. Carlos Castañeda, *Journey to Ixtlan* (New York: Simon and Schuster, 1972) 54–55.

34. Julia Cameron, *Vein of Gold: A Journey to Your Creative Heart* (New York: Putnam, 1996), 264.

35. Brown, *Having It All*, 104 (emphasis in original).

36. Robbins, *Unlimited Power*, 22–24.

37. Robert H. Schuller, *Tough Times Never Last, but Tough People Do* (New York: Bantam, 1984 [1983]), 43–44.

38. See, for example, Covey, *Seven Habits*, 68–73.

39. Anthony Robbins, *Personal Power II: The Driving Force* (San Diego, Calif.: Robbins Research International, 1996 [1993]), audio compact disc.

40. Covey, *Seven Habits*, 70.

41. Ibid., 73.

42. Ibid., 69, 103–4, 88.

43. Arendt, *Human Condition*, 207.

44. Covey, *Seven Habits*, 73.

45. Foucault, "Genealogy of Ethics," 241–42.

46. A topic fruitfully elaborated in Toby Miller, *The Well-Tempered Self: Citizenship, Culture, and the Postmodern Subject* (Baltimore: Johns Hopkins University Press, 1993).

47. Robbins, *Awaken the Giant Within*, 65.

48. Covey, *Seven Habits*, 162–79; Robbins, *Awaken the Giant Within*, 204.

49. Anthony Robbins and Joseph McClendon III, *Unlimited Power: A Black Choice* (New York: Simon and Schuster, 1997), 172.

50. Brown, *Sex and the Single Girl*, 6–7 (emphasis added).

51. Brown, *Having It All*, 71.

52. Ibid., 118 (emphasis in original).

53. Ibid., 24 (emphasis in original).

54. Books that were solely focused on diet and fitness were excluded from those sampled for this study because there was ample concern with diet and fitness in the general conduct-of-life literature.

55. Covey, *Seven Habits*, 296.

56. Ibid., 103–104.

57. Foucault, "Genealogy of Ethics," 253–80.

58. Foucault, "Genealogy of Ethics," 246–47.

59. Ibid., 246.

60. See, for example, Julia Cameron, *The Right to Write* (New York: Putnam, 1998); Henriette Anne Klauser, *Put Your Heart on Paper: Staying Connected in a Loose-Ends World* (New York: Bantam, 1995); Henriette Anne Klauser, *Write It Down, Make It Happen: Knowing What You Want and Getting It!* (New York: Scribner, 2000).

61. Alexander Nehamas, *The Art of Living: Socratic Reflections from Plato to Foucault* (Berkeley: University of California Press, 1998), 8.

62. Cameron, *Artist's Way*, 11.

63. Ibid., 146–147.

64. Ibid., 147.

65. Kassorla, *Go for It*, 5.

66. During the period of speculation in internet and other technology stocks, Robbins also developed a site called dreamlife.com that included forms one could use to track one's personal progress in a series of areas. Since the collapse of the internet industries, the dreamlife.com site has been closed, Tony Robbins, "Tony Robbins: Practicing What He Preaches." Interview by Beverly Schuch, *Pinnacle*, CNN-FN, March 10, 2001. Transcript available online at: http://www.cnn.com/TRANSCRIPTS/0103/10/pin.00.html. Last viewed: August 14, 2003 .

67. Cameron, *Artist's Way*, 39–40 (emphasis added).

68. Rorty, *Contingency*, 20.

69. Robbins, *Awaken the Giant Within*, 209–239.

70. Anthony Robbins, *Notes from a Friend* (New York: Simon and Schuster, 1995), 86 (bold and italics in original).

71. Gabriel Tarde, "The Public and the Crowd," in *On Communication and Social Influence: Selected Papers* (Chicago: University of Chicago Press, 1969 [1893]), 312.

72. See, for example, Eisenstein, *Printing Press as an Agent of Change*; Marshall McLuhan, *The Gutenberg Galaxy: The Making of Typographic Man.* (Toronto: University of Toronto Press, 1962); McLuhan, *Understanding Media: The Extensions of Man*; Ong, *Orality and Literacy.*

73. See, for example, Jacques Ellul, *The Humiliation of the Word*, trans. Joyce Main Hanks (Grand Rapids, Mich.: Eerdmans, 1985); Lash, "Discourse or Figure," Lyotard, *Discours, Figure*; Mitchell Stephens, *The Rise of the Image, the Fall of the Word* (New York: Oxford University Press, 1998).

74. Gawain, *Creative Visualization*, 2–3.

75. Ibid., 106.

76. Cheryl Richardson, *Take Time for Your Life* (New York: Broadway Books, 1998), 165.

77. Breathnach, *Simple Abundance*, January 29.

78. Ibid., January 28.

79. Robbins, *Unlimited Power*, 90.

80. Walter Benjamin, "The Work of Art in the Age of Mechanical Reproduction," in *Illuminations* (New York: Schocken Books, 1968 [1935]), 229.

81. Warren Susman, *Culture as History: The Transformation of American Society in the Twentieth Century* (New York: Pantheon Books, 1984), 271–85.

82. As the cultural historian Hillel Schwartz points out, Benjamin never quite makes the connection between mechanical reproduction and the emergence of a cultural preoccupation with authenticity. Rather, he imagines that the aura—the phenomenon of uniqueness and presence—was diminished when in fact it seems to have grown increasingly important to us as it has been threatened with an array of replicas. *The Culture of the Copy: Striking Likenesses, Unreasonable Facsimiles* (New York: Zone Books, 1996), 140–141. As with so many cultural developments, the concern with authenticity is multiply determined, emerging not only from the possibility of ready replication, but also from changes in the nature of social life, where communities are increasingly replaced with marketplaces, Lionel Trilling, *Sincerity and Authenticity* (Cambridge, Mass.: Harvard University Press, 1971).

83. Teresa Brennan and Martin Jay, eds., *Vision in Context: Historical and Contemporary Perspectives on Sight* (New York: Routledge); Jay, "Scopic Regimes of Modernity," 178–95.

84. See John Berger, *Ways of Seeing* (London: Penguin Books, 1972), 47; de Beauvoir, *Second Sex*, xv–xxxiv; Du Bois, *Souls of Black Folks*, 1–9.

85. Brown, *Having It All*, 139.

86. Ibid., 209.

87. Peters, "The Brand Called You," 83.

88. Tom Peters, *Liberation Management: Necessary Disorganization for the Nanosecond Nineties* (New York: Fawcett Columbine, 1992), 738.

89. Amy M. Spindler, "It's a Face-Lifted, Tummy-Tucked Jungle Out There," *New York Times*, June 9, 1996.

90. As has been argued elsewhere by Decker, *Made in America*; Ewen, *All Consuming Images*.

91. An interview with Peters by John Grossman notes that by one count there were no exclamation marks in *In Search of Excellence* until p. 152, while there were fourteen before the end of the table of contents in Peters's more recent *The Brand You Fifty: Fifty Ways to Transform Yourself from an "Employee" into a Brand That Shouts Distinction, Commitment, and Passion!* (New York: Knopf, 1999). John Grossmann, "Tom Peters' Exclamation Point World," *SKY*, October 2000, 95.

92. Grossman, "Tom Peter's World," 95.

93. Peters, *Liberation Management: Necessary Disorganization for the Nanosecond Nineties*, 17 (emphasis in original).

94. Tom Peters, *The Pursuit of Wow: Every Person's Guide to Topsy-Turvy Times* (New York: Vintage, 1994), 113 (emphasis added; bold in original).

95. Peters, *Pursuit of Wow*, 87–88.

96. Ibid., 116.

97. Stanton, "Aren't You Glad You're Anthony Robbins," 103.

98. Robbins, *Unlimited Power*, 149–50.

99. Ibid., 159–60.

100. Ibid., 160.

101. Hochschild, *Managed Heart*, 192.

102. The very idea of creating or inventing oneself generates a variety of ontological problems—that is, such a task appears to be inherently contradictory and thus an impossible undertaking. Who, one might ask, would be the self that is constructing the self? Alexander Nehamas rightly suggests that such questioning steers us in the direction of the philosopher Immanuel Kant's "transcendental unity of apperception"—or an a priori self or soul. *The Art of Living*, 4. For much of the literature of self-improvement and its readers this is not a problem, as the existence of a given soul is assumed. The goal, in this literature, is to create a self that is harmonious or reconciled with this a priori self.

103. Some might argue that the sponsorship feature of the anonymous groups offers an example of emotional labor and nurturance being valued in this

contest. And indeed it may. But the original work of nurturance and support provided by the family of origin is devalued.

104. While certainly there are numerous experiences/injuries in life that need to be grappled with and incorporated into a sense of self, the idea that one is largely engaged in a reclamation or restoration project, in recovering from injury when developing the self, assumes, as does the psychology of liberation, that one must recuperate from socialization itself.

105. Arendt, *Human Condition*, 184.

106. See, for example, parts 1 and 2 in Craig Calhoun and John McGowan, eds., *Hannah Arendt and the Meaning of Politics*, vol. 6, *Contradictions of Modernity* (Minneapolis: University of Minnesota Press, 1997).

107. Nancy Hartsock argues that we ought to be concerned about the fact that the decline in the idea of individual agency and authority (suggested in post-structuralist and postmodern accounts of social life) occurs at precisely the moment when formerly marginalized groups demand power and authority: "Foucault on Power: A Theory for Women?" in *Feminism/Postmodernism*, ed. Linda J. Nicholson, *Thinking Gender* (New York: Routledge, 1990 [1987]), 163–64. And African American feminist bell hooks argues that the embracing a culture of self-fulfillment is an important step forward for African Americans. bell hooks, *Sisters of the Yam: Black Women and Self-Recovery* (Boston: South End Press, 1993), 47.

Chapter 6

Epigraph from T. J. Jackson Lears, *No Place of Grace: Antimodernism and the Transformation of American Culture, 1880–1920* (New York: Pantheon, 1981), 306.

1. Thus it does not surprise that the slogan also animated one of the most successful advertising campaigns of the late twentieth century, the U.S. Army recruitment campaign developed by the advertising agency A. W. Ayers. Advertising Age, *The Advertising Century* (New York: Crain's International, 1999), 24.

2. Diana Meyers offers an eminently clear account of this development in "Feminist Perspectives on the Self."

3. Whether the singular self is indeed a notion that will, as Michel Foucault suggests, fade like a face drawn in the sand, remains to be seen. I am inclined to think that the notion of a unified self, if it is to erode, will dissipate more like a face carved in sandstone than one traced in sand. Even with God long ago pronounced dead, the preponderance of

Americans continue to pledge their allegiance to this theistic tradition, Michel Foucault, *The Order of Things: An Archaeology of the Human Sciences*, 1st American ed. (New York: Pantheon Books, 1970), 387.

4. This may, in part, explain the enormous popularity of the Twelve-Step groups, as these groups call for an admission of powerlessness in the face of diverse contingencies. The groups' use of the "Serenity Prayer" encourages individuals to accept what they cannot change, to find courage to change what they can change, and to seek wisdom in discerning the difference between these. This would seem the most obvious of points, but in a culture laden with an ideology of self-control and self-mastery, such an admission actually goes against the grain of a self-mastering world. And some even identify this idea as danger to democratic notions of citizenship, for example, Kaminer, *I'm Dysfunctional, You're Dysfunctional.*

5. See, for example, Sara Ruddick, *Maternal Thinking* (Boston: Beacon Press, 1995 [1989]).

6. See, for example, Susan Douglas and Meredith Michaels, *The Mommy Myth: The Idealization of Motherhood and How It Has Undermined Women* (New York: Free Press, 2004).

7. Although I first heard this observation made in a mothers' support group, I subsequently encountered this idea in the memoir of the sociologist and life coach Martha Beck, *Expecting Adam* (New York: Times Books, 1999), 43.

8. Friedrich Nietzsche, *Thus Spoke Zarathustra*, trans. Walter Kaufmann (New York: Viking Penguin, 1954 [1892]), 96 (emphasis in original). My thanks to Joline Blais for bringing this quotation to my attention.

9. Nietzsche, *Human, All Too Human*, 218.

10. Whitman's "Song of Myself," 51.1326. The parallels between Nietzsche and Whitman—the philosopher of the body and the poet of the body— certainly warrant further consideration. While Nietzsche writes: "body am I entirely and nothing else; and soul is only a word for something about the body," in *Thus Spoke Zarathustra*, Whitman writes, "I have said that the soul is not more than the body," Song of Myself," 48.1269.

11. Marvin Minsky, *The Society of Mind* (New York: Simon and Schuster, 1988).

12. Colin Campbell describes the limits of our notions of self-control and "agency" in "Detraditionalization, Character and the Limits to Agency," in *Detraditionalization: Critical Reflections on Authority and Identity*, eds. Paul Heelas, Scott Lash, and Paul Morris (Oxford: Blackwell, 1996), while Thomas Davenport and John C. Beck describe the idea of a bio-*logical,* but not rational, approach to human organizations, 63. *The Attention Economy: Understanding the New Currency of Business* (Cambridge, Mass.: Harvard Business School Press, 2002).

13. Thomson, *In Conflict No Longer: Self and Society in Contemporary America* (Lanham, Md.: Rowman and Littlefield, 2000).

14. Ibid., 133.

15. Steinem, *Revolution from Within*; Robert Wuthnow, *Sharing the Journey* (New York: Free Press, 1994).

16. In this sense my argument follows Jameson's notion of a "political unconscious," Jameson, *Political Unconscious*. Elaine Showalter's biographies of feminists in her *Inventing Herself* (New York: Scribner, 2001) offers numerous examples of how creating a life can, but does not necessarily, necessitate social change.

17. Kaminer, *I'm Dysfunctional, You're Dysfunctional*; Rapping, *Culture of Recovery*; Reinarman, "Twelve-Step Movement and Advanced Capitalist Culture"; Rice, *Disease of One's Own*. The classification of the recovery movement as a social movement depends on how you define social movements. Some social movement theorists, for example, Doug McAdam, *Political Process and the Development of Black Insurgency* (Chicago: University of Chicago Press, 1982), define social movements as efforts "on the part of excluded groups, to promote or resist changes in the structure of society that involve recourse to noninstitutional forms of political participation"; cited in James M. Jaspers, *The Art of Moral Protest* (Chicago: University of Chicago Press, 1997), 34.

18. Richard Rorty, *Achieving Our Country: Leftist Thought in Twentieth-Century America* (Cambridge, Mass.: Harvard University Press, 1998), 88; Richard Rorty, *Against Bosses, Against Oligarchies* (Chicago: Prickly Paradigm Press, 2002), 32–33.

19. Campbell, "Detraditionalization."

20. Wendy Brown, *States of Injury: Power and Freedom in Late Modernity* (Princeton, N.J.: Princeton University Press, 1995).

21. Taylor, *Rock-a-by Baby*, 152.

22. Lichterman, "Self-Help Reading as Thin Culture," 421.

23. Philip C. McGraw, *Life Strategies: Doing What Works, Doing What Matters* (New York: Hyperion, 1999), 76.

24. McGee, "Hooked on Higher Education," 73–74 and "The Over-Extended Family," in *Reframing the Family*, eds. Cornelia Butler and Micki McGee (New York: Artists Space, 1991), 22–30.

25. McGee, "Hooked on Higher Education," 74.

26. The political philosopher Nancy Fraser describes this as the necessity for a pairing of a politics of identity or mutual recognition with a politics of equitable distribution or redistribution. Without a commitment to an equitable distribution of resources, the politics of identity stumbles into fractious divisions and fails to address the fundamental material concerns

that go hand-in-hand with issues of recognition. Nancy Fraser, "Recognition Without Ethics," *Theory, Culture and Society* 18, nos. 2–3 (2001): 21–42; Nancy Fraser, "Social Justice in the Knowledge Society," keynote address at the conference of the same name sponsored by the Heinrich Böll Foundation, Berlin, May 4, 2001. http://www.bildung2010.de/gutzuwissen/thesen/thesen_fraser.html

27. For an early consideration of this, see Nancy Fraser and Linda Gordon, "Contract Versus Charity: Why Is There No Social Citizenship in the United States? " *Socialist Review* 22, no. 3 (1992): 45–68. Examples in self-help culture abound, with Oprah Winfrey's Angel Network charity and the Anthony Robbins Foundation as just two cases.

28. Theresa L. Ebert, *Ludic Feminism: Postmodernism, Desire, and Labor* (Ann Arbor: University of Michigan Press, 1996); Melucci, *Nomads*. Hillel Schwartz's analysis of the historical contexts of the phrase "social problems" demonstrates that the singular social problem of early nineteenth-century Europe—the inequitable distribution of wealth—gradually gave way to an understanding of social problems as varied and multiple—subject to the expertise of particular academic disciplines and interest groups. Similarly, but in the contemporary context, a politics of economic justice has been supplanted by various politics of representation. "On the Origin of the Phrase "Social Problems," *Social Problems* 44, no. 2 (1997): 276–96.

29. The Italian social theorist Alberto Melucci put this succinctly: "every conflict that transgresses a system of shared rules concerning the distribution of material or symbolic resources is a conflict of identity." Melucci, *Nomads*, 46.

30. Fraser, "Communication, Transformation, and Consciousness-Raising," in *Hannah Arendt and the Meaning of Politics*, eds. Craig Calhoun and John McGowan (Minneapolis: University of Minnesota Press, 1997); Fraser, "Social Justice in the Knowledge Society."

31. Reinarman, "Twelve-Step Movement and Advanced Capitalist Culture"; Rice, *Disease of One's Own.*

32. These factors are discussed by Irvine, *Codependent Forevermore*; Rapping, *Culture of Recovery*; Reinarman, "Twelve-Step Movement and Advanced Capitalist Culture"; Rice, *Disease of One's Own.*

33. Giddens, *Transformation of Intimacy*, 184.

34. Irvine, *Codependent Forevermore*; Rapping, *Culture of Recovery*; Reinarman, "Twelve-Step Movement and Advanced Capitalist Culture"; Rice, *Disease of One's Own.*

35. Of course it was precisely this feature of the recovery movement—an admission of powerlessness—that Wendy Kaminer found most objection-

able. Kaminer's ideal of a rational citizen, in charge of his or her destiny, is at odds with the idea that admitting powerlessness can become a source of strength. Kaminer, *I'm Dysfunctional, You're Dysfunctional*, 151.

36. Rorty, *Contingency*, 53.

37. Bloom quoted in ibid., 29.

38. The political philosopher Ernesto Laclau asks:

> Is the realm of personal self-realization really a *private* realm? It would be so if that self-realization took place in a neutral medium in which individuals could seek unimpeded the fulfilment [*sic*] of their own aims. But this medium is, of course, a myth. A woman searching for her self-realization will find obstacles in the form of male oriented rules which will limit her *personal* aspirations and possibilities. The feminist struggles tending to change those rules will constitute a collective "we" different from the "we" of abstract public citizenship, but the space which these struggles create—remember the motto "the personal is political"—will be no less communitarian and public space that the one in which politic parties intervene and in which elections are found.

Emancipation(s) (New York: Verso, 1996), 120 (emphasis in original).

39. Barbara Epstein, *Political Protest and Cultural Revolution: Nonviolent Direct Action in the 1970s and 1980s* (Berkeley: University of California Press, 1991), Taylor, *Rock-a-by Baby*.

40. In Miller's formulation, the individual strives not to harmonize aspects of the self into an ethical subject (what Foucault calls *rapport a soi*) but rather for an articulation of the disjunctions between one's own experience and normative socially prescribed categories, what Miller calls a *différends a soi*. "The différend," Miller notes, quoting the French theorist François Lyotard, "is an unstable condition, a moment in language where something that must be put into words cannot yet be." Phenomena and experiences that fall outside the "taken for granted" categories of normative thought offer the most fruitful sites for exemplary self-invention. *Well Tempered Self*, 180.

41. The exemplary case that Miller describes are the agitprop political performances of a group of Australian gay activists, the Sisters of Perpetual Indulgence. *Well-Tempered Self*, 202–213. Other examples of these sorts of interventions would be the agitprop work of Andrew Boyd and his group Billionaires for Bush. The Billionaires staged numerous media events during the 2000 and 2004 U.S. presidential elections. Andrew Boyd, "Irony, Meme Warfare, and the Extreme Costume Ball," in *From ACT UP*

to the WTO: Urban Protest and Community Building in the Era of Global-
ization, ed. Benjamin Shepard and Ronald Hayduk (London: Verso,
2002), 245–53; Andrew Boyd, "Truth Is a Virus: Meme Warfare and the
Billionaires for Bush (or Gore)," in *The Cultural Resistance Reader,* ed.
Stephen Duncombe (London: Verso, 2002), 369–78.

42. The possible exception to this was the interesting transposition in Anne
Wilson Schaef, *When Society Becomes an Addict* (San Francisco: Harper
and Row, 1987), where the addiction metaphor is moved from the register
of the individual to the collectivity.

43. Fraser, "Communication, Transformation, and Consciousness-Raising,"
166–75; Fraser, "Social Justice in the Knowledge Society."

44. For a more detailed discussion of these ideas, see Fraser, "Communication,
Transformation, and Consciousness-Raising."

45. I am indebted to the analysis and argument offered by the community
organizer Tema Okun, "They Should Be Our People," *Social Policy* 23, no.
2 (1992): 44–48. The Italian social theorist and sociologist Alberto Melucci
observed a similar trend: when there was no longer any space in organizations for personal needs, individuals tended to drop out, finding opportunities for personal growth more available in religious sects and, to some
extent, in drug culture. Melucci, *Nomads,* 59.

46. Ibid., 205.

47. Epstein, *Political Protest and Cultural Revolution: Nonviolent Direct Action
in the 1970s and 1980s;* Taylor, *Rock-a-by Baby.*

48. See, for example, Joshua Gamson, "Silence, Death, and the Invisible
Enemy: AIDS, Activism and Social Movement 'Newness,'" *Social Problems*
36 no. 43 (1989): 351–67; Shepard and Hayduk, *From ACT UP to the
WTO.*

49. Andrew Boyd, "The Web Rewires the Movement," *Nation* 277, no. 4,
August 4, 2003, 13–18.

50. While a thorough consideration of the various factors that contribute to
the success of social movements is beyond the scope of this project, it is
worth considering what social movement theorists have observed. The
most critical point is that the development of an effective social movement
requires much more than simply an aggrieved community. If grievances
and deprivation were all that were required, effective protest movements
would abound. Rather, what seems to be required for a successful
movement is a convergence of factors, among them: (1) the identification
of opportunities in the political environment; (2) the presence of existing
organizations in the aggrieved community; (3) the population's assessment
of its chances for success (assessment of benefits of participation outweigh
the costs of participating); and (4) an array of other resources, including

the availability of recruitment networks, effective methods of funding, and the participation of experienced, even professional, organizers. The development of social movements requires the identification of a social problem, the development of shared interest among a group of individual actors, and then the collective actions of this group. See, for example, Jaspers, *Art of Moral Protest*; Melucci, *Nomads*.

Appendix

1. Lichterman, "Self-Help Reading as Thin Culture," 435; Simonds, *Women and Self-Help Culture*, 1, 49, 66; Starker, *Oracle*, 8.

2. Schneider and Dornbusch, *Popular Religion*.

3. John W. Santrock, Ann M. Minnett, and Barbara D. Campbell, *The Authoritative Guide to Self-Help Books* (New York: Guilford Press, 1994), xv–xvi.

4. Starker, *Oracle*, 118–20.

5. Simonds, *Women and Self-Help Culture*, 5, 138–39.

6. Schor, *Overworked American*, xv. Deborah Tannen's objections to being categorized as self-help reading are discussed in Deborah Cameron, *Verbal Hygiene* (London: Routledge, 1995), 194. The sociologist Neil McLaughlin observes that writing a book that becomes a popular success, along with working in a crossdisciplinary fashion, all but ensures that one's work will lose its long-term legitimacy. "How to Become a Forgotten Intellectual: Intellectual Movements and the Rise and Fall of Erich Fromm," *Sociological Forum* 13, no. 2 (1998): 215–46. Similarly, C. Wright Mills was criticized as a "popularizer" rather than a "professional sociologist." Kevin Mattson, *Intellectuals in Action: The Origins of the New Left and Radical Liberalism* (University Park: Pennsylvania State University Press, 2002), 57.

7. For example, Hochschild, "Commerical Spirit of Intimate Life," and Simonds, *Women and Self-Help Culture*.

8. Hochschild, "Commerical Spirit of Intimate Life"; Simonds, *Women and Self-Help Culture*; Starker, *Oracle*.

9. Randy Martin considers this development in *Financialization of Daily Life*.

Bibliography

Advertising Age. *The Advertising Century*. New York: Crain's International, 1999.

Alger, Horatio Jr. *Struggling Upward or Luke Larkin's Luck*. Philadelphia: Porter and Coates, 1890.

Allison, Tammy Tierney. "'Self-Help' Satisfies Need for Quick Fix." *Business First*. Buffalo, September 14, 1998, v. 14, no. 49, B2, Available online at: http://buffalo.bcentral.com/buffalo/stories/1998/09/14/editorial2.html. Last viewed: January 5, 2005.

Althusser, Louis. "Ideology and Ideological State Apparatuses: Notes Toward an Investigation." In *Lenin and Philosophy and Other Essays*. New York: Monthly Review Press, 1971.

Anthony, Carolyn. "Story Behind the Bestseller: The Long, Winding and Happy Fate of *the Road Less Traveled*." *Publishers Weekly* 228, no. 13 (1985): 76–77.

Arendt, Hannah. *The Human Condition*. Chicago: University of Chicago Press, 1958.

Aronowitz, Stanley, and William DiFazio. *The Jobless Future: Sci-Tech and the Dogma of Work*. Minneapolis: University of Minnesota Press, 1994.

Arthur, Michael B., and Denise M. Rousseau, eds. *The Boundaryless Career: A New Employment Principle for a New Organizational Era*. New York: Oxford University Press, 1996.

Babbitt, Dave. *Downscaling: Simplify and Enrich Your Lifestyle*. Chicago: Moody Press, 1993.

Babcock, Marguerite, and Christine McKay, eds. *Challenging Codependency: Feminist Critiques.* Toronto: University of Toronto Press, 1995.

Barton, Bruce. *The Man Nobody Knows.* Indianapolis: Bobbs-Merrill, 1924.

Bateson, Mary Catherine. *Composing a Life.* New York: Penguin, 1990 [1989].

Bauder, Don. "Dreamlife Has Trouble Making Its Dreams Come True." *San Diego Union-Tribune*, January 21, 2001, H2.

———. "Robbins Donates Millions of Shares Back to Ailing Dot-Com." *San Diego Union-Tribune*, February 3, 2001, C3.

Bauman, Zygmunt. *Community.* Cambridge: Polity Press, 2001.

———. *Liquid Modernity.* Cambridge: Polity Press, 2000.

Beattie, Melody. *Beyond Codependency: And Getting Better All the Time.* San Francisco: Harper, 1989.

———. *Codependent No More: How to Stop Controlling Others and Start Caring for Yourself.* New York: Harper, 1987.

Beck, Martha N. *Expecting Adam.* New York: Times Books, 1999.

Beigel, Greta. "The Path to the Person Inside." *Los Angeles Times*, July 23, 1995, E1.

Bell, Daniel. *The Cultural Contradictions of Capitalism.* New York: Basic Books, 1976.

Bellah, Robert N., Richard Madsen, William M. Sullivan, Ann Swidler, and Steven M. Tipton. *Habits of the Heart: Individualism and Commitment in American Life.* New York: Harper and Row, 1985.

Benjamin, Jessica. *The Bonds of Love: Psychoanalysis, Feminism, and the Problem of Domination.* New York: Pantheon Books, 1988.

Benjamin, Walter. "The Work of Art in the Age of Mechanical Reproduction." In *Illuminations* (pp. 217–52). New York: Schocken Books, 1968 [1935].

Berenson, Alex. "Motivating Investors: Anthony Robbins Makes an Internet Play." *New York Times*, January 8, 2000, C-1, C-4.

Berger, John. *Ways of Seeing.* London: Penguin Books, 1972.

Berger, Leslie. "*Our Bodies* Is Recast for Latina Culture." *New York Times*, February 13, 2000, F-8.

Berman, Marshall. *The Politics of Authenticity: Radical Individualism and the Emergence of Modern Society.* Edited by Michael Walzer. 1st ed. New York: Atheneum, 1970.

Bersani, Leo. *Baudelaire and Freud.* Berkeley: University of California Press, 1977.

Blanchard, Kenneth, and Spencer Johnson. *The One Minute Manager.* New York: Berkley Books, 1981.

Boldt, Laurence G. *Zen and the Art of Making a Living: A Practical Guide to Creative Career Change.* New York: Penguin, 1992.

Bolles, Richard Nelson. *What Color Is Your Parachute? A Practical Manual for Job-Hunters and Career-Changers.* Berkeley: Ten Speed Press, 1972. Reprint, revised annually since 1975. The following editions are cited or referred to herein: 1977, 1979, 1981, 1982, 1987, 1988, 1989, 1990, 1992, 1996, 1997, 2000, 2001, 2002.

Bolotin, Susan. "God and Freud: What Makes a Bestseller?" *Vogue*, December 1985, 317.

Boyd, Andrew. *Daily Afflictions: The Agony of Being Connected to Everything in the Universe*. New York: Norton, 2002.

———. "Irony, Meme Warfare, and the Extreme Costume Ball." In *From ACT UP to the WTO: Urban Protest and Community Building in the Era of Globalization*, edited by Benjamin Shepard and Ronald Hayduk (pp. 245–53). London: Verso, 2002.

———. "Truth Is a Virus: Meme Warfare and the Billionaires for Bush (or Gore)." In *The Cultural Resistance Reader*, edited by Stephen Duncombe (pp. 369–78). New York: Verso, 2002.

———. "The Web Rewires the Movement," *Nation* 277, no. 4, August 4, 2003, 13–18.

Bradshaw, John. *Homecoming: Reclaiming and Championing Your Inner Child*. New York: Bantam, 1990.

Braverman, Harry. *Labor and Monopoly Capital: The Degradation of Work in the Twentieth Century*. New York: Monthly Review Press, 1974.

Breathnach, Sarah Ban. *Simple Abundance: A Daybook of Comfort and Joy*. New York: Warner Books, 1995.

Brennan, Teresa. *Exhausting Modernity: Grounds for a New Economy*. London: Routledge, 2000.

———. *Globalization and Its Terrors: Daily Life in the West*. London: Routledge, 2003.

Brennan, Teresa, and Martin Jay, eds. *Vision in Context: Historical and Contemporary Perspectives on Sight*. New York: Routledge.

Bronson, Po. *What Should I Do with My Life?* New York: Random House, 2002.

Brooks, David. *Bobos in Paradise: The New Upper Class and How They Got There*. New York: Simon and Schuster, 2000.

Brown, Helen Gurley. *Having It All*. New York: Pocket Books, 1982.

———. *I'm Wild Again: Snippets from My Life and a Few Brazen Thoughts*. New York: St. Martin's Press, 2000.

———. *Sex and the Single Girl*. New York: Avon Books, 1962.

Brown, Mason. *Who Cut the Cheese?: A Cutting-Edge Way of Surviving Change by Shifting the Blame*. New York: Simon and Schuster, 2000.

Brown, Wendy. *States of Injury: Power and Freedom in Late Modernity*. Princeton, N.J.: Princeton University Press, 1995.

Bryan, Mark, with Julia Cameron and Catherine Allen. *The Artist's Way at Work: Riding the Dragon*. New York: Morrow, 1998.

Butler, Judith. *Gender Trouble: Feminism and the Subversion of Identity.* New York: Routledge, 1990.

Calhoun, Craig, ed. *Habermas and the Public Sphere.* Cambridge, Mass.: MIT Press, 1992.

Calhoun, Craig, and John McGowan, eds. *Hannah Arendt and the Meaning of Politics.* Edited by Craig Calhoun. Vol. 6, *Contradictions of Modernity.* Minneapolis: University of Minnesota Press, 1997.

Cameron, Deborah. *Verbal Hygiene.* London: Routledge, 1995.

Cameron, Julia. *The Artist's Way: A Spiritual Path to Higher Creativity.* New York: Tarcher, 1992.

———. *The Right to Write.* New York: Putnam, 1998.

———. *Vein of Gold: A Journey to Your Creative Heart.* New York: Putnam, 1996.

Campbell, Colin. "Detraditionalization, Character and the Limits to Agency." In *Detraditionalization: Critical Reflections on Authority and Identity*, edited by Paul Heelas, Scott Lash and Paul Morris (pp. 149–69). Oxford: Blackwell, 1996.

———. *The Romantic Ethic and the Spirit of Modern Consumerism.* Cambridge: Blackwell, 1987.

Canetti, Elias. *Crowds and Power [Masse und Macht].* Translated by Carol Stewart. New York: Seabury Press, 1978.

Carlin, George. "People Who Oughta Be Killed: Self-Help Books." *Complaints and Grievances.* Atlantic, 2001. Audio compact disc.

Carlson, Richard. *Don't Sweat the Small Stuff . . . And It's All Small Stuff.* New York: Hyperion, 1997.

———. *Don't Sweat the Small Stuff for Teens.* New York: Hyperion, 2000.

Carnegie, Andrew. *The Empire of Business.* New York: Doubleday Page, 1902.

Carnegie, Dale. *How to Win Friends and Influence People.* New York: Simon and Schuster, 1936.

Castañeda, Carlos. *Journey to Ixtlan.* New York: Simon and Schuster, 1972.

Cawelti, John G. *Apostles of the Self-Made Man.* Chicago: University of Chicago Press, 1988 [1965].

Chast, Roz. "The Last Word: Mom's World." *Ladies Home Journal,* May 1997, 192.

Chenoweth, Lawrence. *The American Dream of Success: The Search for Self in the Twentieth Century.* North Scitutate, Mass.: Duxbury Press, 1974.

Chernin, Kim. *The Hungry Self: Women, Eating and Identity.* New York: Perennial Library, 1985.

Chodorow, Nancy. *The Reproduction of Mothering: Psychoanalysis and the Sociology of Gender.* Berkeley: University of California Press, 1978.

Chopra, Deepak. *Ageless Body, Timeless Mind.* New York: Harmony Books, 1993.

———. *Creating Affluence: Wealth Consciousness in the Field of All Possibilities.* San Rafael, Calif.: New World, 1993.

———. *The A-to-Z Steps to a Richer Life*. New York: Barnes and Noble Books, 1993.

———. *The Seven Spiritual Laws of Success*. San Rafael, Calif.: New World Library, 1994.

Coeyman, Marjorie. "Everybody Can Use a Little Help." *Christian Science Monitor*, August 8, 2000, 13. online ed.

Cohen, Herb. *You Can Negotiate Anything*. New York: Bantam, 1980.

Colapinto, John. "M. Scott Peck at the End of the Road." *Rolling Stone*, October 19, 1995, 80–82, 86, 164.

Conwell, Russell H. *Acres of Diamonds*. New York: Harper, 1915.

Covey, Sean. *The Seven Habits of Highly Effective Teens*. New York: Simon and Schuster, 1998.

Covey, Stephen R. *The Divine Center*. Salt Lake City: Bookcraft Publishers, 1982.

———. *How to Succeed with People*. Salt Lake City: Deseret Books, 1971.

———. *Principle-Centered Leadership*. New York: Summit, 1990.

———. *The Seven Habits of Highly Effective People*. New York: Simon and Schuster, 1989.

———. *Spiritual Roots of Human Relations*. Salt Lake City: Deseret Books, 1976.

Covey, Stephen R., and Truman G. Madsen. *Marriage and Family: Gospel Insights*. Salt Lake City: Deseret Books, 1983.

Covey, Stephen R., A. Roger Merrill, and Rebecca R. Merrill. *First Things First*. New York: Simon and Schuster, 1994.

Cowan, Connell, and Melvyn Kinder. *Smart Women, Foolish Choices: Finding the Right Men, Avoiding the Wrong Ones*. New York: Signet, 1985.

———. *Women Men Love, Women Men Leave*. New York: Signet, 1987.

Creative America: A Report to the President. Washington, D.C.: President's Committee on the Arts and the Humanities, 1997.

Csikszentmihalyi, Mihaly. *The Evolving Self: A Psychology for the Third Millennium*. New York: HarperCollins, 1993.

———. *Flow: The Psychology of Optimal Experience: Steps toward Enhancing the Quality of Life*. New York: HarperPerennial, 1990.

Cushman, Philip. *Constructing the Self, Constructing America: A Cultural History of Psychotherapy*. Reading, Mass.: Addison-Wesley, 1995.

———. "Why the Self Is Empty: Toward a Historically Situated Psychology." *American Psychologist* 45, no. 5 (1990): 599–611.

Davenport, Thomas H., and John C. Beck. *The Attention Economy: Understanding the New Currency of Business*. Cambridge, Mass.: Harvard Business School Press, 2002.

Dean, Carolyn J. *The Self and Its Pleasures: Bataille, Lacan, and the History of the Decentered Subject*. Ithaca, N.Y.: Cornell University Press, 1992.

de Beauvoir, Simone. *The Second Sex*. Translated by H. M. Parshley. New York: Vintage Books, 1974 [1952].

Decker, Jeffrey Louis. *Made in America: Self-Styled Success from Horatio Alger to Oprah Winfrey*. Minneapolis: University of Minnesota Press, 1997.

de Graaf, John, ed. *Take Back Your Time: Fighting Overwork and Time Poverty in America*. San Francisco: Berrett-Koehler, 2003.

de Lauretis, Teresa. *Alice Doesn't: Feminism, Semiotics, Cinema*. Bloomington: Indiana University Press, 1984.

Derrida, Jacques. "Structure, Sign and Play in the Discourse of the Human Sciences." In *Writing and Difference* (pp. 278–93). Chicago: University of Chicago Press, 1978 [1967].

Dinnerstein, Dorothy. *The Mermaid and the Minotaur: Sexual Arrangements and Human Malaise*. New York: Harper and Row, 1976.

Donohue, John W. "The Book Much Read." *America*, April 19, 1997, 26–29.

Donzelot, Jacques. "Pleasure in Work." In *The Foucault Effect: Studies in Governmentality*, edited by Graham Burchell, Colin Gordon and Peter Miller (pp. 251–80). Chicago: University of Chicago Press, 1991 [1980].

Douglas, Susan, and Meredith Michaels. *The Mommy Myth: The Idealization of Motherhood and How It Has Undermined Women*. New York: Free Press, 2004.

Dreyfus, Hubert L. and Paul Rabinow. *Michel Foucault: Beyond Structuralism and Hermeneutics*. Chicago: University of Chicago Press, 1983.

Drucker, Peter F. *Post-Capitalist Society*. New York: HarperCollins, 1993. Reprint, Harper Business, 1994.

Du Bois, W. E. B. *The Souls of Black Folks*. New York: Bantam, 1989 [1903].

Dyer, Wayne. *Pulling Your Own Strings*. New York: Crowell, 1978.

———. *Your Erroneous Zones*. New York: Funk and Wagnalls, 1976.

Ebert, Theresa L. *Ludic Feminism: Postmodernism, Desire, and Labor*. Ann Arbor: University of Michigan Press, 1996.

Economic Report of the President. Washington, D.C.: U.S. Government Printing Office, 2000, 2003.

Ehrenreich, Barbara, Elizabeth Hess, and Gloria Jacobs. *Re-Making Love: The Feminization of Sex*. Garden City, N.Y.: Anchor Press, 1986.

Eisenstein, Elizabeth L. *The Printing Press as an Agent of Change*. 2 vols. Vol. 1. Cambridge: Cambridge University Press, 1979.

Elgin, Duane. *Voluntary Simplicity: Toward a Way of Life That Is Outwardly Simple, Inwardly Rich*. New York: Quill, 1993.

Elias, Norbert. *The Civilizing Process*. Translated by Edmund Jephcott. New York: Urizen Press, 1978.

Eliasoph, Nina. *Avoiding Politics: How Americans Produce Apathy in Everyday Life*. Cambridge: Cambridge University Press, 1998.

Ellul, Jacques. *The Humiliation of the Word*. Translated by Joyce Main Hanks. Grand Rapids, Mich.: Eerdmans, 1985.

Elster, Jon, ed. *The Multiple Self: Studies in Rationality and Social Change*. Cambridge: Cambridge University Press, 1985.

Emerson, Ralph Waldo. *Self Reliance*. 1841. Reprinted in *Self-Reliance and Other Essays*. New York: Dover, 1993.

———. *Success, Greatness, Immortality*. Boston: Houghton, Osgood, 1880 [1870].

Epstein, Barbara. *Political Protest and Cultural Revolution: Nonviolent Direct Action in the 1970s and 1980s*. Berkeley: University of California Press, 1991.

Ewen, Stuart. *All Consuming Images: The Politics of Style in Contemporary Culture*. New York: Basic Books, 1988.

———. *Captains of Consciousness: Advertising and the Social Roots of the Consumer Culture*. New York: McGraw-Hill, 1976.

———. *PR! A Social History of Spin*. New York: Basic Books, 1996.

Fabunmi, Constance, Loretta Frederick, and Mary Jarvis Bicknese. "The Codependency Trap." In *Challenging Codependency: Feminist Critiques*, edited by Marguerite Babcock and Christine McKay (pp. 88–92). Toronto: University of Toronto Press, 1995.

Faludi, Susan. *Backlash: The Undeclared War Against American Women*. New York: Crown, 1991.

Featherstone, Mike. "Postmodernism and the Aestheticization of Everyday Life." In *Modernity and Identity*, edited by Scott Lash and Jonathan Friedman (pp. 265–90). Oxford: Blackwell, 1992.

Fellman, Anita Clair, and Michael Fellman. *Making Sense of Self: Medical Advice Literature in Late Nineteenth-Century America*. Philadelphia: University of Pennsylvania Press, 1981.

Fisher, Roger, and William Ury. *Getting to Yes: Negotiating Agreement without Giving In*. New York: Penguin, 1981.

Florida, Richard. *The Rise of the Creative Class*. New York: Basic Books, 2002.

Forward, Susan, with Craig Buck. *Toxic Parents: Overcoming Their Hurtful Legacy and Reclaiming Your Life*. New York: Bantam, 1989.

Forward, Susan, and Joan Torres. *Men Who Hate Women and the Women Who Love Them: When Loving Hurts and You Don't Know Why*. New York: Bantam, 1986.

Foucault, Michel. *Ethics, Subjectivity and Truth*. Translated by Robert Hurley. Edited by Paul Rabinow. 3 vols. Vol. 1, *Essential Works of Michel Foucault, 1954–1984*. New York: The New Press, 1994.

———. "How We Behave: Sex, Food and Other Ethical Matters." Interview by Hubert L. Dreyfus and Paul Rabinow. *Vanity Fair* 46, no. 9 (1983): 60–69.

———. *Madness and Civilization: A History of Insanity in the Age of Reason*. Translated by Richard Howard. New York: Vintage, 1973 [1965].

———. "On the Geneaology of Ethics: An Overview of a Work in Progress." In *Michel Foucault: Beyond Structuralism and Hermeneutics*, 2nd ed. Hubert L.

Dreyfus and Paul Rabinow (pp. 229–52). Chicago: University of Chicago Press, 1983.

———. *Madness and Civilization: A History of Insanity in the Age of Reason.* Translated by Richard Howard. New York: Vintage, 1973 [1965].

———. *The Order of Things: An Archaeology of the Human Sciences.* New York: Pantheon Books, 1970.

Franklin, Benjamin. "The Autobiography of Benjamin Franklin." In *The Autobiography and Other Writings* (pp. 3–197). New York: Penguin, 1986 [1791].

Fraser, Nancy. "Communication, Transformation, and Consciousness-Raising." In *Hannah Arendt and the Meaning of Politics*, edited by Craig Calhoun and John McGowan (pp. 166–75). Minneapolis: University of Minnesota Press, 1997.

———. "Recognition Without Ethics." *Theory, Culture and Society* 18, nos. 2–3 (2001): 21–42.

———. "Rethinking the Public Sphere: A Contribution to the Critique of Actually Existing Democracy." In *Habermas and the Public Sphere*, edited by Craig Calhoun (pp. 109–42). Cambridge, Mass.: MIT Press, 1992.

———. "Social Justice in the Knowledge Society." Keynote address at the Social Justice in the Knowledge Society conference, sponsored by the Heinrich Böll Foundation, Berlin, May 4, 2001. Available online at: http://www.bildung2010. de/gutzuwissen/thesen/thesen_fraser.html. Last viewed, January 16, 2005.

———. *Unruly Practices: Power, Discourse, and Gender in Contemporary Social Theory.* Minneapolis: University of Minnesota Press, 1989.

Fraser, Nancy, and Linda Gordon. "Contract Versus Charity: Why Is There No Social Citizenship in the United States?" *Socialist Review* 22, no. 3 (1992): 45–68.

Freud, Sigmund. "The Interpretation of Dreams." In *The Standard Edition of the Complete Psychological Works of Sigmund Freud*, edited by James Strachey vol. 4–5, pp. xi–338, 99–627. London: Hogarth Press, 1900.

———. "The Psychopathology of Everyday Life." In *The Standard Edition.* Vol. 6, pp. 1–290. London: Hogarth Press, 1901.

Friedan, Betty. *The Feminine Mystique.* New York: Norton, 1974 [1963].

Fulghum, Robert. *All I Really Need to Know I Learned in Kindergarten.* New York: Villard, 1988 [1986].

———. *It Was on Fire When I Lay Down on It.* New York: Villard Books, 1988.

Gal, Susan. "A Semiotics of the Public/Private Distinction." *Differences* 13, no. 1 (2002): 77–95.

Gamson, Joshua. "Silence, Death, and the Invisible Enemy: AIDS Activism and Social Movement 'Newness.'" *Social Problems* 36, no. 4 (1989): 351–67.

Garfinkel, Harold. *Studies in Ethnomethodology.* Englewood Cliffs, N.J.: Prentice-Hall, 1967.

Gartner, Alan, and Frank Riessman, ed. *The Self-Help Revolution*. Edited by Bernard L. Bloom series ed. Vol. 10, *Community Psychology Series*. New York: Human Sciences Press, 1984.

Gawain, Shakti. *Creative Visualization*. New York: Bantam, 1985 [1979].

——. *Living in the Light*. Mill Valley, Calif.: Whatever Publishing, 1986.

Gergen, Kenneth J. *The Saturated Self: Dilemmas of Identity in Contemporary Life*. New York: Basic Books, 1991.

Giddens, Anthony. *The Transformation of Intimacy: Sexuality, Love and Eroticism in Modern Societies*. Stanford: Stanford University Press, 1992.

Glaser, Connie, and Barbara Steinberg Smalley. *Swim with the Dolphins: How Women Can Succeed in Corporate America on Their Own Terms*. New York: Warner Books, 1995.

Gleick, James. *Faster: The Acceleration of Just about Everything*. New York: Random House, 1999.

Golden, Lonnie, and Deborah M. Figart, eds. *Working Time: Internal Trends, Theory and Policy Perspectives*. London: Routledge, 2000.

Griffin, N. "The Charismatic Kid." *Life*, March 1985, 41–44.

Grimes, William. "Mega-Seller, Great Gift." *New York Times*, November 8, 1992, sec. 9, 11.

Grossmann, John. "Tom Peters' Exclamation Point World." *SKY*, October 2000, 92–97.

Habermas, Jürgen. *The Structural Transformation of the Public Sphere*. Translated by Thomas Burger and Frederick Lawrence. Cambridge, Mass.: MIT Press, 1992.

Hagen, Kay. "Codependency and the Myth of Recovery: A Feminist Scrutiny." In *Challenging Codependency*, edited by Marguerite Babcock and Christine McKay (pp. 198–206). Toronto: University of Toronto Press, 1995.

Hall, Catherine. "The Early Formation of Victorian Domestic Ideology." In *Fit Work for Women*, edited by Sandra Burman (pp. 15–32). London: Croom Helm, 1981.

Hardt, Michael, and Antonio Negri. *Empire*. Cambridge, Mass.: Harvard University Press, 2000.

——. *Labor of Dionysus: A Critique of the State-Form*. Minneapolis: University of Minnesota Press, 1994.

Hartsock, Nancy. "Foucault on Power: A Theory for Women?" In *Feminism/Postmodernism*, edited by Linda J. Nicholson (pp. 157–75). New York: Routledge, 1990 [1987].

Harvey, David. *The Condition of Postmodernity: An Enquiry into the Origins of Cultural Change*. Cambridge, Mass.: Blackwell, 1989.

Heelas, Paul, Scott Lash, and Paul Morris, eds. *Detraditionalization: Critical Reflections on Authority and Identity*. Oxford: Blackwell, 1996.

Heilbrun, Carolyn G. *The Education of a Woman: The Life of Gloria Steinem*. New York: Dial Press, 1995.

Heintz, James, Nancy Folbre, and the Center for Popular Economics. *The Ultimate Field Guide to the U.S. Economy*. New York: New Press, 2000.

Herr, Edwin L. "The Emerging History of Career Education: A Summary View Prepared for the National Advisory Council on Career Education." Washington, D.C., 1976.

Hewlett, Sylvia Ann. *A Lesser Life: The Myth of Women's Liberation in America*. New York: Morrow, 1986.

Hilkey, Judy. *Character Is Capital: Success Manuals and Manhood in Gilded Age America*. Chapel Hill: University of North Carolina Press, 1997.

Hobbes, Thomas. *Leviathan*. Indianapolis: Hackett, 1994 [1651].

Hobsbawm, Eric. *Primitive Rebels*. New York: Norton, 1959.

Hochberg, Ilene. *Who Stole My Cheese? An A-Mazing Way to Make More Money from the Poor Suckers That You Cheated in Your Work and in Your Life*. New York: Union Square Press, 2002.

Hochschild, Arlie Russell. *The Commercialization of Intimate Life: Notes from Home and Work*. Berkeley: University of California Press, 2003.

———. "The Commercial Spirit of Intimate Life and the Abduction of Feminism: Signs from Women's Advice Books." *Theory, Culture and Society* 11, no. 2 (1994): 1–24.

———. *The Managed Heart: The Commercialization of Human Feeling*. Berkeley: University of California Press, 1983.

———. *The Time Bind: When Work Becomes Home and Home Becomes Work*. New York: Metropolitan, 1997.

Hochschild, Arlie Russell, with Anne Machung. *The Second Shift*. New York: Avon, 1990 [1989].

hooks, bell. *Sisters of the Yam: Black Women and Self-Recovery*. Boston: South End Press, 1993.

Huizinga, Johan. *Homo Ludens*. London: Routledge and Kegan Paul, 1949.

Hyde, Lewis. *The Gift: Imagination and the Erotic Life of Property*. New York: Vintage Books, 1979.

Irvine, Leslie. *Codependent Forevermore: The Invention of Self in a Twelve Step Group*. Chicago: University of Chicago Press, 1999.

Isaacson, Walter. *Benjamin Franklin: An American Life*. New York: Simon and Schuster, 2003.

James, Henry. *The Portrait of a Lady*. New York: Oxford University Press, 1999 [1880].

James, William. *The Letters of William James*. Boston: Little, Brown, 1926.

Jameson, Fredric. *The Political Unconscious: Narratives as a Socially Symbolic Act*. Ithaca, N.Y.: Cornell University Press, 1981.

———. *Postmodernism, or, the Cultural Logic of Late Capitalism.* Durham, N.C.: Duke University Press, 1991.

Jaspers, James M. *The Art of Moral Protest.* Chicago: University of Chicago Press, 1997.

Jay, Martin. "Scopic Regimes of Modernity." In *Modernity and Identity*, edited by Scott Lash and Jonathan Friedman (pp. 178–95). Oxford: Blackwell, 1992.

Johnson, Spencer. *Who Moved My Cheese?: An Amazing Way to Deal with Change in Your Work and in Your Life.* New York: Putnam, 1998.

Jones, Laurie Beth. *Jesus CEO: Using Ancient Wisdom for Visionary Leadership.* New York: Hyperion, 1996.

———. *The Path: Creating Your Mission Statement for Work and Life.* New York: Hyperion, 1996.

Kaminer, Wendy. *I'm Dysfunctional, You're Dysfunctional.* Reading, Mass.: Addison-Wesley, 1992.

Kassorla, Irene C. *Go for It! How to Win at Love, Work and Play.* New York: Delacorte, 1984.

———. *Nice Girls Do—and Now You Can Too!* Los Angeles: Stratford Press, 1980.

Katz, Alfred H., and Eugene I. Bender. *The Strength in Us: Self-Help Groups in the Modern World.* New York: Franklin Watts, 1976.

Kaufman, Gershen, Lev Raphael and Pamela Espeland. *Stick Up for Yourself: Every Kid's Guide to Personal Power and Positive Self-Esteem.* Minneapolis, Minn.: Free Press, 1999.

Kaufman-Rosen, Leslie. "Getting in Touch with Your Inner President." *Newsweek*, January 16, 1995, 72.

Kelley, Mary. "Petitioning with the Left Hand: Educating Women in Benjamin Franklin's America." In *Benjamin Franklin and Women*, edited by Larry E. Tise (pp. 83–101). University Park: Pennsylvania State University Press, 2000.

Kerber, Linda K. "Separate Spheres, Female Worlds, Woman's Place: The Rhetoric of Women's History." *Journal of American History* 75, no. 1 (1988): 9–39.

Klauser, Henriette Anne. *Put Your Heart on Paper: Staying Connected in a Loose-Ends World.* New York: Bantam, 1995.

———. *Write It Down, Make It Happen: Knowing What You Want and Getting It!* New York: Scribner, 2000.

Klein, Julia M. "A Noodler's Chicken Soup." *Nation* 272, no. 10 (2001): 31–34.

Korda, Michael. *Power! How to Get It, How to Use It.* New York: Ballantine, 1975.

Krestan, Jo-Ann, and Claudia Bepko. "Codependency: The Social Reconstruction of Female Experience." In *Challenging Codependency: Feminist Critiques*, edited by Marguerite Babcock and Christine McKay (pp. 93–110). Toronto: University of Toronto Press, 1995.

Kushner, Harold S. *When All You've Ever Wanted Isn't Enough.* New York: Simon and Schuster, 1986.

Lacan, Jacques. *Écrits: A Selection*. Translated by Alan Sheridan. New York: Norton, 1977 [1966].

Laclau, Ernesto. *Emancipation(s)*. London: Verso, 1996.

Laing, R. D. *The Divided Self: An Existential Study in Sanity and Madness*. Middlesex, England: Penguin Books, 1965.

Lakoff, George, and Mark Johnson. *Metaphors We Live By*. Chicago: University of Chicago Press, 1980.

———. *Philosophy in the Flesh: The Embodied Mind and Its Challege to Western Thought*. New York: Basic Books, 1999.

Langstaff, Margaret. "Beating Those Workplace Blues." *Publishers Weekly* 241, no. 15 (1994): 35–40.

Lasch, Christopher. *The Culture of Narcissism: American Life in an Age of Diminishing Expectations*. New York: Warner Books, 1979.

———. *The Minimal Self: Psychic Survival in Troubled Times*. New York: Norton, 1984.

Lash, Scott. "Discourse or Figure? Postmodernism as a 'Regime of Signification.'" *Theory, Culture and Society* 5 (1988): 311–36.

Lash, Scott, and John Urry. *The End of Organized Capitalism*. Madison: University of Wisconsin Press, 1987.

Lasswell, Mark. "Habit Former." *People*, June 12, 1995, 81–82.

Lazzarato, Maurizio. "Immaterial Labor." In *Radical Thought in Italy: A Potential Politics*, edited by Paolo Virno and Michael Hardt (pp. 133–47). Minneapolis: University of Minnesota Press, 1996.

Le Bon, Gustave. *The Crowd: A Study of the Popular Mind*. London: Unwin, 1896.

Lears, T. J. Jackson. *Fables of Abundance: A Cultural History of Advertising in America*. New York: Basic Books, 1994.

———. *No Place of Grace: Antimodernism and the Transformation of American Culture 1880–1920*. New York: Pantheon, 1981.

Leerhsen, Charles. "Peck's Path to Inner Peace." *Newsweek*, November 18, 1985, 79.

Lefebvre, Henri. *Everyday Life in the Modern World*. Translated by Sacha Rabinovitch. New York: Harper and Row, 1971.

Levine, Art. "Peak Performance Is Tiring." *U.S. News and World Report*, February 24, 1997, 53–55.

Lewis, Michael. "The Artist in the Grey Flannel Pajamas." *New York Times Magazine*, March 5, 2000, 45–48.

Lichterman, Paul. "Self-Help Reading as Thin Culture." *Media, Culture and Society* 14, no. 3 (1992): 421–47.

"Lifestyle Makeovers: Energy Drains." *The Oprah Winfrey Show*. June 12, 2000. Burrell's transcripts.

Lifton, Robert Jay. *The Protean Self*. Chicago: University of Chicago Press, 1993.

Lind, Richard E. *The Seeking Self: The Quest for Self Improvement and the Creation of Personal Suffering*. Grand Rapids, Mich.: Phanes Press, 2000.

Lockwood, Georgene Muller. *The Complete Idiot's Guide to Simple Living*. Indianapolis: Alpha, 2000.

Lopez, Claude-Anne, and Eugenia W. Herbert. *The Private Franklin: The Man and His Family*. New York: Norton, 1975.

Lyotard, Jean François. *Discours, Figure*. Paris: Klincksieck, 1971.

Mackay, Harvey B. *Swim with the Sharks Without Being Eaten Alive*. New York: Ballantine, 1988.

Maddox, Brenda. *Rosalind Franklin: The Dark Lady of DNA*. New York: HarperCollins, 2002.

Mandel, Ernest. *Late Capitalism*. Translated by Joris De Bres. Atlantic Highlands, N.J.: Humanities Press, 1975.

Marcuse, Herbert. *An Essay on Liberation*. Boston: Beacon Press, 1969.

Margolis, Diane Rothbard. *The Fabric of Self: A Theory of Ethics and Emotions*. New Haven: Yale University Press, 1998.

Martin, Randy. *Financialization of Daily Life*. Philadelphia: Temple University Press, 2002.

Marx, Karl. *Capital*. Vol., 1, Translated by Ben Fowkes. New York: Vintage, 1997 [1867].

Marx, Karl, and Friedrich Engels. "Manifesto of the Communist Party." In *The Marx-Engels Reader*, edited by Robert C. Tucker (pp. 469–500). New York: Norton, 1978 [1848].

Maslow, Abraham H. *Eupsychian Management: A Journal*. Homewood, Ill.: Dorsey Press, 1965.

———. *The Farther Reaches of Human Nature*. New York: Viking Press, 1971.

———. *Religions, Values and Peak Experiences*. New York: Viking, 1964.

———. *Toward a Psychology of Being*. 3rd ed. New York: Wiley, 1999 [1968].

Mather, Cotton. *Bonifacius: An Essay . . . To Do Good*. Gainesville, Fl.: Scholar's Facsimiles and Reprints, 1967 [1710].

———. "A Christian at His Calling." In *The American Gospel of Success*, edited by Moses Rischin (pp. 23–30). Chicago: Quadrangle Books, 1965 [1701].

Mattson, Kevin. *Intellectuals in Action: The Origins of the New Left and Radical Liberalism*. University Park: Pennsylvania State University Press, 2002.

McAdam, Doug. *Political Process and the Development of Black Insurgency*. Chicago: University of Chicago Press, 1982.

McGee, Micki. "The Artist's Way? Self-Help and Self-Subsidy in an Era of Declining Public Funding for the Arts." In *Trends and Strategies in the Arts and Culture Industries*, edited by Susanne Janssen, Marlite Halbertsma, Teunis Ijdens, and Karlijn Ernst (pp. 381–96). Rotterdam: Barjesteh Van Waalwijk Doorn, 2001.

———. "Hooked on Higher Education and Other Tales from Adjunct Faculty Organizing." *Social Text*, vol. 70 (2002): 61–80.

———. "The Over-Extended Family." In *Reframing the Family*, edited by Cornelia Butler and Micki McGee (pp. 22–30). New York: Artists Space, 1991.

McGinn, Daniel. "Self Help U.S.A." *Newsweek*, January 10, 2000, 42.

McGraw, Jay. *Life Strategies for Teens*. New York: Fireside, 2000.

McGraw, Philip C. *Life Strategies: Doing What Works, Doing What Matters*. New York: Hyperion, 1999.

McLaughlin, Neil. "How to Become a Forgotten Intellectual: Intellectual Movements and the Rise and Fall of Erich Fromm." *Sociological Forum* 13, no. 2 (1998): 215–46.

McLuhan, Marshall. *The Gutenberg Galaxy: The Making of Typographic Man*. Toronto: University of Toronto Press, 1962.

———. *Understanding Media: The Extensions of Man*. Cambridge, Mass.: MIT Press, 1994 [1964].

McManus, Kevin. "Making a Career of Careers." *Forbes*, March 15, 1982, 144.

Mead, George Herbert. *Mind, Self, and Society from the Standpoint of a Social Behaviorist*. Chicago: University of Chicago Press, 1934.

Melucci, Alberto. *Nomads of the Present*. Philadelphia: Temple University Press, 1989.

———. *The Playing Self: Person and Meaning in the Planetary Society*. Edited by Jeffrey C. Alexander and Steven Seidman. *Cambridge Cultural Social Studies*. Cambridge: Cambridge University Press, 1996.

Merchant, Carolyn. *The Death of Nature: Women, Ecology, and the Scientific Revolution*. San Francisco: Harper and Row, 1980.

Merton, Robert K. *Social Theory and Social Structure*. New York: Free Press, 1968.

Meyer, Donald B. *The Positive Thinkers*. Middlebury, Conn.: Wesleyan University Press, 1988 [1965].

Meyers, Diana. "Feminist Perspectives on the Self." In *The Stanford Encyclopedia of Philosophy*, edited by Edward N. Zalta, 2000. Available online at: http://plato. stanford.edu/archives/sum2000/entries/feminism-self/. Last viewed: January 5, 2005.

Miller, Perry. *Jonathan Edwards, American Men of Letters Series*. New York: Sloane, 1949.

Miller, Toby. *The Well-Tempered Self: Citizenship, Culture and the Postmodern Subject*. Baltimore: Johns Hopkins University Press, 1993.

Mills, C. Wright. *White Collar*. London: Oxford University Press, 1951.

Minsky, Marvin. *The Society of Mind*. New York: Simon and Schuster, 1988.

Moskowitz, Eva S. *In Therapy We Trust: America's Obsession with Self-Fulfillment*. Baltimore: Johns Hopkins University Press, 2001.

Muller, René J. *The Marginal Self: An Existenial Inquiry into Narcissism*. Atlantic Highlands, N.J.: Humanities Press International, 1987.

Nehamas, Alexander. *The Art of Living: Socratic Reflections from Plato to Foucault.* Berkeley: University of California Press, 1998.

Neumark, David, ed. *On the Job: Is Long-Term Employment a Thing of the Past?* New York: Russell Sage Foundation, 2000.

Newman, Mildred, and Bernard Berkowitz. *How to Be Your Own Best Friend.* New York: Random House, 1971.

Nietzsche, Friedrich. "Ecce Homo." In *Basic Writings of Nietzsche* (pp. 655–791). New York: Modern Library, 1992 [1908].

———. *The Gay Science.* Translated by Walter Kaufman. New York: Vintage, 1974 [1882, 1887].

———. *Human, All Too Human.* Translated by R. J. Hollingdale. Cambridge: Cambridge University Press, 1996 [1878].

———. *Thus Spoke Zarathustra.* Translated by Walter Kaufmann. New York: Viking Penguin, 1954 [1892].

Norwood, Robin. *Women Who Love Too Much: When You Keep Wishing and Hoping He'll Change.* New York: Pocket Books, 1985.

Okun, Tema. "They Should Be Our People." *Social Policy* 23, no. 2 (1992): 44–48.

Ong, Walter J. *Orality and Literacy: The Technologizing of the Word.* New York: Routledge, 1991 [1982].

Orman, Suze. *The Nine Steps to Financial Freedom.* New York: Crown, 2000 [1997].

Osterman, Paul. *Securing Prosperity, the American Labor Market: How It Has Changed and What to Do About It.* Princeton, N.J.: Princeton University Press, 1999.

Peck, M. Scott. *The Road Less Traveled: Spiritual Growth in an Age of Anxiety.* New York: Simon and Schuster, 1978.

Pennino, Dorothy E. "Engendering the Text: Self-Reliant Women in American Self-Help Literature (1848–1896)." Ph.D. diss., George Washington University, 1991.

Peters, Thomas J., and Robert H. Waterman, Jr. *In Search of Excellence: Lessons from America's Best-Run Companies.* New York: Harper and Row, 1982.

Peters, Tom. "The Brand Called You." *Fast Company,* August 1997, 83. Available online at: www.fastcompany.com/online/10/brandyou.html. Last viewed: January 15, 2005.

———. *The Brand You Fifty: Fifty Ways to Transform Yourself from an 'Employee' into a Brand That Shouts Distinction, Commitment, and Passion!* New York: Knopf, 1999.

———. *Liberation Management: Necessary Disorganization for the Nanosecond Nineties.* New York: Fawcett Columbine, 1992.

———. *The Pursuit of Wow: Every Person's Guide to Topsy-Turvy Times.* New York: Vintage, 1994.

———. *Thriving on Chaos.* New York: Knopf, 1987.

Peterson, V. Spike. "Rereading Public and Private: The Dichotomy That Is Not One." *SAIS Review* 20, no. 2 (2000): 11–29.

Pogrebin, Letty Cottin. "Can Women Really Have It All? Should We?" *Ms.*, March 1978, 47–48.

Polanyi, Karl. *The Great Transformation: The Political and Economic Origins of Our Time.* Boston: Beacon Press, 1957 [1944].

Ponder, Catherine. *The Dynamic Laws of Prosperity: Forces That Bring Riches to You.* Englewood Cliffs, N.J.: Prentice-Hall, 1962.

Potter, Beverly. *Finding a Path with a Heart: How to Go from Burnout to Bliss.* Berkeley: Ronin, 1995.

Potter, David M. *People of Plenty: Economic Abundance and the American Character.* Chicago: University of Chicago Press, 1954.

Rabinow, Paul, ed. *The Foucault Reader.* New York: Pantheon, 1984.

Rapping, Elayne. *The Culture of Recovery: Making Sense of the Self-Help Movement in Women's Lives.* Boston: Beacon Press, 1996.

Ray, Paul H., and Sherry Ruth Anderson. *The Cultural Creatives: How Fifty Million People Are Changing the World.* New York: Harmony Books, 2000.

Reich, Charles. *The Greening of America.* New York: Random House, 1970.

Reinarman, Craig. "The Twelve-Step Movement and Advanced Capitalist Culture: The Politics of Self-Control in Postmodernity." In *Cultural Politics and Social Movements,* edited by Marcy Darnovsky, Barbara Epstein, and Richard Flacks (pp. 90–109). Philadelphia: Temple University Press, 1995.

Rice, John Steadman. *A Disease of One's Own: Psychotherapy, Addiction, and the Emergence of Co-Dependency.* New Brunswick, N.J.: Transaction, 1996.

Richardson, Cheryl. *Take Time for Your Life.* New York: Broadway Books, 1998.

Rieff, Philip. *The Triumph of the Therapeutic: Uses of Faith after Freud.* New York: Harper and Row, 1966.

Rifkin, Jeremy. *The End of Work: The Decline of the Global Labor Force and the Dawn of the Post-Market Era.* New York: Putnam, 1995.

———. *Time Wars: The Primary Conflict in Human History.* New York: Holt, 1987.

Ringer, Robert J. *Looking Out for Number One.* Beverly Hills, Calif.: Los Angeles Book Corp., distributed by Funk and Wagnalls, 1977.

———. *Winning Through Intimidation.* 2nd ed. New York: Funk and Wagnalls, 1974 [1973].

Robbins, Anthony. *Awaken the Giant Within.* New York: Simon and Schuster, 1991.

———. *Notes from a Friend.* New York: Simon and Schuster, 1995.

———. *Personal Power II: The Driving Force.* San Diego, Calif.: Robbins Research International, 1996 [1993]. Audio compact disc.

———. "Tony Robbins: Practicing What He Preaches." Interview by Beverly Schuch. Pinnacle, CNN-FN, March 10, 2001. Transcript available online at http://www.cnn.com/TRANSCRIPTS/0103/10/pin.00.html. Last viewed: August 14, 2003.

———. *Unlimited Power*. New York: Fawcett Columbine, 1986.

Robbins, Anthony, and Joseph McClendon III. *Unlimited Power: A Black Choice*. New York: Simon and Schuster, 1997.

Robbins, Bruce, ed. *The Phantom Public Sphere*. Vol. 5, *Cultural Politics*. Minneapolis: University of Minnesota Press, 1993.

Robinson, John P., and Geoffrey Godbey. *Time for Life: The Surprising Ways Americans Use Their Time*. University Park, Pa.: University of Pennsylvania Press, 1997.

Rorty, Richard. *Achieving Our Country: Leftist Thought in Twentieth-Century America*. Cambridge, Mass.: Harvard University Press, 1998.

———. *Against Bosses, Against Oligarchies*. Chicago: Prickly Paradigm Press, 2002.

———. *Contingency, Irony and Solidarity*. Cambridge: Cambridge University Press, 1989.

Rosaldo, Michelle Zimbalist. "The Use and Abuse of Anthropology: Reflections on Feminism and Cross-Cultural Understanding." *Signs* 5 (Spring 1980): 389–417.

Rose, Nikolas. *Governing the Soul: The Shaping of the Private Self*. 2nd ed. London: Free Association Books, 1989.

———. *Inventing Our Selves: Psychology, Power, and Personhood*. Edited by Mitchell G. Ash and William R. Woodward. *Cambridge Studies in the History of Psychology*. Cambridge: Cambridge University Press, 1998 [1996].

Rosenberg, Rosalind. *Beyond Separate Spheres*. New Haven: Yale University Press, 1982.

Ross, Andrew. "The Mental Labor Problem." *Social Text #63* (2000): 1–31.

———. *No Collar: The Humane Workplace and Its Hidden Costs*. New York: Basic Books, 2003.

Ruddick, Sara. *Maternal Thinking*. Boston: Beacon Press, 1995 [1989].

Ryan, Mary P. *Cradle of the Middle Class: The Family in Oneida County, New York, 1790–1865*. Cambridge: Cambridge University Press, 1981.

———. "Gender and Public Access: Women's Politics in Nineteenth Century America." In *Habermas and the Public Sphere*, edited by Craig Calhoun (pp. 259–288). Cambridge, Mass.: MIT Press, 1992.

Sabel, Charles. "Mobius-Strip Organizations and Open Labor Markets: Some Consequences of the Reintegration of Conception and Execution in a Volatile Economy." In *Social Theory for a Changing Society*, edited by Pierre Bourdieu and James S. Coleman (pp. 23–61). Boulder, Colo.: Westview Press, 1991.

Santrock, John W., Ann M. Minnett, and Barbara D. Campbell. *The Authoritative Guide to Self-Help Books*. New York: Guilford Press, 1994.

Schaef, Anne Wilson. *When Society Becomes an Addict*. San Francisco: Harper and Row, 1987.

Schick, Elizabeth A., ed. *1998 Current Biography Yearbook*. New York: Wilson, 1998.

Schneider, Louis, and Sanford M. Dornbusch. *Popular Religion: Inspirational Books in America*. Chicago: University of Chicago Press, 1958.

Schor, Juliet B. *The Overworked American: The Unexpected Decline of Leisure*. New York: Basic Books, 1991.

———. "Working Hours and Time Pressure: The Controversy about Trends in Time Use." In *Working Time: International Trends, Theory and Political Perspectives*, edited by Lonnie Golden and Deborah M. Figart (pp. 73–86). London: Routledge, 2000.

Schuller, Robert H. *The Be (Happy) Attitudes*. Waco, Tex.: Word, 1985.

———. *Be Happy You Are Loved*. Nashville: Nelson, 1986.

———. *Tough-Minded Faith for Tender-Hearted People*. New York: Bantam, 1985.

———. *Tough Times Never Last, but Tough People Do*. New York: Bantam, 1984 [1983].

Schwartz, Hillel. *The Culture of the Copy: Striking Likenesses, Unreasonable Facsimiles*. New York: Zone Books, 1996.

———. *Never Satisfied: A Cultural History of Diets, Fantasies and Fat*. New York: Doubleday, 1986.

———. "On the Origin of the Phrase 'Social Problems,'" *Social Problems* 44, no. 2 (1997): 276–96.

Scott, Hilda. *Working Your Way to the Bottom: The Feminization of Poverty*. London: Pandora Press, 1984.

Scott, Joan W. "Comment: Conceptualizing Gender in American Business History." *Business History Review* 72, no. 2 (1998): 242–49.

Seldon, Philip. *The Complete Idiot's Guide to Wine*. Indianapolis, Ind.: Alpha Group, 1997.

Sennett, Richard. *The Corrosion of Character: The Personal Consequences of Work in the New Capitalism*. New York: Norton, 1998.

———. *The Fall of Public Man: On the Social Psychology of Capitalism*. New York: Vintage, 1974.

Servin, James. "Is Nice Back?" *Harper's Bazaar*, January 1997, 100–101, 133.

Shaw, George Bernard. *Man and Superman: A Comedy and a Philosophy*. Edinburgh: Penguin Books, 1946 [1903].

Shepard, Benjamin, and Ronald Hayduk, eds. *From ACT UP to the WTO: Urban Protest and Community Building in the Era of Globalization*. London: Verso, 2002.

Sher, Barbara, with Annie Gottlieb. *Wishcraft: How to Get What You Really Want*. New York: Ballantine, 1979.

Sher, Barbara, with Barbara Smith. *I Could Do Anything, If I Only Knew What It Was*. New York: Delacorte, 1994.

Shi, David E. *The Simple Life: Plain Living and High Thinking in American Culture*. New York: Oxford University Press, 1985.

Showalter, Elaine. *Inventing Herself*. New York: Scribner, 2001.

Sidel, Ruth. *Women and Children Last*. New York: Penguin, 1986.

Simonds, Wendy. *Women and Self-Help Culture: Reading between the Lines*. New Brunswick, N.J.: Rutgers University Press, 1992.

Sinetar, Marsha. *Do What You Love, the Money Will Follow: Discovering Your Right Livelihood*. Mahwah, N.J.: Paulist Press, 1987.

Skow, John. "The Fairway Less Traveled." *Time*, September 19, 1994, 91.

Smith, Adam. *An Inquiry into the Nature and Causes of the Wealth of Nations*. 2 vols. Vol. 2. Oxford: Oxford University Press, 1976 [1776].

———. *The Theory of Moral Sentiments*. Oxford: Claredon Press, 1976 [1759].

Smith, Dorothy E. "A Sociology for Women." In *The Prism of Sex*, edited by Julia A. Sherman and Evelyn Torton Beck (pp. 135–87). Madison, Wis.: University of Wisconsin Press, 1977.

Smith, Timothy K. "What's So Effective about Stephen Covey?" *Fortune*, December 12, 1994, 116–26.

Spindler, Amy M. "It's a Face-Lifted, Tummy-Tucked Jungle Out There." *New York Times*, June 9, 1996, sec. 3, 1, 8–9.

St. James, Elaine. *Inner Simplicity: One Hundred Ways to Regain Peace and Nourish Your Soul*. New York: Hyperion, 1995.

———. *Living the Simple Life: A Guide to Scaling Down and Enjoying More*. New York: Hyperion, 1996.

———. *Simplify Your Life: One Hundred Ways to Slow Down and Enjoy the Things That Really Matter*. New York: Hyperion, 1994.

Stanton, Doug. "Aren't You Glad You're Anthony Robbins?" *Esquire*, April 1994, 100–107.

Starker, Steven. *Oracle at the Supermarket: The American Preoccupation with Self-Help Books*. New Brunswick, N.J.: Transaction, 1989.

Steinem, Gloria. *Revolution from Within: A Book of Self-Esteem*. New York: Little, Brown, 1992.

Stephens, Mitchell. *The Rise of the Image, the Fall of the Word*. New York: Oxford University Press, 1998.

Stewart, James B. "Bestseller: The Agent from Texas That New York Can't Ignore." *New Yorker*, September 8, 1997, 44–49.

Susman, Warren. *Culture as History: The Transformation of American Society in the Twentieth Century*. New York: Pantheon Books, 1984.

Szasz, Thomas S. *The Manufacture of Madness: A Comparative Study of the Inquisition and the Mental Health Movement*. New York: Harper and Row, 1977 [1970].

———. *The Myth of Mental Illness: Foundations of a Theory of Personal Conduct*. New York: Hoeber-Harper, 1961.

Tallen, Bette S. "Codependency: A Feminist Critique." In *Challenging Codependency: Feminist Critiques*, edited by Marguerite Babcock and Christine McKay (pp. 169–76). Toronto: University of Toronto Press, 1995.

Tarde, Gabriel. "The Public and the Crowd." In *On Communication and Social Influence: Selected Papers*. Edited by Terry N. Clark (pp. 277–94). Chicago: University of Chicago Press, 1969 [1893].

Tavris, Carol. *The Mismeasure of Woman*. New York: Simon and Schuster, 1992.

Taylor, Charles. *The Ethics of Authenticity*. Cambridge, Mass.: Harvard University Press, 1991.

———. *Sources of the Self*. Cambridge, Mass.: Harvard University Press, 1989.

Taylor, Verta. *Rock-a-by Baby: Feminism, Self-Help and Postpartum Depression*. New York: Routledge, 1996.

Theroux, Phyllis. "A Psychotherapist's Guide for Living." Review of *The Road Less Traveled*, by M. Scott Peck. *Washington Post*, September 29, 1978, A-1.

Thomson, Irene Taviss. *In Conflict No Longer: Self and Society in Contemporary America*. Lanham, Md.: Rowman and Littlefield, 2000.

Tiede, Tom. *Self-Help Nation*. New York: Atlantic Monthly Press, 2001.

Tipton, Steven M. *Getting Saved from the Sixties: Moral Meaning in Conversion and Cultural Change*. Berkeley: University of California Press, 1982.

Tolle, Eckhart. *The Power of Now*. Novato, Calif.: New World Library, 1999.

Tracy, Diane. *Take This Job and Love It: A Personal Guide to Career Empowerment*. New York: McGraw-Hill, 1994.

Trilling, Lionel. *Sincerity and Authenticity*. Cambridge, Mass.: Harvard University Press, 1971.

Trine, Ralph Waldo. *The Best of Ralph Waldo Trine*. Indianapolis, Ind.: Bobbs-Merrill, 1957.

———. *In Tune with the Infinite, or Fullness of Peace, Power, and Plenty*. New York: Crowell, 1897.

Tyson, Eric. *Personal Finance for Dummies*. San Mateo, Calif.: IDG Books Worldwide, 1994.

Van Steenhouse, Andrea with Doris A. Fuller. *A Woman's Guide to a Simpler Life*. New York: Harmony Books, 1996.

Wallulis, Jerald. *The New Insecurity: The End of the Standard Job and Family*. Albany, N.Y.: State University of New York Press, 1998.

Walters, Ray. "Paperback Talk." *New York Times Book Review*, February 18, 1979, 41–42.

Warhol, Andy. *The Philosophy of Andy Warhol (from A to B and Back Again)*. New York: Harcourt Brace Jovanovich, 1975.

Warren, Rick. *The Purpose Driven Life: What on Earth Am I Here For?* Grand Rapids, Mich.: Zondervan, 2002.

Weber, Max. *The Protestant Ethic and the Spirit of Capitalism.* Translated by Talcott Parsons. New York: Scribner's, 1958 [1904].

———. "Religious Rejections of the World and Their Directions." In *From Max Weber,* edited by Hans H. Gerth and C. Wright Mills (pp. 343–49). New York: Oxford University Press, 1946 [1915].

Weiss, Richard. *The American Myth of Success.* Urbana, Ill.: University of Illinois Press, 1988 [1969].

Whelan, Christine B. *Self-Help Books and the Quest for Self-Control in the United States 1950–2000.* Ph.D. diss. Oxford University, 2004.

Whitman, Walt. *Complete Poems.* New York: Penguin, 2004.

Whitmyer, Claude, ed. *Mindfulness and Meaningful Work.* Berkeley, Calif.: Parallax, 1994.

Whyte, David. *The Heart Aroused: Poetry and the Preservation of the Soul in Corporate America.* New York: Doubleday, 1994.

Whyte, William H., Jr. *The Organization Man.* Garden City, N.Y.: Doubleday, 1957 [1956].

Williams, Raymond. *Keywords: A Vocabulary of Culture and Society.* New York: Oxford University Press, 1976.

Winfrey, Oprah. "What I Know for Sure." *O, The Oprah Magazine,* November 2000, 298.

Woititz, Janet Geringer. *Adult Children of Alcoholics.* Deerfield Beach, Fla.: Health Communications, 1983.

Wolfe, Alan. "White Magic in America." *New Republic,* February 23, 1998, 26–34.

Wood, Leonard. "The Gallup Survey: Self-Help Buying Trends." *Publishers Weekly* 234, no. 16 (1988): 33.

Wood, Michael R., and Louis A. Zurcher, Jr. *The Development of a Postmodern Self.* Vol. 70, *Contributions in Sociology.* New York: Greenwood Press, 1988.

Wuthnow, Robert. *Sharing the Journey: Support Groups and America's New Quest for Community.* New York: Free Press, 1994.

Wyllie, Irvin G. *The Self-Made Man in America: The Myth of Rags to Riches.* New York: Free Press, 1966 [1954].

Yankelovich, Daniel. *New Rules: Searching for Self-Fulfillment in a World Turned Upside Down.* New York: Random House, 1981.

Zerner, Donna. "The Artist's Way." *Yoga Journal,* March–April 1995, 96–100.

Zurcher, Louis A., Jr. *The Mutable Self: A Self-Concept for Social Change.* Vol. 59, *Sage Library of Social Research.* Beverly Hills: Sage, 1977.

Index

AA. *See* Alcoholics Anonymous

Abbott, Lyman, 58

abundance, 35, 63, 70–71, 79, 101–103, 125
  as antidote to economic insecurity, 102
  and gratitude, 146–148
  "simple abundance," 95–96, 101, 109, 147, 163–164

Acres of Diamonds. See Conwell, Russell H.

ACT UP. *See* AIDS Coalition to Unleash Power

acting, theatrical versus film, 165

Actor's Equity, 125

addiction, 89, 186. *See also* codependence

Adult Children of Alcoholics. See Woititz, Janet

advertising
  deregulation of television, 62
  and social anxiety, 17, 204
  for U.S. Army recruitment ("be all you can be"), 175n2

advice manuals
  career, 57, 112–128, 196 (*see also* career advice)
  in the nineteenth century, 34, 49, 58

aesthetic values
  as alternative to instrumental rationality, 21–22
  merged with market values, 21–22
  in nineteenth-century Romantic tradition, 21
  role of in secular society, 47, 52, 94
  as substitute for moral values, 21, 47, 94

affluence, 71–72, 76, 92, 102
  "inner affluence," 125
  See also abundance

African Americans, 184
  alternative position on self-recovery, 174n107
  as representatives of enthusiasm (Peters), 168
  unemployment among, 131

Ageless Body, Timeless Mind. See Chopra, Deepak

agency, human, 38, 172, 182
  limits to, 178n12

Aid to Families with Dependent Children, 232
  See also social safety net

AIDS Coalition to Unleash Power, 190

civic contributions
 of Benjamin Franklin, 31
 of Harvey MacKay, 73
civil rights movement, 14, 54, 100
 See also social movements
civility, 88
Coach University, 104
coaching, life. *See* life coaching
coaching, personal. *See* life coaching
coalcoholism, 89. *See also* codependence
codependence, 21, 50, 82, 88–91, 195,
 225
 as application of market values to
 intimate life, 88–89, 185
 conservative political efficacy, 90, 160,
 188
 popularizers of term, 147
 Steinem and, 97
 and "women who love too much,"
 109–110, 177
collective action, 23
 as context for personal change, 98
 imagining, 160, 190–191, 194
 in the 1960s, 54
 supposed futility of, 54
college teaching, as self-promotion
 opportunity, 135
Collier, Robert, 163
commercial sphere, 21, 24, 28, 30
community service, 31
competition
 for jobs, 15, 50, 73, 83–86, 191
 as consequence of globalization, 41,
 83–85
 and gender, 84
Complete Idiot's Guide to Wine, The, 18
Composing a Life. *See* Bateson, Mary
 Catherine
conflict, 179
 aversion to in Covey, 68–70, 179–180
 individual vs. society, 180
 and negotiation, 8
 as opposed to congruence, 170, 179
 between personal and professional
 life, 68–70, 87
consciousness
 collective, 63
 dual or split nature of in response to
 oppression, 45, 165
consciousness-raising, 100, 187
consumerism, role of aesthetics in
 promoting, 22, 46

consumption, 22, 45, 102–103, 164
 as labor, 29
 separation from production, 37–38
contingencies, 142, 151, 166, 173
contingent labor. *See* labor, contingent
Conwell, Russell H., 34–35, 58
corporations, vertical integration of, 14
Cosmopolitan Magazine, 85
cost-benefit analysis, in intimate life, 21,
 29, 91, 110, 139
Cotham, Frank, *137*
Coué, Emile, 36
Courage to be Rich, The. *See* Orman,
 Suze
Covenant of Grace, 27, 56
Covenant of Works, 27, 56
Covey Leadership Center, 6n11, 59n38
Covey, Maria, 3–9, 80, 178, 204
Covey, Stephen R.
 accounting metaphor in, 85
 advice to his daughter, 3–9, 45
 aversion to conflict, 68–70, 179–180
 Christian themes in writing by, 5, 48,
 66
 comparison with Cotton Mather, 66–
 68, 149
 computer metaphor in, 66
 and continuous work on self, 143
 daughter of (*see* Covey, Maria)
 funeral fantasy exercise in, 66–68,
 149
 gendered solutions to social problems
 in, 3–9, 79–81, 179
 ideas regarding character, 61–62, 64
 ideas of self-mastery in, 142, 152, 153–
 154
 on the importance of writing, 156, 159
 influence of Fisher and Ury, 55
 inward turn in, 84
 metonyms of clock and compass, 4–5,
 65
 and Mormonism, 5n15
 normative roles in, 179
 privileging of reason in, 142, 155, 176,
 179
 rhetoric of natural laws in, 59, 64
 scheduling by social role, 153–*154*
 time management systems of, 153–154
Creating Affluence. *See* Chopra, Deepak
Creative America, 126
Creative Visualization. *See* Gawain,
 Shakti

enthusiasm, 167–169
entrepreneur, artist as, 22, 111, 136–138
entrepreneurship, 131
   and enthusiasm, 168, 191
   ethics and, 168
   and exhaustion, 169
   and loneliness, 168
Epstein, Barbara, 190
ethic, Protestant. *See* Protestant ethic
ethics
   absence of, 54
   entrepreneurship as impediment to, 168
etiquette books, 5
evil, as laziness, 56
   See also work ethic
Ewen, Stuart, 17n21
excellence, 128, 130, 132–133
exercise, 86–87, 121, 150, 153, 155, 169
   See also fitness
expressive individualism. *See*
      individualism, expressive
Extreme Makeover. See makeover
      television

False Promises. See Aronowitz, Stanley
Faludi, Susan, 88n37, 194
family, dysfunctional, 89, 188
family man, 135
family wage, 8, 109
   See also wages
fat, loathing of, 37, 154–155
   See also body types; fitness
Federal Communications Commission
      (FCC), 62
Feminine Mystique, The. See Friedan,
      Betty
femininity, associated with weakness,
      37
   See also masculinity
feminism, 50, 54, 90–91, 98, 109, 187
   See also women's movement
"feminization of poverty" (Sidel), 82
financial compensation
   decline in, 131
   separation of work from, 22, 40–43,
      112, 125–126, 129, 130, 135–136
financial counselors
   as personal coaches, 104
financial planners, 104, 104n97
financialization of daily life, 109n111,
      185
First Great Awakening, 28
   See also religious revivalism

First Things First. See Covey, Stephen R.
Fisher, Robert, 55
fitness, 37, 59, 86, 195
   as sign of self-discipline, 86, 153
   as source of energy, 86–87
flexible accumulation. *See* capital, flexible
      strategies for accumulation of
*Flow: The Psychology of Optimal
      Experience. See* Csikszentmihalyi,
      Mihaly
flows, 35–36, 52, 63, 72–73, 222. *See also*
      liquidity, metaphors of
Ford, Henry, 36
Fordism, 40
Forward, Susan, 89
Fosdick, Harry Emerson, 58
Foucault, Michel
   on death of the subject, 177
   on Greek practices of self-cultivation,
      95, 139, 152, 156–157
   idea of governmentality in, 23n37
   idea of life as a work of art in, 94, 139,
      166, 172
   and Nietzsche, 94
   and rejection of authenticity, 94, 171
Fox, Emmet, 58
Frankl, Victor, 152
Franklin, Benjamin, 13, 27, 31, 59,
   as "avant-garde of one," 28, 136, 209
   book of virtues of, 6
   commitment to social goods, 31
   daughter of (*see* Bache, Sarah "Sally"
      Franklin)
   and rise of literacy, 31, 211
   use of schedules by, 6, 199
   wife of (*see* Franklin, Deborah Read)
Franklin, Deborah Read, 7–9
   compared with Maria Covey, 8
Franklin, Rosalind, 99, 99n70
FranklinCovey Company, 6, 59, 65–66,
      153–154
   clock and compass as trademarks of,
      65
   merger that created, 6n11, 59n38
   website of, 159
Franklin Furnace, 128
Franklin Planner. *See* day planners;
      Franklin Quest Company
Franklin Quest Company, 6n11, 59n38
Fraser, Nancy, 183n26
freedom, 38, 141, 171–174
Freud, Sigmund, 91
Freudian slips, as metaphors, 91

imagination, 20, 162–163, 189, 191
  paucity of in self-help literature, 160, 188
  See also sociological imagination
imitation, 169
impression management, 87, 162, 165–166
In Search of Excellence (Peters and
      Waterman), 132–133, 167
In Tune with the Infinite. See Trine,
      Ralph Waldo
individualism, 19
  expressive, 29, 51
  utilitarian, 29, 51
industrial reserve army, 130
industrialization
  and emergence of separate spheres, 30
  and erosion of rural life, 33
infomercials, use of, 62
initiative, in the workplace, 135
"inner child," 97, 127, 148, 178
"inner corpse" (Boyd), 148
insecurity, economic sources of, 9, 12, 43
  See also anxiety
instrumental rationality, 22, 29, 35, 47,
      61, 72, 110
insufficiency, perception of, 18
interdependence, 177–179
internet, 62, 128, 128n51, 159, 190
  See also websites
Interpretation of Dreams, The. See Freud,
      Sigmund
intimate sphere, 4, 24, 30
  blurring of boundaries with
      commercial sphere, 20, 21, 86,
      90, 176, 185, 189
  labor in, 13
"invisible hand" (Smith), 55, 70
"inward turn" (Taylor), 47, 49–51, 76–
      77, 84, 96, 165, 178
It Was on Fire When I Lay Down On It.
      See Fulghum, Robert

James, William, 38n49
Jameson, Fredric, 5n10, 180n16
Japanese management techniques, 132, 199
Jesus Christ, as salesman, 50n4, 58
job market, changes in, 93
  See also labor market
job security, 132
  lack of, 112, 131
  as necessity for motivating workers, 133
job skills
  exercises to assess, 115, 124
  as "transferable skills," 115

job-hunting, 112, 113, 121
  with passion, 121
  and religion, 119
  while working full-time, 113
"jobless future" (Aronowitz), 15
  See also unemployment
Johnson, Mark, 62
Johnson, Spencer, 73–76, 183
journal writing, 96, 127, 146–148, 156,
      159, 164
  as exercise among ancient Greek
      citizens, 95, 156
  See also self-help exercises; writing
      exercises
*Journey to Ixtlan: The Lessons of Don
      Juan. See* Castañeda, Carlos
justice, economic, 183, 188–190

Kaizen (pursuit of perfection), 132–133
  See also Japanese management
      techniques
Kaminer, Wendy, 23n37, 89n42, 177n4
Kant, Immanuel, ethical imperatives of,
      51, 64, 171n102
Kassorla, Irene C., 83, 149, 158
  as Monica Lewinsky's
      psychotherapist, 171n12
Kerber, Linda K., 28n13
Klein, Melanie, 38n51
Korda, Michael, 52–55, 76, 83, 87
Kushner, Harold S., 58

labor
  associated with bodily exertion, 140–
      141
  in caring for others, 9, 13, 16, 24, 88,
      169, 172, 176, 178
  contingent, 15, 30, 40, 49, 132–133
  discounted, 109, 126
  doctrine of dignity of all, 35, 125,
      125n37
  domestic, 9, 13, 16, 23, 136 (*see also*
      labor in caring for others)
  emotional, 170
  etymology of, 140
  expectation of compensation, 18
  flexible, 18, 49
  forced, 9, 24, 183 (*see also* workfare)
  gendered division of, 13, 37, 80, 130, 179
    in nineteenth century, 28, 37
    in the home, 136, 181 (*see also* labor,
        domestic; labor, discounted;
        work, without compensation)

"luck and pluck," 32
Lyotard, François, 46n40, 162n73, 188n40

Macbeth, 165
Mackay, Harvey, 73–74, 76
Madonna. See Ciccione, Madonna Maria, 17n19
makeover television, 17, 20
makeovers, 17. See also makeover television
of "lifestyle," 105–106
Malcolm X (Little, Malcolm), 23, 105
Maltz, Maxwell, 60
Man Nobody Knows, The. See Barton, Bruce
Man and Superman. See Shaw, George Bernard
managed heart, 170
management advice books, as self-help for organizations, 134
manners. See etiquette
Marcuse, Herbert, 22n36
market values, 21, 29, 58, 82, 90, 101
Martin, Randy, 109n111
Marx, Karl, 72, 141, 142, 191
biological metaphors in work by, 234
masculinity, 13, 23
characteristics of, 13, 37
and images of success, 37
See also femininity; gender roles
Maslow, Abraham H., 42–43, 131, 183
his hierarchy of human needs, 43, 131
Mather, Cotton, 26–30, 33, 43, 66–68, 68n72, 117–119, 149
Maudlin Exemplar, 150–153, 185
McGraw, Philip C. ("Dr. Phil"), 182
McKinsey & Company, 133
Mead, George Herbert, 68
Mead, Margaret, 94
mechanization, 63
See also "jobless future"
medication, antidepressant, 120
medicine, Ayurvedic, 71
meditation, 18, 95–96, 97, 101, 127, 145, 149, 156
Men Who Hate Women and the Women Who Love Them. See Forward, Susan
mental illness, 120
meritocracy, 13, 31
Merrill, A. Roger, 81, 143
Merrill, Rebecca R., 81, 143
mesmerism, 36, 38, 60

metaphor
accounting, 64, 69, 85, 87, 90
of ascent, 51–84 (see also metaphor, of climbing)
biological, 98; in Marx, 234
of the body, 98–99
business, 21–22, 51m 52, 83–84, 91, 139, 174
of climbing (see metaphor, of ascent)
computer, 51, 52, 60, 64, 66 (see also cybernetic self; metaphor of machine)
contagion, 98–99
of farming, 64
of filmmaking, 164
game, 51–53, 139
journey, 5, 6, 44, 47, 51, 53, 56, 64, 66, 93–94
gendered nature of, 44, 93–94, 44n67
in Nietzsche, 95
jungle, 52–54, 76, 87 (see also survivalism)
maternal, 178
organic, 98 (see also metaphors, biological)
path (see metaphor, of journey)
race, 53
of ripples in a pond, 68; in Mather, 68n73
sport, 51, 52–54, 83, 116–117
as structure of thought, 62
of war or battle, 51, 68
metonym
of animals (see animals in self-help literature)
of clock, 5, 65
of compass, 4, 5, 65
Meyer, Donald, 36n37, 38
Miller, Jan, 59
Miller, Toby, 188, 23n40, 188n40
Mills, C. Wright, 182
mind over matter, 60, 99, 103, 155, 162, 185
See also mind-power
mind-cure, 36, 38
See also mind-power
mindfulness, 125
mind-power, 35, 48, 60–64, 70, 102, 185
Minsky, Marvin, 179
Mismeasure of Woman, The (Tavris)
mischaracterized as self-help book, 194
mission, 40, 44–47, 65–66, 117–120, 158–159, 168
See also calling, vocation

"organization man" (Whyte), 49, 130
Organization Man, The. See Whyte,
    William H.
organizational behavior, 69
Orman, Suze, 36, 104, 107–109
Our Bodies, Ourselves, 19
    See also Nuestros Cuerpos, Nuestras Vidas
outsourcing, 30, 40
Over-Soul, 35, 71
overtime. *See* labor, overtime
overtime labor, 135
    and entrepreneurship, 169
    mandatory, 132
    as vital to success, 87
Oxford English Dictionary, 34, 45, 88, 116

parachute, images of, 113–115, *114*
parapraxis. *See* Freudian slips, 91
parenting, 4
    as obstacle to career success, 136,
        17n19
    See also childrearing
passion, work as expression of, 116, 121–
    122
Paulist Press, 122
Peale, Norman Vincent, 36, 57, 60, 102
Peck, M. Scott, 48, 83, 195
    constant work in, 143
    gender roles in, 80
    Road Less Traveled, The, sales figures
        for, 56, 127
    therapeutic theism, 56–59, 79–80, 83
People magazine, 158
perfection, 145. *See also* Kaizen
Personal Finance for Dummies, 18
personal life, in conflict with work, 16,
    68, 75, 105, 136
Personal Power II. See Robbins, Anthony
    "Tony"
personality, as distinct from character, 64
perspective, aerial, 117
Peters, Tom (Thomas J.), 128
    on "Brand You," 134–135, 166
    CEO of Me, Inc., 22, 134–136, 170
    enthusiasm in, 167–168
    as managing self-actualizing worker,
        42–43, 97
    on motivating workers, 132–133
    search for "excellence," 128, 131–132
    shift to writing self-help books, 134
    and total quality management, 21
pirates, image of, 163
plagiarism, in self-help books, 50n4

play, 29, 83, 92, 123, 125, 168, 29l
    board games, *115*
    enthusiasm and, 168
pleasure, 19, 122, 162, 168
    in childrearing, 130
    sexual, 39
    in work, 25, 39, 42–43, 47, 112, 129, 168
plenty. *See* abundance
poetry, 128
poetry workshops, 128
Pogrebin, Letty Cottin, 79
poker, 52–53, 76
    See also metaphor of games, 53
Polanyi, Karl, 120
polis, 139
political dialogue
    avoidance of in makeover television, 107
    avoidance of in Twelve-Step groups,
        186
political opportunity, 12, 16, 24, 180
politics, identity, 184, 189
Ponder, Catherine, 102
positive thinking, 36, 57, 64, 162
post-capitalism, 14
postmodernity, 162
poverty
    among the middle-class, 107
    as sign of lack of attunement, 63, 72, 102
    as sign of spiritual estrangement, 63, 183
    as sign of vice, 35, 102
    among women and children, 82, 102
    (*see also* "feminization of
        poverty")
Power! How to Get It, How to Use It. See
    Korda, Michael
Power of Now, The. See Tolle, Eckhart
Power Through Constructive Thinking.
    See Fox, Emmet
predatory behavior, 21, 52, 73
predestination, doctrine of, 26–27, 130,
    150
President's Committee on the Arts and
    the Humanities, 126
print culture, 5, 63, 77, 165. *See also*
    literacy
private sphere. *See also* separate spheres
    democratization of, 186, 38n41
    in nineteenth century, 30, 38
productivity, 109
    development of human potential as
        key to, 132
    expectations of, 112
professions. *See* work

Ringer, Robert J.
  advice for women, 79–80
  and collective action, 54
  life as a battle, 53, 68
  life as a game, 53
  Looking Out for Number One, 52–55,
    58, 68, 74, 76, 176
  Screwor-Screwee Theory, 80, 84
  and survivalism, 52–55, 83, 87, 101, 176
Road Less Traveled, The. See Peck, M.
    Scott
Robbins, Anthony "Tony"
  and continuous work, 142, 146
  cybernetic metaphors in, 60–61
  focus on individual success in, 161
  idea of "congruence," 169–171, 179
  and inward turn, 76
  and Maudlin Exemplar, 150–151
  metaphor of filmmaking in, 164–165
  mind over matter in, 155
  and mind-power, 48, 59–61
  and rhetoric of scientific legitimacy,
    59–62, 70
  and televangelists, 59
  use of infomercials, 62
  use of internet technology, 159, 220
Robbins Research International. *See*
    Robbins, Anthony "Tony"
roles, normative, 179
Romantic ethic, 20–21, 25, 28, 32, 47, 91,
    96, 110, 130
  and attunement with nature, 176
Romanticism, 28–29, 130
Rorty, Richard, 91, 160, 187
Rose, Nikolas, 20n26, 51, 23n37, 42n59
Ross, Andrew, 21n31, 129
Ryan, Mary P., 33, 37

Sabel, John, 69–70
Sadat, Anwar, 152
salvation, 26–27, 30, 41, 47
  secular, 142
  and self-realization, 111
salvation religions, in competition with
    aesthetics, 47
sampling error, in Weber, 28
sampling methods, 193–195
scarcity, 52
  as imaginary, 101–102 (*see also*
    abundance)
schedules. *See* time management
Schor, Juliet B., 12n10, 112n2, 195
Schuller, Robert H., 57, 150–151

Schwartz, Hillel, 37n45, 165n82
Schwarzenegger, Arnold, 13, 37
scientific principles, rhetoric of, 59, 60–
    63
Scott, Joan W., 28n13
scripts, 66, 156, 179
Second Great Awakening, 33
  See also religious revivalism
"second shift" (Hochschild), 50
Second Shift, The (Hochschild),
    mischaracterized as self-help
    book, 194
Secret of the Ages, The. See Collier,
    Robert
self
  authenticity of, 9, 16, 94–96, 122, 127,
    166–169
    Brown's disavowal of, 166
    Foucault's disavowal of, 94–95
  authentic (*see* self, authenticity of)
  belabored (*see* belabored self)
  as business, 22, 83–84, 87
  calculating, 4, 179
  as combatants, 51
  as computer, 51, 60–61, 64, 66
  as corporation, 22 (*see also* self, as
    business; CEO of Me, Inc.)
  decentered, 15
  enterprising, 15, 51
  as entrepreneur, 51 (*see also*
    enterprising)
  ethical, 68
  as explorer, 51
  as game player, 51
  invention of, 7, 11
  as manager, 51, 69, 179
  minimal, 15, 16n18
  multiple, 178, 190
  mutable, 15
  narcissistic, 77
  persuasive, 169–170
  rational, 179
  relational, 180, 190
  as salesperson, 51
  as servant, 51
  theories of the, 15
  well-tempered, 15, 23n40
  as a work of art (*see* life as work of art)
self-actualization, 40–43, 99, 125, 131, 183
    (*see also* self-fulfillment, self-
    realization)
  managing workers in pursuit of, 97,
    131–136

Steinem, Gloria, 96–100, 110, 180, 190
Stewart, Martha, 17n19, 101
"strong poets" (Bloom), 160, 187
Struggling Upward, or Luke Larkin's Luck. See Alger, Jr., Horatio
subject, crisis of the, 177
subjectivity, 15. *See also* subject, crisis of the
subordination, strategic, 81, 84
success, 13, 142
    balance and proportion as criteria for, 46
    changing criteria for, 19, 34, 46
    external measures of, 19
    female allegory of as "Bitch Goddess," 38n49
    internal criteria for, 19
    masculine metaphors of, 14–15, 37
    power as measure of, 19, 54
    self-fulfillment as criterion for, 19
    social status as measure of, 19, 32, 85
    wealth as measure of, 19, 34–35, 54 (*see also* wealth)
Success. See Emerson, Ralph Waldo, 33
surgery, cosmetic, 60, 166
survivalism, 48, 49–54, 73–75, 83, 86–87, 139, 203
Swim with the Sharks without Being Eaten Alive. See Mackay, Harvey

Take This Job and Love It: A Personal Guide to Career Empowerment. See Tracy, Diane
Take Time for Your Life. See Richardson, Cheryl
talents, biblical parable of, 119
Tannen, Deborah, 195
Tarde, Gabriel, 161
Tavris, Carol, 194
Taylor, Charles
    on authenticity and democratic polities, 23n40
    on self as computer, 61
Taylor, Verta, 23n40, 190
telecommunication technology
    as putative source of stress, 106
    use of in self-help culture, 58, 220
    See also internet
television, deregulation of advertising on, 62
Ten Speed Press, 113
testimony, 168, 186
theism, therapeutic, 55–57

Theroux, Phyllis, 56
Think and Grow Rich. See Hill, Napoleon
"third shift" (Hochschild), 103
Thomson, Irene Taviss, 180
Thriving on Chaos. See Peters, Tom (Thomas J.)
time
    equation of with money, 107
    as illusion, 145
    present moment in, 144–145
    pressure on working parents, 103
time and space, substitution of space for time, 5, 5n10
"time bind" (Hochschild), 50, 103–104
Time Bind, The. See Hochschild, Arlie Russell
time management, 18, 59
    in Covey, 4, 66, 68, 81, 153, 156
    Franklin's emphasis on, 6–7
to-do lists, 144. *See also* time management
Tolle, Eckhart, 142, 145
Torre, Joan, 89
total quality management, 21, 132
Tough-Minded Faith for Tender-Hearted People. See Schuller, Robert H.
Tough Times Never Last, But Tough People Do. See Schuller, Robert H.
Tracy, Diane, 151
Trading Spaces. See makeover television
Transcendentalism, as reaction to industrialization, 32–33
Trine, Ralph Waldo, 35–36, 63, 71–72
"triumph of the therapeutic" (Rieff), 20, 43
Triumph of the Therapeutic, The. See Rieff, Philip
"true north"
    in Cameron, 158
    in Covey 65
"true womanhood," 29
Twelve-Step Groups, 89, 97–98, 180–181, 186, 188, 190
    conservative political efficacy of, 188
    prohibition on political positions in, 186

unemployment, 9, 12, 15, 57, 113
    as crisis of identity, 120–121
    as economic crisis, 120
    of mid-level managers, 133
    rates of in early 1980s, 131
    retraining to avoid, 12, 133

winners, 53, 56
women as, 83
See also losers
Winning Through Intimidation. See
Ringer, Robert J.
*Wishcraft: How to Get What You Really
Want. See* Sher, Barbara
Woititz, Janet Geringer, 89
women
career expectations of, 8, 5, 14, 39, 81
labor force participation of (*see* labor
force, women's participation in
paid)
as readers of self-help literature, 45,
45n69
role of in making self-made man, 37–38
self-made, 17n19
supporting role of, 7, 37–38, 81
as wives, 9, 37–38, 79, 109, 140
Women and Self-Help Culture. See
Simonds, Wendy
Women Who Love Too Much. See
Norwood, Robin
women's movement, 14, 79–80. *See also*
social movements
Wood, Phil, 117
work ethic. *See also* Protestant ethic;
right livelihood
fusion of Buddhist and Protestant
beliefs in, 123–125
work
as art, 128
in conflict with family life, 68, 75, 105,
136
continuous, 135, 142–143, 146
etymology of, 140
without financial compensation, 40–
42, 4, 85, 112, 125–126, 129–130,
131, 135, 136 (*see also* labor,
uncompensated)

freelance (*see* self-employment)
and mortality, 141
as place to meet men, 39
satisfaction in, 43, 109 122, 130
on self, 41, 43, 57, 133, 136
continuous nature of, 142–143
as an investment, 143
as a requirement for employability,
138
as source of identity, 39–40, 42,
214
as source of pleasure, 25, 39, 42–43,
47, 112, 129, 168
as source of self-fulfillment, 8, 39, 42–
43, 111, 121
use of term in association with art,
140
See also labor
workfare. *See* labor, forced
Working Today, 107n106
workplace
humane, 21
sexuality in the, 85–86
writing
and identity, 157
as source of authority, 155
writing exercises
among ancient Greeks, 156–157
in Cameron, 157–158
in Covey, 156–158
in Robbins, 161
Wuthnow, Robert, 180

Yankelovich, Skelly, and White, 91
You Can Negotiate Anything, 55
Your Erroneous Zones. See Dyer,
Wayne W.

Zen and the Art of Making a Living. See
Boldt, Laurence G.